THE KEY
STUDENT STUDY GUIDE

English 12

THE KEY student study guide is designed to help students achieve success in school. The content in each study guide is 100% aligned to the provincial curriculum and serves as an excellent source of material for review and practice. To create this book, teachers, curriculum specialists, and assessment experts have worked closely to develop the instructional pieces that explain each of the key concepts for the course. The practice questions and sample tests have detailed solutions that show problem-solving methods, highlight concepts that are likely to be tested, and point out potential sources of errors. *THE KEY* is a complete guide to be used by students throughout the school year for reviewing and understanding course content, and to prepare for assessments.

Published 2008
Copyright © 2008 Castle Rock Research Corporation

Rao, Gautam, 1961 –
THE KEY – English 12 (2009 Edition) British Columbia

1. English – Juvenile Literature. I. Title

Published by
Castle Rock Research Corp.
2340 Manulife Place
10180 – 101 Street
Edmonton, AB T5J 3S4

1 2 3 FP 10 09 08

Printed in Canada

Publisher
Gautam Rao

Contributors
George Biggs
Brigitta Braden
Murray Chambers

Dedicated to the memory of Dr. V. S. Rao

THE KEY—ENGLISH GRADE 12

THE KEY Study Guide for English Grade 12 is designed to complement classroom instruction and assist in preparation for unit tests and final exams.

THE KEY is a compilation of teacher-generated questions and answers that are correlated to the English Grade 12 curriculum. Questions have been grouped by concepts so you can use this resource to study throughout the year. The strategies and suggestions presented are intended to be used in conjunction with the curriculum concepts and content you have studied in the classroom.

THE KEY for English Grade 12 includes a Class Focus section and two tests that reflect the expectations of a year-end assessment. Detailed solutions are provided for each question. Solutions examine the choices provided and explain why the correct answer is the most suitable response. It is hoped that you can improve your performance in each section of the test by studying problem areas and by using the suggestions offered to address these difficulties.

THE KEY is organized into the following sections:

I **KEY Tips for Being Successful at School** provides you with examples of study and review strategies. Information is included on learning styles, study schedules, and developing review notes.

II **Class Focus** provides a breakdown of the English Grade 12 course by topic. Curriculum expectations are presented unit by unit. Within each unit, instructional pieces explain key concepts and skills, practice questions test your knowledge of the unit content in a variety of ways, and a unit test measures your level of understanding. At the beginning of every unit, there is a Table of Correlations that lists all applicable curriculum expectations for that unit.

III **KEY Strategies for Success on Tests** explores topics such as common test question formats and strategies for response, commonly used directing words, how to begin the test, and managing test anxiety.

IV **Practice Tests** section includes two tests. You may use these as practice tests to become familiar with the format and rigour of an English Grade 12 year-end assessment. Answers and sample solutions are provided.

For the complete curriculum document visit www.bced.gov.bc.ca/irp/ela

For information about any of our resources or services, please call Castle Rock Research at 250.868.8384 or visit our website at http://www.castlerockresearch.com.

At Castle Rock Research, we strive to produce a resource that is error-free. If you should find an error, please contact us so that future editions can be corrected.

TABLE OF CONTENTS

KEY Tips for Being Successful at School

KEY FACTORS CONTRIBUTING TO SCHOOL SUCCESS

In addition to learning the content of your courses, there are some other things that you can do to help you do your best at school. Some of these strategies are listed below:

KEEP A POSITIVE ATTITUDE. Always reflect on what you can already do and what you already know.

BE PREPARED TO LEARN. Have ready the necessary pencils, pens, notebooks, and other required materials for participating in class.

COMPLETE ALL OF YOUR ASSIGNMENTS. Do your best to finish all of your assignments. Even if you know the material well, practice will reinforce your knowledge. If an assignment or question is difficult for you, work through it as far as you can so that your teacher can see exactly where you are having difficulty.

SET SMALL GOALS for yourself when you are learning new material. For example, when learning the parts of speech, do not try to learn everything in one night. Work on only one part or section each study session. When you have memorized one particular part of speech and understand it, then move on to another one, continue this process until you have memorized and learned all the parts of speech.

REVIEW YOUR CLASSROOM WORK regularly at home to be sure that you understand the material that you learned in class.

ASK YOUR TEACHER FOR HELP when you do not understand something or when you are having a difficult time completing your assignments.

GET PLENTY OF REST AND EXERCISE. Concentrating in class is hard work. It is important to be well-rested and have time to relax and socialize with your friends. This helps you to keep a positive attitude about your school work.

EAT HEALTHY MEALS. A balanced diet keeps you healthy and gives you the energy that you need for studying at school and at home.

HOW TO FIND YOUR LEARNING STYLE

Every student has a certain manner in which it seems easier for him or her to learn. The manner in which you learn best is called your learning style. By knowing your learning style, you can increase your success at school. Most students use a combination of learning styles. Do you know what type of learner you are? Read the following descriptions. Which of these common learning styles do you use most often?

Linguistic Learner: You may learn best by saying, hearing, and seeing words. You are probably really good at memorizing things such as dates, places, names, and facts. You may need **to write and then say out loud** the steps in a process, a formula, or the actions that lead up to a significant event.

Spatial Learner: You may learn best by looking at and working with pictures. You are probably really good at puzzles, imagining things, and reading maps and charts. You may need to use strategies like **mind mapping and webbing** to organize your information and study notes.

Kinaesthetic Learner: You may learn best by touching, moving, and figuring things out using manipulation. You are probably really good at physical activities and learning through movement. You may need to **draw your finger over a diagram** to remember it, **"tap out" the steps** needed to solve a problem, or **"feel" yourself writing** or typing a formula.

SCHEDULING STUDY TIME

You should review your class notes regularly to ensure that you have a clear understanding of all the new material you learned. Reviewing your lessons on a regular basis helps you to learn and remember ideas and concepts. It also reduces the quantity of material that you need to study prior to a test. Establishing a study schedule will help you to make the best use of your time.

Regardless of the type of study schedule you use, you may want to consider the following suggestions to maximize your study time and effort:

- Organize your work so that you begin with the most challenging material first.

- Divide the subject's content into small, manageable chunks.

- Alternate regularly between your different subjects and types of study activities in order to maintain your interest and motivation.

- Make a daily list with headings like "Must Do," "Should Do," and "Could Do."

- Begin each study session by quickly reviewing what you studied the day before.

- Maintain a routine of eating, sleeping, and exercising to help you concentrate better for extended periods of time.

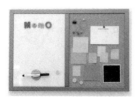

CREATING STUDY NOTES

MIND-MAPPING OR WEBBING

• Use the key words, ideas, or concepts from your reading or class notes to create a *mind map* or *web* (a diagram or visual representation of the given information). A mind map or web is sometimes referred to as a *knowledge map*.

• Write the key word, concept, theory, or formula in the centre of your page.

• Write down related facts, ideas, events, and information and then link them to the central concept with lines.

• Use coloured markers, underlining, or other symbols to emphasize important information, such as relationships between ideas or specific aspects of a timeline.

The following mind map is an example of an organization tool that could help you develop an essay:

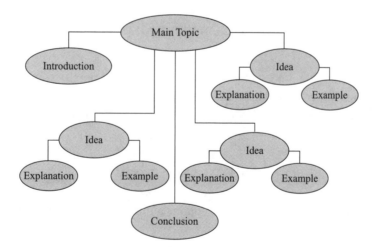

INDEX CARDS

To use index cards while studying, follow these steps:

- Write a key word or question on one side of an index card.

- On the reverse side, write the definition of the word, answer to the question, and any other important information that you want to remember.

> # What are synonyms?

> **What are synonyms?**
>
> Synonyms are words that have the same or almost the same meaning.
> E.g., coarse = rough

SYMBOLS AND STICKY NOTES—IDENTIFYING IMPORTANT INFORMATION

- Use symbols to mark your class notes. For example, an exclamation mark might be used to point out something that must be learned well because it is a very important idea. A question mark may highlight something that you are not certain about, and a diamond (◊) or asterisk (*) could highlight interesting information that you want to remember.

- Use sticky notes when you are not allowed to put marks in books.

- Use sticky notes to mark a page in a book that contains an important diagram, formula, explanation, etc.

- Use sticky notes to mark important facts in research books.

MEMORIZATION TECHNIQUES

- **ASSOCIATION** relates new learning to something you already know. For example, to remember the spelling difference between *dessert* and *desert*, recall that the word *sand* has only one -*s*. So, because there is sand in a desert, the word *desert* only has one -*s*.

- **MNEMONIC DEVICES** are sentences that you create to remember a list or group of items. For example, the first letter of each word in the phrase "**E**very **G**ood **B**oy **D**eserves **F**udge" helps you to remember the names of the lines on the treble clef staff (E, G, B, D, and F) in music.

- **ACRONYMS** are words that are formed from the first letters or parts of the words in a group. For example, *radar* is an actually acronym for <u>Ra</u>dio <u>D</u>etection <u>an</u>d <u>R</u>anging, and *MASH* is an acronym for <u>M</u>obile <u>A</u>rmy <u>S</u>urgical <u>H</u>ospital. **HOMES** helps you to remember the names of the five Great Lakes (**H**uron, **O**ntario, **M**ichigan, **E**rie, and **S**uperior).

- **VISUALIZING** requires you to use your mind's eye to imagine a chart, list, map, diagram, or sentence as it is in your textbook or notes, on the chalkboard or computer screen, or in a display.

- **INITIALISMS** are abbreviations that are formed from the first letters or parts of the words in a group. Unlike acronyms, initialisms cannot be pronounced as a word themselves. For example, IBM is an initialism for International Business Machines, and PRC is an initialism for the People's Republic of China..

KEY STRATEGIES FOR REVIEWING

Reviewing textbook material, class notes, and handouts should be an ongoing activity. Spending time reviewing becomes more critical when you are preparing for tests. You may find some of the following review strategies useful when studying during your scheduled study time.

- Before reading a selection, preview it by noting the headings, charts, graphs, and chapter questions.
- Read the complete introduction to identify the key information that is addressed in the selection.
- Read the first sentence of the next paragraph for the main idea.
- Skim the paragraph and make note of key words, phrases, and information.
- Read the last sentence of the paragraph.
- Repeat this process for each paragraph and section until you have skimmed the entire selection.

KEY STRATEGIES FOR SUCCESS: A CHECKLIST

Review, review, review: review is a huge part of doing well at school and preparing for tests. Here is a checklist for you to keep track of how many suggested strategies for success you are using. Read each question and then put a check mark (✓) in the correct column. Look at the questions where you have checked the "No" column. Think about how you might try using some of these strategies to help you do your best at school.

KEY Strategies for Success	Yes	No
Do you know your personal learning style—how you learn best?		
Do you spend 15 to 30 minutes a day reviewing your notes?		
Do you study in a quiet place at home?		
Do you clearly mark the most important ideas in your study notes?		
Do you use sticky notes to mark texts and research books?		
Do you practise answering multiple-choice and written-response questions?		
Do you ask your teacher for help when you need it?		
Are you maintaining a healthy diet and sleep routine?		
Are you participating in regular physical activity?		

Class Focus
Reading and Viewing

TABLE OF CORRELATIONS			
General Outcome	**Specific Outcome**	**Practice Questions**	**Unit Test**
B Reading and Viewing (Purpose)	B1 read, both collaboratively and independently, to comprehend a wide variety of literary text		
	B2 read, both collaboratively and independently, to comprehend a wide variety of information and persuasive texts with increasing complexity and subtlety of ideas and form		
	B3 view, both collaboratively and independently, to comprehend a variety of visual texts with increasing complexity and subtlety of ideas and form		
	B4 independently select and read, for sustained periods of time, texts for enjoyment and to increase fluency		
	B5 before reading and viewing, select, adapt, and apply a range of strategies to anticipate content and construct meaning		
	B6 during reading and viewing, select, adapt, and apply a range of strategies to construct, monitor, and confirm meaning	5, 7, 16, 22, 23, 24, 25, 26, 27, 29, 30, 34, 35, 36, 39, 44, 50	5, 6, 13, 14, 20, 27, 29, 30, 31, 34, 35
	B7 after reading and viewing, select, adapt, and apply a range of strategies to extend and confirm meaning, and to consider author's craft	2, 8, 38, 40, 42, 43	9, 11, 12, 16, 22, 24, 38, 40

B	Reading and Viewing (Thinking)	B8	explain and support personal responses to texts		
		B9	interpret, analyse, and evaluate ideas and information from texts	14, 18, 31, 37, 49	23, 28, 36, 39, 41, 42
		B10	synthesize and extend thinking about texts	17	19, 33, 37
		B11	use metacognitive strategies to reflect on and assess their reading and viewing		
B	Reading and Viewing (Features)	B12	recognize and explain how structures and features of text shape readers' and viewers' construction of meaning and appreciation of author's craft	1, 3, 4, 6, 9, 10, 11, 13, 19, 21, 28, 32, 41, 46, 47, 48	1, 2, 3, 4, 7, 8, 10, 15, 18, 21, 26, 32
		B13	demonstrate increasing work skills and vocabulary knowledge	12, 15, 20, 33, 45	17, 25

READING AND VIEWING

All forms of communication, be they seen, heard, or read, seek to impart information. The task of the effective viewer, listener, or reader is to apply a series of basic skill sets in order to extract, interpret, and evaluate the information received. Each of these communication modes conveys information in one of two general ways: directly, or explicitly, and indirectly, or implicitly. Of the two, directly revealed facts are easiest to extract. Information that is implied requires a greater degree of analysis or translation, which requires you to reason more carefully. Familiarizing yourself with the forms and techniques used in different types of communication is the first step to effective viewing and reading. Using a set of common strategies to interpret each form is the next essential step. For the purposes of this *KEY*, written text is the central form to be reviewed. However, you should keep in mind that all forms of communication seek to impart information: first by gaining the audience's attention and second by using a variety of techniques to maintain that attention while communicating the desired message. With that in mind, there are several basic strategies that any audience can apply when receiving information, and more specifically, while reading text.

What you do before starting to read can make or break your reading experience. First of all, decide what purpose your reading serves. Are you researching information for an essay? Answering questions for an assignment? Getting instructions for assembling a new bicycle? Escaping into the latest best-selling novel? Reading an advertisement for a product you are interested in purchasing? Deciding your purpose for reading will determine your attitude toward the text you read, the time you take to read it, the strategies you use to interpret that text, and what you do with the information you have taken from it. Having a purpose when reading is like having a road map when driving: once you know your destination, you can make use of a number of signposts along the way to help you reach your destination.

B1   read, both collaboratively and independently, to comprehend a wide variety of literary texts

LITERARY PROSE AND VERSE

ESTABLISHING A PURPOSE FOR READING

Unlike non-literary informational texts, which typically serve a practical purpose, the reading of literature is a leisure activity and as such is as a vehicle of entertainment and recreation. Mindful of this, some people argue that reading literature (fiction) is an impractical and time-consuming task. Of course, the same thing can be said of listening to music, watching television, looking at art, playing sports, viewing movies, or even sleeping. For what reason do people pursue any of these activities? The answer is simple. By participating in these supposed "useless activities," you are in one way or another recreating yourself and the world around you. Like most forms of recreation, the arts satisfy several basic human needs. They satisfy a hunger for self-expression, give a framework for ordering a seemingly random and confusing world, and often provide insight into what it means to be a human being. However, not all activities are equally beneficial, for there is a great difference between what you can gain from active as opposed to passive involvement. Just as the sports enthusiast derives a variety of physical, emotional, and intellectual rewards from playing the game he or she loves, the individual who chooses to read fiction rather than simply viewing it derives similar tangible benefits. The same cannot be said of the fan that sits on the sidelines and watches others play the game. Similarly, those who watch stories unfold on a television or movie screen restrict the imaginative process and in doing so, rob themselves of any significant growth and satisfaction.

Fiction or literary text falls into two main categories: prose and verse. Since each is approached somewhat differently, this section of this *KEY* will look first at verse forms and then discuss approaches to short stories and novels separately.

POETRY

Poets tackle the same "big ideas" that other forms of fiction address, but like graphic text, poetry is an abbreviated form of communication that requires you to be far more intuitive than you would be if you were reading prose. Because poetry is frequently written in fragmented syntax and employs figurative language, much is implied by the poet, who paints word pictures. As a result, you will need to develop your ability to infer—to reason by way of association. Poems come in a variety of forms and, like all things, have changed in form over time. Some generalizations can be made when comparing traditional verse forms with modern poetic forms.

Although any sort of strict categorization is likely to include exceptions, one might type poems of the 19th century and earlier as "traditional" and those written in the 20th century or later as "modern."

Traditional Verse—Traditional poetic techniques include rhythmic patterns, rhyme schemes, and closed structures. Examples of typical traditional verse forms are the sonnet, epic, ballad, and villanelle.

Modern Verse—Unlike the more restrictive traditional forms, modern verse is less encumbered by metric patterns and rhyme schemes. The modern poet is more likely to write in free verse and may develop his or her ideas in stanzas of irregular length, since modern poets seem to prefer working with an open structure rather than a closed one. Although any of the traditional forms can be used in modern poetry, the desire to follow a pre-determined pattern seems to be less important to modern poets. The lyric, a short poem that expresses the emotions or thoughts of a writer, is the most common type of modern poem you will study.

B5   *before reading and viewing, select, adapt, and apply a range of strategies to anticipate content and construct meaning*

B6   *during reading and viewing, select, adapt, and apply a range of strategies to anticipate content and construct meaning*

B7   *after reading and viewing, select, adapt, and apply a range of strategies to extend and confirm meaning, and to consider author's craft*

READING STRATEGIES

Reading poetry in some respects is the same as reading any other kind of text. Ideas can be developed through narration, description, exposition, or a combination of these styles. Once alerted to the style of development, you can anticipate the use of various techniques. You must also be aware of what you wish to take from the poem. Are you reading for enjoyment or is your purpose to study a passage to gain insight? Most students will initially read poetry as a course requirement rather than a form of entertainment, so the same steps taken when reading prose should be employed while reading poetry.

PRE-READING

- Remind yourself for what reason you are reading and preview the form of the poem you are about to read. Take note of any hints that may indicate whether the poem is a traditional or modern poem. Are the line lengths even or uneven? Are the stanzas uniform or irregular in line number? Has the poet used an unorthodox arrangement of text or varied font type or size?
- Note the name of the writer as well as the title of the poem. If you are familiar with the poet's work and era, you may have some idea of the poet's style and possible themes. The title of the poem will usually give you some idea of what the poem is about and may later play a role in determining the writer's theme. Look for allusions, or plays on words, that may provide you with some insight.

ACTIVE READING AND COMPREHENSION

- As you read the first few lines or stanzas, determine which of the developmental patterns the poet has chosen for his or her text (narrative, descriptive, expository) and note the writer's diction. Is it dated or current, simple or challenging? Has the writer employed a metric pattern or a rhyme scheme? Identify the speaker—the voice that conveys the ideas or tells the story. Note the poet's tone if it can be inferred from the speaker's comments. Note information that establishes the writer's subject, and refer back to the title for confirmation of any predicted pattern of idea development.
- Not all poetry rhymes, but nearly all poetry has strong rhythm. Finding the rhythm will allow you to read the poem as the writer intended it to be read. The rhythm will often provide clues to meaning, especially if the poet has used irregular syntax or complicated imagery.
- Take note of all punctuation marks that are used to direct the flow and meaning of ideas. Keep in mind that a line of poetry is not like a sentence. It may not contain a complete thought—that thought may spill over into the next line.
- As you work your way through the poem, look for methods of idea blocking. For example, stanzas are poetic units often used to build one idea upon another. They can also serve to frame contrasting ideas or to indicate shifts in time, space, or point of view. Highlight phrases that convey the main idea in each stanza or section of the poem.
- Read figurative language very carefully. The writer has fashioned these phrases to express a significant idea in a unique way. The writer wants you to visualize what he or she has imagined. Record your impressions of these idea blocks and comment on how each contributes to the writer's developing theme.
- As you approach the end of the poem, look for the poet to draw conclusions. These conclusions may contain a direct statement of the writer's theme or thoughts that lead you to an implied theme.

POST-READING: SYNTHESIS AND REFLECTION

- Review the poet's pattern of idea development and study the details the poet has used to make his or her point. Consider how each element of the unfolding pattern contributes to the whole (title, initial statements, idea blocks, figurative language, concluding statements).
- If the theme has not been stated directly, state what you believe the writer has implied, and review the details you have noted to determine whether they confirm your interpretation.
- Taking into consideration your interpretation of the poem, whatever you know about the poet, and the era in which it was written, evaluate the worth of the passage. What effect has the poem had on you? Do you agree or disagree with any assertions the poet has made? Are the ideas or sentiments outdated or still useful?
- Consider what conditions (historical, social or personal) may have influenced the poet or motivated the poet to express his or her particular theme. Consider other poems on the same theme and compare them.

B8   *explain and support personal responses to texts*

B9   *interpret, analyse, and evaluate ideas and information from texts*

B10   *synthesize and extend thinking about texts*

SKILLS APPLICATION

The poem "That time of year thou may'st in me behold" written by William Shakespeare is a good example of a traditional poem. Read it and consider the accompanying notes, which model a reader's response.

SONNET VIII

That time of year thou may'st in me behold
When yellow leaves, or none, or few, do hang
Upon those boughs which shake against the cold-
Bare ruin'd choirs where late the sweet birds sang,
In me thou see'st the twilight of such day
As after Sunset fadeth in the West,
Which by and by black night doth take away,
Death's second self, that seals up all in rest.
In me thou see'st the glowing of such fire
That on the ashes of his youth doth lie,
As the death-bed whereon it must expire,
Consumed with that which it was nourish'd by.
     This thou perceiv'st, which makes thy love more strong
     To love that well which thou must leave ere long

—*by* William Shakespeare

Sample Notes for "That Time of Year Thou May'st in Me Behold"

Pre-Reading Notes

- Since the writer is Shakespeare, archaic word choices will appear in this text.
- The poem is 14 lines long and as such is a sonnet—closed form.
- Shakespeare's syntax is Elizabethan in style and therefore convoluted or irregular when compared with modern phrasing. Subject/verb placement is typically reversed to facilitate end rhymes.
- Shakespeare uses familiar subjects to develop his imagery.
- Shakespeare's sonnets are written in iambic pentameter.
- The sonnet form has a standard rhyme scheme.
- The traditional sonnet is divided into an 8 line octave followed by a 6 line sestet.
- The octave typically raises an issue, and the sestet draws a conclusion.
- There is a break in the arrangement of text: the last two lines have been deliberately indented, perhaps to signal their importance.

Active Reading and Comprehension Notes

- The title of this poem is the opening line.
- The word *mayst* is the archaic form of *may*.
- The first four lines make up one full sentence: "You may see in me the time of year when very few if any yellow leaves hang onto branches and struggle against the cold that has forced the song birds to migrate to a warmer climate."
- The writer is referring to autumn, the season when trees shed their leaves and brace for winter. This season is likened to the time in the speaker's life when he is losing his youthful vitality.
- The four seasons are representative of life's stages: spring—birth/childhood, summer —youth and young adulthood, autumn—maturity/age, and winter—old age/death.
- The rhyme scheme in the first four lines is abab, and the metre in each line is iambic pentameter.
- Shakespeare is using both description and exposition to develop his poem. The speaker, possibly Shakespeare himself, is describing what someone sees in him (perhaps a close friend or wife).
- The phrase, "In me thou see'st" is repeated and consequently connects the first 12 lines of the poem.
- What is seen is a gradual weakening of vitality, and this diminishing life force is captured in three common images: the leafless autumn trees, the fading daylight at dusk, and the fading embers of a fire that is all but burnt out.
- The forth line in each successive image comments on the age the speaker has chosen to describe:
  - "bare ruined choirs" suggests a loss of harmony and happiness at that age
  - "death's second self" suggests that death, like sleep, is part of a natural cycle
  - "consumed with that which it was nourished by" suggests that by living, the very life force one associates with youth consumes the life it enjoys
- The last two lines of the poem draw a conclusion about what the viewer apparently understands about the age in question: "You understand this and consequently love me more deeply now since you realize I will not be with you much longer."
- "This" refers back to the diminishing life force, which is exemplified by each of the three central images.

Post-Reading Notes

- The poem, like a dramatic monologue, appears to be addressing a loved one who is being told why he or she apparently loves the speaker more strongly now than ever before.
- By telling a loved one what motivates him or her to love, the speaker seems self-centered, immodest, and presumptuous.
- Despite the speaker's immodest tone, the poem hits upon a truth: people seem to appreciate and love far more fervently that which they are about to lose than they do when the subject of their affections remains unthreatened.
- Shakespeare's use of natural cycles like the changing of seasons and the daily cycle of day to night to day suggests that death is part of a grand design that you should not fear.
- What Shakespeare wrote about in the late 15th and early 16th century is as useful to people today as it would have been when he first penned this sonnet.
- The use of a closed-form poem is effective because it reinforces the notion of harmony within the life cycle and the limits placed upon life on Earth (both themes that Shakespeare touches upon in this poem).

METRICAL OR TRADITIONAL POETRY

The elements of the rhythm of metrical poetry, such as sonnets, should be understood. Recall how dictionary words are divided into syllables and how the stressed syllables are marked with accents: re·mem'·ber, com'·men·tar·y.[1] In metrical poetry, the regular alternation of stressed and unstressed syllables produces the regular rhythm. The rhythm of poetry is called *metre*, and a unit of rhythm is called a *foot*.

Certain metrical feet have names. Here are the two most common names and some single-word examples for each.

> iambic foot: unstressed, stressed (to day', ab stain', re cruit', re turn')
> trochaic foot: stressed, unstressed (coun' ter, chem' ist, wick' er, sim' ple)

A line of metrical poetry is usually made up of a fixed number of feet. Thus, a poem written in iambic pentameter has lines of five iambs. (Recall that *penta* means five and that an iamb has two syllables. Thus, each line usually has ten syllables.) Because poets pattern words into a regular rhythm, that rhythm can be indicated with stress marks above syllables: a "—" above an unaccented syllable (weak stress) and a "/" above an accented syllable (strong stress). Such a careful examination of the rhythm of a poem is called *scansion*.

Here are two lines of Shakespeare's blank verse (unrhymed iambic pentameter).

> Why, what a candy deal of courtesy
> This fawning greyhound then did proffer me![2]

Notice the use of *candy* as an adjective to modify *deal* (quantity, amount). This is Shakespeare being free with his parts of speech.

Here are the same lines scanned (marked to show the metrical feet).

—	/	—	/—	/	—	/—
Why	**what**	a	**can**dy	**deal**	of	**court**esy
1	2	3	4–5	6	7	8–9–10

—	/—	/—	/	—	/—	/
This	**fawn**ing	**grey**hound	**then**	did	**pro**ffer	**me!**
1	2–3	4–5	6	7	8–9	10

Notice that the last two syllables of the first line are unstressed. Iambic pentameter is very forgiving of slight variations. In fact, poets often add slight variations deliberately so as to avoid monotony.

FREE VERSE

Free verse also contains rhythm, although it is not as regular. Here is a short poem by Walt Whitman. Try reading it aloud. Notice the definite, but irregular, rhythm. This kind of rhythm is sometimes called *cadence*, and it is closer to ordinary speech than is the regular rhythm of Shakespeare's blank verse.

WHEN I HEARD THE LEARN'D ASTRONOMER

When I heard the learn'd astronomer,
When the proofs, the figures, were ranged in columns before me,
When I was shown the charts and diagrams, to add, divide, and measure them,
When I sitting heard the astronomer where he lectured with much applause in the lecture-room,
How soon unaccountable I became tired and sick,
Till rising and gliding out I wander'd off by myself,
In the mystical moist night-air, and from time to time,
Look'd up in perfect silence at the stars.

—*by* Walt Whitman

Notice how Whitman turns the two-syllable word *learned* into the one syllable word *learn'd*. In writing free verse, Whitman is just as careful with rhythm as Shakespeare, only his rhythms are different. When reading free verse, read with the rhythm and "hear" how it contributes to the poet's intention. In this example, lines 3 to 5 are long and written with a repetitive rhythm that echoes Whitman's boredom and dislike. The rhythms of the concluding lines change as the speaker escapes from the lecture room.

Be aware that some poetry can only be recognized by the arrangement of lines. Some poetry reads exactly like prose that has been cut up into irregular pieces. Work with the poetic imagery in such poems.

The poem, "Before Two Portraits of my Mother" by Emile Nelligan provides an interesting contrast to Shakespeare's sonnet. Nelligan, a French-Canadian poet writing at the beginning of the 20th century, also addresses the subject of aging, but unlike Shakespeare, he uses a more open version of the traditional sonnet. Read the poem and its accompanying notes and consider the questions that follow.

---

[1] The second example has primary and secondary stress. Both may be regarded simply as stressed syllables.
[2] from *Henry IV Part I.*

BEFORE TWO PORTRAITS OF MY MOTHER

I love the beautiful young girl of this
Portrait, my mother, painted years ago
When her forehead was white, and there was no
Shadow in the dazzling Venetian glass
Of her gaze. But this other likeness shows
The deep trenches across her forehead's white
Marble. The rose poem of her youth that
Her marriage sang is far behind. Here is
My sadness: I compare these portraits, one
Of a joy-radiant brow, the other care-
Heavy: sunrise—and the thick coming on
Of night. And yet how strange my ways appear,
For when I look at these faded lips my heart
Smiles, but at the smiling girl my tears start.

—by Emile Nelligan

Sample Notes for "Before Two Portraits of My Mother"

Pre-Reading Notes

- The title suggests a comparison will be made between the two pictures.
- The poem's stanzas are not uniform, although there is a clear pattern: the first two stanzas are comprised of four lines, while the last two stanzas are comprised of three lines each. The total number of lines is 14—a sonnet form.
- Perhaps the stanza groupings are designed to reflect a difference between the two pictures or suggest some form of diminishment, which is reflected in the movement from four lines to three.

Active Reading and Comprehension Notes

- The first stanza introduces a phrasing structure more typical of prose than the more fragmented style of poetry. The lines are incomplete and flow into each other; there is no attempt to terminate a thought at the end of a line or stanza.
- The first stanza contains several images: the mother's self-portrait is the central image, while her forehead, one element of the portrait, is further described as "white," showing "no shadow," and her gaze is likened to "dazzling Venetian glass." Each of these images associated with the "beautiful young girl" is positive. The colour white is associated with purity and innocence, the lack of "shadows" also suggests a lightness or goodness, and the comparison of her gaze to "Venetian glass" suggests a kind of beauty associated with a much-valued and famous product.
- The second stanza introduces the anticipated comparison with the word *but*, which signals a change in the flow of thought. The imagery used here is clearly negative. The phrase "deep trenches" used to describe the mother's wrinkles is hyperbolic, as it brings to mind something far larger and more disfiguring than "age lines." Similarly, the expression "white marble" alters the purity of the white mentioned in the preceding stanza and suggests a blotchy or grainy appearance created by age spots, which are far less flattering than clear, youthful skin.

- The observation that her youth, likened to a "rose poem," is "far behind her" clearly states that she has lost her beauty (the rose poem of her youth), which was celebrated in her happy marriage ("her marriage sang"). Here, the rose and the song are both used as contrasting images to the negative images at the beginning of the stanza.

- Note that stanzas three and four (two stanzas involving reflection) are only three lines long, and each begins with a far "darker" word choice than that which began stanzas one and two ("my sadness" and "of night"). It would appear that stanza length reflects a change in thought process (observation to evaluation).

- The third stanza (including the bleeding into stanza four) clarifies the difference between the two portraits, both literally and figuratively. The youthful image has a "joy-radiant brow" and is likened to sunrise, while the aged image has a "care-heavy" expression and is likened to "the thick coming on of night."

- The last stanza of the poem reveals the speaker's thoughts, having compared the young with the old. He expresses a degree of ambivalence or confusion after having viewed both portraits. The portrait of his aging mother brings him joy ("my heart smiles"), but the portrait of his mother as a young girl makes him cry ("but at the smiling girl my tears start").

- The concluding stanza raises a question—why would a son be touched by one picture of his mother but be saddened by the other? If the pattern established in Shakespeare's sonnet has been used in this "modern sonnet," the answer to this question likely reveals the writer's theme.

Post-Reading Notes

- The writer has used contrasting images to compare his mother's appearance as a youth to her appearance as an aging woman.

- The portrait of his aging mother brings a smile to his face, while the portrait of her as a youth brings tears. This suggests that he is closer to his aging mother since she has sacrificed far more for him than her "youthful self."

- Alternatively, he cries when he sees the youthful image because he is forced to accept the fact that she is growing older and will inevitably die. The picture of the aging mother might also suggest a life of struggle that the son appreciates only after looking at her youthful face.

- The reader might draw his or her own conclusions: life is fleeting, so one must savor whatever form it takes. Youth and age are all the same—a time to appreciate the existence people have.

Study Questions: "That Time of Year" and "Before Two Portraits of My Mother"

When answering questions on these and subsequent poems, collaborate with one or more students in order to compare and discuss differences in interpretation and emotional response to text.

1. Compare the syllabic formation in the first stanza of each poem. Does each stanza employ iambic pentameter?

2. Is Nelligan's use of "bleeding lines," lack of rhyme scheme, and incomplete thought development within his stanzas more or less effective than Shakespeare's more rigid form? Explain. For what reason is the phrase "the rose poem of her youth" an effective metaphor?

3. Nelligan uses contrasting images, while Shakespeare's imagery is uniform. What are the advantages and disadvantages of using contrasting imagery?

4. Explain the paradox Shakespeare creates when he writes, "Consumed with that which it was nourished by."

5. Use the Internet to research Emile Nilligan's life, and determine whether there was any special reason for his feeling as he does while viewing two portraits that frame his mother's life.

IRONY IN POETRY

While most of the poems studied to this point develop their themes in an unequivocal or straightforward manner, poets can also put on an ironic mask, which allows the writer to pretend to champion one belief while actually supporting its opposite. The writer creates this incongruity by expressing the thoughts of a speaker whose beliefs are contrary to those which the poet wishes expressed.

The poetry question on the provincial exam consists of two types of questions: a short answer, multiple-choice set and a paragraph-response question. The series of multiple-choice questions tests your knowledge of stylistic techniques, literary devices, and comprehension of both literal and implied meanings within the text.

DRAMATIC VERSE (SHAKESPEARE'S PLAYS)

A play is a story told through action and dialogue that is brought to life by actors performing on a stage. Like novels and short stories, the elements of a drama include characters, setting, plot, mood, and theme. However, the essential difference between plays and texts is that a play is written by a playwright to be performed by actors on a stage in front of an audience.

A play's four essential elements of expression, plot, character, and theme make up the play's structure and are always presented through the action and dialogue (the conversation among the characters). Setting is alternatively presented through dialogue or exposition, the process by which the playwright lets the audience know the type of play being presented (tragedy, comedy, etc.), the setting (time and place), the leading characters, and the situations and conflicts in which the leading characters find themselves. For example, the prologues that begin some of Shakespeare's plays directly provide needed background information at the beginning of the play.

Example

—*from* the prologue to *Romeo and Juliet*

Two households, both alike in dignity,
In fair Verona, where we lay our scene,
From ancient grudge break to new mutiny,
Where civil blood makes civil hands unclean.
From forth the fatal loins of these two foes
A pair of star-crossed lovers take their life;
Whose misadventured piteous overthrows
Doth with their death bury their parents' strife.
The fearful passage of their death-marked love,
And the continuance of their parents' rage,
Which, but their children's end, naught could remove,
Is now the two hours' traffic of our stage;
The which of you with patient ears attend,
What here shall miss, our toil shall strive to mend.

In *Hamlet*, the setting and background information are presented indirectly through the dialogue between several guards and Horatio, who has been invited onto the platform to bare witness to the existence of a ghost. In this way the audience of Shakespeare's day was responsible for creating the scene suggested by a dialogue laced with imagery.

Example

Marcellus conjures up the image of a city frantically arming itself in preparation for war:

—*from Hamlet*

Good now, sit down, and tell me, he that knows,
Why this same strict and most observant watch
So nightly toils the subject of the land,

And why such daily cast of brazen cannon,
And foreign mart for implements of war,
Why such impress of shipwrights, whose sore task
Does not divide the Sunday from the week,
What might be toward, that this sweaty haste
Doth make the night joint-labourer with the day:
Who is't that can inform me?

By requiring the audience to imagine what could not be easily presented (constantly changing sets, lavish costumes, and special effects), Shakespeare relied on the power of imagery to bring his plays to life. It is his ability to paint such powerful "word pictures" that makes his plays powerful, poetic, but problematic for a modern audience used to having everything brought to life for them. The Shakespearean drama is as much a play to be heard as it is a play to be seen, for in the verse, the words bring the play to life. The audience can fully feel a character's passion only if they can appreciate Shakespeare's poetry. For example, after hearing the news of his wife's death, Macbeth summarizes his attitude toward life and in doing so, invites his audience to relate to his dejected state.

Example

MacBeth, Act V, scene 5—**Macbeth to Seyton**

She should have died hereafter:
There would have been a time for such a word.
To-morrow, and to-morrow, and to-morrow,
Creeps in this petty pace from day to day,
To the last syllable of recorded time;
And all our yesterdays have lighted fools
The way to dusty death. Out, out brief candle!
Life's but a walking shadow, a poor player
That struts and frets his hour upon the stage,
And then is heard no more; it is a tale
Told by an idiot, full of sound and fury,
Signifying nothing.

The verse in Shakespeare's plays also provides character insight that is frequently noted by a narrator in short stories or novels. Here again, the use of figurative language requires the audience to listen carefully in order to accurately conjure up the character being described.

Example

Julius Caesar, Act I, scene 2—**Caesar to Antony**

Yond Cassius has a lean and hungry look.
He thinks too much. Such men are dangerous.
…He reads much,
He is a great observer, and he looks
Quite through the deeds of men. He loves no plays

As thou dost Antony; he hears no music.
Such men as he be never at heart's ease
Whiles they behold a greater than themselves,
And therefore are they very dangerous.

Another technique used by the dramatist to reveal character is the soliloquy, which allows a character to expose aspects of his or her own character as well as those of others. When reading or viewing any Shakespeare play, you are well advised to study with care each of these speeches, for they are focal points used as vehicles of insight into character and theme. For example, in Act III, scene 3 of *Hamlet*, Claudius is found struggling with his conscience as he attempts to pray for forgiveness for killing his brother. The audience is treated to a powerful moment of insight, for Claudius reveals himself to be sensitive, morally aware, but pragmatic. He also acknowledges his faith and the inevitability of divine judgment. Trapped as he is, you are moved to feel some sympathy for him.

Example

Hamlet, Act III, scene 3—King Claudius to himself

O! My offence is rank, it smells to heaven;
It hath the primal eldest curse upon't;
A brother's murder! Pray can I not,
Though inclination be as sharp as will:
My stronger guilt defeats my strong intent;
And like a man to double business bound,
I stand in pause where I shall first begin,
And both neglect. What if this cursed hand
Were thicker than itself with brother's blood,
Is there not rain enough in the sweet heavens
To wash it white as snow? Whereto serves mercy
But to confront the visage of offence?
And what's in prayer but this two-fold force,
To be forestalled, ere we come to fall,
Or pardon'd, being down? Then I'll look up;
My fault is past. But, O! what form of prayer
Can serve my turn? 'Forgive me my foul murder?'
That cannot be since I am still possess'd
Of those effects for which I did the murder,
My crown, mine own ambition, and my queen.
May one be pardoned and retain the offence?
In the corrupted currents of this world
Offence's gilded hand may shove by justice,
And oft 'tis seen the wicked prize itself
Buys out the law; but 'tis not so above;
There is no shuffling, there the action lies
In his true nature, and we ourselves compell'd
Even to the teeth and forehead of our faults
To give in evidence.

Each of Shakespeare's plays is comprised of five acts that, like chapters in a novel or stanzas in a poem, contribute to your understanding of plot, character, and above all, theme. Be mindful that the repetition of selected images is also used to reinforce theme. For example, Hamlet's first soliloquy likens his environment to an "unweeded garden." This metaphor initiates a series of similar images of corruption and decay that remind you that Hamlet, the tragic hero, also has flaws that will bring about his downfall. In this way, the play is like an elaborate poem filled with rich imagery designed to drive home the playwright's theme. Note also that the last act of the play, like the concluding stanza of a poem, contains either explicit or implicit theme statements. For example, although Hamlet struggles with his own inability to act decisively through much of the play, by the final act, he has arrived at the understanding that one does not need to take on life alone; there is a higher power that arbitrates between warring foes and ultimately has the last word. This is made clear in two speeches by Hamlet, both spoken to his confidante, Horatio, near the end of the play.

Examples

Hamlet, Act V, scene 2

Hamlet explains to Horatio what moved him to discover the letters carried by Rosencrantz and Guildenstern.

> Sir, in my heart there was a kind of fighting
> That would not let me sleep; methought I lay
> Worse than the mutines in the bilboes[3]. Rashly,-
> And prais'd be rashness for it, let us know,
> Our indiscretions sometimes serves us well
> When our deep plots do pall; and that should teach us
> There's a divinity that shapes our ends,
> Rough-hew them how we will.

Hamlet, Act V, scene 2

In response to Horatio's concern that Hamlet not get involved in a duel with Laertes, Hamet responds by saying

> ...we defy augury[4]; there's a special
> Providence in the fall of a sparrow. If it[5] be now,
> 'tis not to come; if it be not to come, it will be now;
> If it be not now, yet it will come; the readiness is all.

---

[3] mutineers imprisoned in chains.
[4] omens.
[5] death.

Skills Application: Dramatic Verse

Study each of the following play extracts collaboratively and discuss how various poetic techniques have been used to convey the character of both the speaker and the individual described.

Julius Caesar, Act II, scene 1

Brutus, in soliloquy, considers the character of Caesar.

> He would be crowned.
> How that might change his nature, there's the question.
> It is the bright day that brings forth the adder,
> And that craves wary walking. Crown him that
> And then I grant we put a sting in him
> That at his will he may do danger with.
> Th'abuse of greatness is, when it disjoins
> Remorse from power. But 'tis common proof
> That lowliness is young ambition's ladder,
> Whereto the climber upward turns his face;
> But when he once attains the upmost round,
> He then unto the ladder turns his back,
> Looks in the clouds, scorning the base degrees
> By which he did ascend. So Caesar may,
> Then lest he may, prevent. And since the quarrel
> Will bear no colour for the thing he is,
> Fashion it thus: that what he is, augmented,
> Would run to these and these extremities;
> And therefore think him as a serpent's egg,
> Which, hatched, would as his kind grow mischievous
> And kill him in the shell.

Hamlet, Act III, scene 3

Hamlet describes Claudius while criticizing his mother's choice of second husband.

Hamlet   This was your husband: look you now, what follows,
    Here is your husband; like a mildew'd ear[6],
    Blasting the wholesome brother. Have you eyes?
    Could you on this fair mountain leave to feed,
    And batten on this moor? Have you eyes?

    …

Queen   O Hamlet! Speak to me no more;
    Thou turns't mine eyes into my very soul;

    …

Hamlet   A murderer and a villain;
    A slave that is not twentieth part the tithe
    Of your precedent lord; a vice of kings;
    A cut-purse of the empire…
    A king of shreds and patches –

---

[6] ear of corn.

Taming of the Shrew, Act IV, scene 3

Petruchio explains to his wife Kate how her character is **best** defined.

Well, come, my Kate; we will unto your father's
Even in these honest mean habiliments[7]:
Our purses shall be proud, our garments poor;
For 'tis the mind that makes the body rich;
And as the sun breaks through the darkest clouds,
So honour peereth in the meanest habit.
What, is the jay more precious than the lark,
Because his feathers are more beautiful?
Or is the adder better than the eel,
Because his painted skin contents the eye?
On no, good Kate; neither art thou the worse
For this poor furniture and mean array.
If you account'st it shame, lay it on me.

Macbeth, Act III, scene 1

Macbeth lectures one of his murderers on what it means to be called a "man."

Ay, in the catalogue ye go for men;
As hounds and greyhounds, mongrels, spaniels, curs,
Shoughs, water-rugs[8], and demi-wolves, are clept
All by the name of dogs; the valu'd file
Distinguishes the swift, the slow, the subtle,
The housekeeper, the hunter, every one
According to the gift which bounteous nature
Hath in him clos'd; whereby he does receive
Particular addition, from the bill
That writes them all alike: and so of men.
Now, if you have a station in the file,
Not i' the worst rank of manhood, say it;

---

[7] simple clothes.
[8] shaggy-haired dogs and rough water dogs.

Romeo and Juliet, Act II, scene 3

Friar Laurence describes Romeo's changing nature.

Holy Saint Francis! What a change is here!
Is Rosaline, that thou dids't love so dear,
So soon forsaken? Young men's love then lies
Not truly in their hearts, but in their eyes.
Jesu Maria! What a deal of brine
Hath washed thy sallow cheeks for Rosaline!
How much salt water thrown away in waste
To season love, that of it doth not taste!
The sun not yet thy sights from heaven clears,
Thy old groans ring yet in mine ancient ears.
Lo, here upon thy cheek the stain doth sit
Of an old tear that is not washed off yet.
If e'er thou wast thyself, and these woes thine,
Thou and these woes were all for Rosaline.
And thou art changed?

FICTIONAL PROSE

THE SHORT STORY AND NOVEL

There is no frigate like a book
To take us lands away,
Nor any coursers like a page
Of prancing poetry:
This traverse may the poorest take
Without oppress of toil;
How frugal is the chariot
That bears the human soul

—*by* Emily Dickinson (1830–1886)

A RATIONALE FOR READING LITERATURE

The intent of literature is to present the reader with values, perspectives, and world views in a way that invites engagement, interpretation, discussion, and comparison. While values are invisible, they are based on beliefs and principles that influence your perspective or point of view on the experiences of your life, on the issues you encounter, and, consequently, the way you view the world. Your world view influences your judgments as well as your feelings toward and treatment of others. Consequently, literature, like life, is an arena of values, perspectives, and world views revealed in the narration of writers, description of settings, and motivation of characters. Characters in literature often become a "voice" for beliefs, perspectives, and world views, and their stories offer you the opportunity to explore your own actions, thoughts, and feelings while reading about others. Analytic skills will develop as you explore and assess ideas, themes, concepts, and arguments. However, it is worth noting at the outset that all elements of a narrative contribute to its theme or the controlling idea, as is indicated in the following diagram.

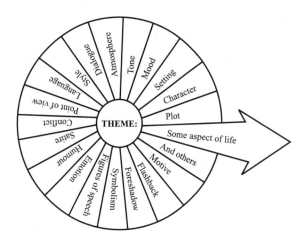

Another consideration worth noting is the prevalence of universal themes in literature. Some frequently-encountered universal themes include

- the fear of the unknown
- the struggle between good and evil
- the desire for meaningful relationships
- the desire for understanding and the search for truth
- the desire to control our environment
- the struggle to meet challenges or overcome adversity

The fact that universal themes recur contributes to the enduring appeal of cross-cultural and classical literature. Charles Dickens' novel *Oliver Twist*, for example, addresses the theme of good struggling against evil. In the novel, written approximately 200 years ago, various aspects contribute to the theme.

Consider some of the following aspects from *Oliver Twist*:

Setting

The dark, dank workhouse environment, the dark, closed casket where Oliver hides at Sowerberry's undertaking establishment, and the dark, seamy underbelly of criminal London contrast sharply with the airy open windows of Mr. Brownlow's home looking out over the sunny square bustling with legitimate human endeavours and business.

Character

The novel is filled with contrasting good and evil characters, most notably Bill Sikes, who represents the very epitome of evil, and Oliver's gracious and benevolent grandfather, Mr. Brownlow.

Mood

The mood of suspense and foreboding that lurks in the deep shadows of the London Bridge at night contrasts with the mood of salvation and anticipation evident in Mr. Brownlow's hurrying steps as he hastens toward his fateful meeting with Nancy.

Conflict

In the climactic struggle under the bridge, evil seems to temporarily triumph over good, as Bill Sikes takes Nancy's life in a fit of rage.

Plot

Many of the episodes comprising the rising action of the novel reflect the theme of good versus evil: the old nurse stealing the locket from Oliver's mother, the struggle for fair treatment in the workhouse that climaxes in Oliver asking for more food, the struggles at the undertaker's, and Fagin's constant indecision between good intentions and his profitable but evil lifestyle.

Point of View

The omniscient narrative viewpoint allows the revelation of the ongoing struggle between good and evil to be revealed through character perspectives, including Nancy's gradual transformation from cynical exploiter (evil) to heroic saviour (good).

Foreshadowing

Bill Sikes' threats against Nancy foreshadow the evil outcome that will result from her courageous choice, while the ironic surrender of a small gold locket to Mr. Brownlow by the greedy Bumbles foreshadows the golden outcome that lies ahead for Oliver.

If you refer back to the theme diagram, you will see that other elements of the narrative also contribute to the universal theme underlying the novel.

Reading Strategies

The reading strategies already mentioned in the study of non-literary text, poetry, and dramatic verse can be applied to the study of short literary fiction (short stories) and novels. However, a quick examination of a writer's biography can be an essential first step when reading any assigned piece of literature. Context and background can provide more information than just the meaning of a word. Remember that context is background information, knowledge, and ideas—anything needed or helpful for understanding. For example, you may wish to know the following about any piece of literature:

- Who was the intended audience?
- What was the writer's purpose in writing?
- When was the piece written?
- Where was the writer living?
- What were the issues of the time period?
- Who is speaking?

B2   read, both collaboratively and independently, to comprehend a wide variety of informational and persuasive texts with increasing complexity and subtlety of ideas and form

B5   before reading and viewing, select, adapt, and apply a range of strategies to anticipate content and construct meaning

B6   during reading and viewing, select, adapt, and apply a range of strategies to anticipate content and construct meaning

B7   after reading and viewing, select, adapt, and apply a range of strategies to extend and confirm meaning, and to consider the author's craft

INFORMATIONAL TEXTS

TYPES OF TEXTS

Since individuals communicate for different reasons—to inform, to persuade, or to entertain, for example—the form and style of text will differ according to the writer's purpose. The following categories are the usual forms of informational text, and each has its unique characteristics.

Exposition—Exposition is writing designed to explain and is used wherever individuals wish to impart information. Magazine articles, newspaper articles, essays, and technical reports are common types of expository writing. In form, expository writing begins by stating its thesis or topic, and then, through a series of supporting ideas, develops the central thesis in subsequent related paragraphs. This type of text is more likely to use evidence and logic.

Persuasion—Persuasion is writing designed to "win over" or convince and is used wherever differences in ideas or feelings compete. Political speeches, critical essays, letters to the editor, and advertisements are common examples of persuasive writing. In form, persuasion, like exposition, begins by establishing a thesis or position and then develops that thesis by providing supportive arguments. This type of text is more likely to include a combination of logic, analogy, statistics, satire, and emotional appeals, which come in the form of loaded language.

Narration—Narration is writing designed to tell a story. Narration can be used like exposition to inform people of a series of events and may also be used either to entertain or teach. Essays, newspaper articles, historical accounts, and travelogues are typical forms of narration. Unlike exposition or persuasion, the form of narration follows a plot that is structured by time and typically involves characters who bring the plot to life. Paragraph structure in this type of writing is controlled by shifts in point of view, time, and plot occurrences.

Description—Description is writing designed to tell how something looks—to freeze it in time. Although all forms of writing usually contain descriptive details, the purpose of description is to have the reader see and/or feel what the writer has experienced. It can be either clinical or factual, as one might find in a scientific report describing the Moon's surface, or it could be a far more artful description of a beautiful scene whereby the writer attempts to translate his or her impressions and create a mood through the use of imagery. Unlike narration, it is organized by space rather than time and makes use of a variety of rhetorical techniques. Paragraph structure is more likely controlled by shifts in spatial point of view.

Graphic Text—Graphic text is writing combined with some type of graphic. At one level it can be a simple form, such as tables, charts, and graphs, which are designed to group information in order to facilitate quick comprehension of factual information. At a more sophisticated level, graphic text adds cartoons, diagrams, drawings, and photographs to written text as aids in communicating both thoughts and feelings. Since pictures can suggest a variety of interpretations, the reading of this type of graphic text requires the reader to interpret connotative language and implicit suggestions associated with the picture or diagram.

READING STRATEGIES

Since reading text is usually a voluntary activity, the reader, anticipating the task, has time to make plans before reading, to employ some previously selected strategies during the reading process, and to take the time to reflect on what he or she has read after reading. The following suggestions are a sample of the types of strategies you can employ at each of these three basic stages.

Pre-Reading

- Remind yourself what you are reading for and preview the type of text you are about to read by taking note of headings, titles, footnotes, the writer's name, the date of publication, reference to the source of the passage (newspaper, novel, journal, essay, etc.), accompanying graphs, diagrams, or pictures and any associated captions. From any of these elements, you may gain some sense of the writer's topic, tone, thesis, or bias.

- Always try to build on your background knowledge (previous understanding and experiences) to help you understand what you are about to read. Is there anything in the material you have scanned that provides you with insight? For example, by determining what type of text it is, you can anticipate the format or method of development the writer will use. Similarly, reading other works by the same writer may give you insight into his or her themes, biases, and writing style. Noting a date and country of origin may provide you with some idea of the trends associated with that place or period of history. A title frequently suggests the writer's tone and reveals the focus of the passage. If you are familiar with the subject you are about to read, ask yourself what you already know about the topic and reflect on any feelings or thoughts you may have about that topic.

Active Reading and Comprehension

- Carefully read the opening paragraph, first few sentences, or an identifiable section of the piece, and note the writer's method of gaining the reader's attention and the writer's thesis or purpose for writing. Although this may not always appear at the beginning of every type of writing, in most informational texts (non-fiction) and frequently in works of fiction, the writer provides his or her readers with some idea of what issues he or she plans to develop. If the thesis is clearly stated, highlight the key words in the sentence. If no thesis is clearly stated, make your own notation in the margin predicting or guessing where you think the passage will go.

- As you move through the text, underline or highlight the building blocks or supporting details that the writer uses to develop his or her central thesis. These may or may not be signaled earlier in the passage. For example, a writer may state that "there are four good reasons to get daily exercise." If they are not formally announced, they may be introduced by signal words or transitional expressions, such as "The first reason for daily exercise is…" followed by "Another effective way to take care of your health…."

- Note each paragraph shift, and ask yourself what added information is provided by each of these building blocks. Watch also for transition words that may signal a change in the writer's thought flow.

- As you come across style elements, such as conventional descriptive details, figurative language, statistical information, italicization, underlining, or other printing techniques, try to determine the reason such techniques have been used. What does each element add to the writer's purpose? Always keep in mind that nothing appears in a crafted text unintentionally. The smart reader is always asking the question, "For what reason is this here?"

- Take time to visualize what the writer has taken the trouble to describe. Although it is a cliché, "a picture is worth a thousand words." That is the reason writers employ imagery. Take the time to construct the picture in your own head and attempt to explain the reason that associated image has been used.

- When you come across unfamiliar vocabulary, attempt to find meaning for it by either looking for context clues or what the word might mean considering the general meaning of the sentence in which it is found. Additionally, you might find the word's meaning by studying the word form—prefix, base, and suffix meanings—that may be familiar to you.

- Monitor for meaning by continually checking your understanding of the material that you read. Think about whether or not the text makes sense to you, and think about the broader meaning of the passage as it unfolds in your mind.

- Active reading means that you should always employ critical thinking skills while reading any text. For example, you may on one level judge the writer's clarity. Is the passage easily read or confusing because of unnecessarily difficult vocabulary? Is the writer's style dry or engaging? Do you agree with the central thesis? Are any of the supporting details vague, contentious, or poorly phrased? Never read without questioning a writer's motives for writing or the worth of the text he or she has produced.

- You should make inferences or educated guesses, associated meanings, or assumptions about the writer and the text. You can make inferences by combining your background knowledge and the information in the text to create meaning beyond what is directly stated in the text. Inferences may include predictions, conclusions, or insights that the writer has only implied.

- Record key definitions, predictions, patterns, questions, and insights somewhere on the document. This should take the form of margin notes, which should be brief but clear enough that when you return to them, you know what you wished to remember. Underlining and highlighting are appropriate for focusing your attention, but they do not allow for analysis. Recording information as it comes to mind ensures that important insights are not forgotten when it comes time to reflect on what you have read. Do not count on your memory.

Post-Reading: Synthesis and Reflection

- Synthesizing what you have read requires you to construct a whole meaning for the passage. It involves a kind of reconstruction of the details you have considered important. What is the writer's purpose, and how has the writer gone about developing or supporting that central idea? How does each of the parts of the passage contribute to its overall effect? Are there any aspects of the piece you failed to fully understand? Have you returned to the passage in an attempt to answer those questions? Have you checked your notes for any clues you might have overlooked?

- Reflection is perhaps the most important reading step, for it requires the reader to create something new from the information he or she has read. Analysis up to this point has been a process of attempting to understand the worth of the elements within the text and how they contribute to the whole. But what effect has the writer's thesis or purpose in writing had on you? Has your thinking changed after reading the passage, and if so, how might this change the way you think or act in the future? If you are not changed by the content of the passage, which of your attitudes or beliefs have been confirmed or strengthened? It is in this last step that the reader fully understands and appreciates what he or she has read.

B8 *explain and support personal responses to texts*

B9 *interpret, analyse, and evaluate ideas and information from texts*

B10 *synthesize and extend thinking about texts*

SKILLS APPLICATION: INFORMATIONAL TEXT

Although informational text or non-fiction can be more rigidly structured than literary pieces, the good reader will make use of many of the strategies outlined above while reading any type of text. In fact, a critical listener and viewer of a TV show, a movie, or a live drama will find many of these strategies equally useful. Read the following passage taken from "The Hard Life," and note the application of a number of the reading strategies outlined above.

—*from The Hard Life*

Why is life in Japan so hard? I don't mean hard for me, with my battered dollars, but hard for the Japanese, who have supposedly won the world's economic wars. Japan, as everyone knows, now has the highest per capita income of any country, apart from, perhaps, a couple of oil baronies. Yet few Europeans or North Americans would willingly trade places in daily life with the average Japanese, whose living conditions are cramped, working hours are long, and material rewards and chances for recreation are slight compared with those in the rest of the industrialized world. One friend from New York, on his first visit to Japan, walked through our neighborhood in Yokohama on a sunny day and saw laundry flapping from every window and porch. "You mean no one has dryers?" he asked. "This is how I expected Seoul to look." Japan now has enough money to do anything it wants. Why do rich people keep living this way?

The answer to this question is crucial, because it essentially determines whether the world's trade battles with Japan will ever end. If most Japanese people agree with the outside view—that Japanese life is needlessly hard—then trade imbalances will start working themselves out. The Japanese government may try to keep markets closed, but the people themselves will eventually rebel. They will find ways to buy cheaper imports, they will take more time off, they will get tired of tightening their belts in order to increase world market share. They will complain about, and finally change, the regulations and government-sanctioned cartels that thwart the consumer's interest in Japan. But if, for whatever reason, the Japanese public feels that its material desires have been satisfied, then trade problems might never solve themselves. Japanese workers and consumers will have little incentive to behave the way market theory says they should, by using their ever increasing wealth to live in ever more comfortable style.

Continued

My impression is that, unfortunately, the second hypothesis is the correct one: the Japanese public is already quite content, or, more precisely, is not unhappy enough to demand a substantial change. Contentment is a plus for any country, but in this case it practically guarantees continued trade friction....

How, then, can anyone call Japanese life mean or hard? Many Japanese have replied with semi-offended astonishment when I've raised my "low living standards" questions with them; they've taken the very premise of the question as a sneer at what they have achieved. In attempting to explain why it's not a sneer, I've come up with three ways in which this ever more affluent country still seems pointlessly austere.

The first is crowded housing, and daily crowding in general. The typical Japanese dwelling is much smaller, much more expensive, and somewhat worse made than its counterpart in Europe or, especially, the United States. The typical Japanese also spends more of his day fighting for survival space in unending crowds. The second is purchasing power. Japanese factories make many products very efficiently, and Japanese exports are famous for giving overseas consumers more for their money. When they spend their yen at home, however, Japanese consumers are shortchanged no matter what they buy. The third is leisure. Certain categories of Japanese— namely, white-collar salarymen and public-school students—have essentially no free time.

The most interesting thing about such "hardships" is the sharply differing conclusions that Japanese and foreign observers draw from them. To me they look like totally unnecessary burdens, and to most outside economists they are all symptoms of an economy biased toward "underconsumption." To many Japanese, however, they're part of the broadly accepted social contract that has allowed the nation to succeed.

The high cost and poor quality of housing are the best-known Japanese problems, and the ones that Japanese themselves are most likely to grumble about. But the grumbling does not appear to be the kind that would lead to a change in behavior. Most Japanese seem to view the tight quarters and high prices as part of their fate, since they live (in the boiler-plate phrase that I have heard times without number) in a "small island nation lacking natural resources...."

In actuality, a variety of commercial and political forces leave [the Japanese] with very little choice but to live in expensive, inelegant houses on small plots. Japan's determination to subsidize its high-cost rice farmers means that tiny, inefficient paddies occupy about a quarter of the nation's nonmountainous land. Tax laws discourage the sale and development of land, and further inflate the price of any land that reaches the market. The cost of land makes the dwelling itself seem a trivial, consumable item. In greater Tokyo the value of a house is typically only a tenth of the value of the land it's built on. This means that many houses are built to be torn down in a decade or two, which discourages heavy investment in sturdiness or finishing touches. One neighborhood near our house exemplifies the modern "Japanese dream": brand-new single-family homes, tastefully landscaped on a small scale, many even with carports to hold the meticulously shined Toyotas and BMWs. It would be obvious to any Japanese that these houses represent a tremendous concentration of wealth; a typical house in the neighborhood, with its land, costs several million dollars. Yet most foreigners, passing by, would think the houses attractive but unexceptional. To me, the neighborhood looks like a new development in Silicon Valley[1] with much smaller lots....

Continued

Besides the housing shortage, there is the general atmosphere of crowding that throws outsiders like me into a panic and must wear down even people who have been used to it all their lives. Nanjing Road, the main street of Shanghai, is celebrated by the Chinese as an extremely crowded thoroughfare, but to me it can't compare in claustrophobic density to any of Tokyo's big train stations or major shopping streets. Each morning between 7:15 and 8:45 the platforms at my neighborhood train station are patrolled by "packers," ready to cram extra riders into each passing commuter train. Every train that pulls in is already full, but commuters who need to make a certain train take their places in specific areas on the platform. As the doors open, the first dozen or so people in each line push their way in under their own power, often entering backward and digging with their heels for extra traction. Then the packers take over and wedge in anyone else in line. Two or three times a week I make the half-hour trip to Tokyo on one of these trains. As I stand with my arms immobilized against my chest, someone's hip jammed into my groin and odd appendages pressed against my other surfaces, I alternately boil with anger and rejoice that I don't have to undergo this indignity every day. When I get off the train, after giving thanks for my survival and trying to smooth out my jacket and tie, I wonder why no one except foreigners seems to think that a rich country should find a less degrading way for its citizens to get to work.

My intention is not to examine the roots of Tokyo's housing and crowding problems but simply to say that they're not likely to change. All the remedies would involve making frontal assaults on the strongest interests in Japanese politics: changing the tax laws to encourage residential development, driving out the rice farmers, moving the central government away from Tokyo. (Prime Minister Noboru Takeshita often talks about moving government offices to the hinterland, but this seems more like a dream than an actual plan.) If ordinary Japanese had more room to live and play in, they might behave more like consumers in the rest of the world. "I can honestly say there's nothing I want that I don't have," a Japanese journalist friend of mine said one night when we were discussing the Japanese contentment with low living standards. "Oh, come on," said another friend, a professor. "You mean there's nothing you want that will fit in your house." They agreed on one thing: neither will ever have a bigger house.

—*by* James Fallows—American journalist

Sample Notes for "The Hard Life"

Pre-Reading Notes

- The writer, James Fallows, is an American journalist.
- This passage is likely part of a travel guide or magazine article.
- The title suggests a serious article.
- The footnote on Silicon Valley suggests an American setting.
- Title associations include thoughts about the Great Depression, manual labour, and hard work.

Active Reading and Comprehension Notes

- In the opening paragraph, the reader's attention is gained by using a rhetorical question to begin the passage.
- The central question is the thesis or point of the article: Why do the Japanese, who are wealthy, live in cramped quarters, work long hours, and accept a simpler lifestyle than they can clearly afford?
- The writer lives in Yokohama and obviously has first-hand knowledge of Japanese life. How long has he lived there?
- The writer's point of view is first person, and he is a foreigner.
- First impression of this writer's style: easy to understand, logical, and factual. He sets the goal of explaining the apparent paradox of rich people living poorly.

Post-Reading Notes

- The writer's central question functions as a kind of thesis statement in that it anticipates an answer.
- The passage explains why the Japanese, while viewed as wealthy people, remain content to live a life that North Americans would consider "unacceptable."
- The writer cites overcrowding, long working hours, and a lack of luxury as the three main symptoms of a lower-than-acceptable standard of living.
- Although he proposed two hypotheses to explain this paradoxical situation (a government out of touch with its people will soon be thrown out or a people realizing the limitations of a resource-poor island accept the sacrifice of protecting what little agricultural land they have), the writer believes that the Japanese people are most willing to make sacrifices in order to save what little land they have.
- The reader is made to realize how important agricultural land is to the Japanese and indeed to the world. In Canada, people are lucky to have an abundance of space.
- The Japanese situation raises an interesting dilemma for all nations to ponder: How far are people willing to go to satisfy their desire for luxury? Are people willing to gamble with the land that grows the food they must have to survive?
- The most moving part of Fallows' passage is his effective description of Tokyo's big train stations and the manner in which individuals are jammed in like sardines and forced to endure an unimaginable 30-minute journey twice daily.
- The reader should gain a renewed respect for the Japanese. This article might explain why citizens of this country are viewed as reserved, hard-working, and proud.

EXPOSITORY PROSE

The expository essay, which allows you to compare and contrast, illustrate, classify, define, or analyze, is the most common type of writing you will use, since its focused and relatively rigid structure provides you with a flexible vehicle for explanation. Unlike descriptive or narrative prose, which usually requires the reader to interpret text, expository prose is designed to impart information directly. Furthermore, while writers of descriptive and narrative pieces frequently use figurative or connotative language to develop impressions, exposition is more likely to use denotation and fact to show, expose, or explain a clearly stated thesis.

PERSUASIVE PROSE

Unlike the narrative essay, which tells a story, the persuasive or argumentative essay seeks to convince the reader to agree with the writer's point of view. The writer presents his or her arguments logically rather than chronologically. The basic text is expository because it uses logical reasoning, comparison and contrast, cause and effect, or definition to argue the thesis.

B3   view, both collaboratively and independently, to comprehend a variety of visual texts, with increasing complexity and subtlety of ideas and form

GRAPHIC TEXT

VIEWING STRATEGIES

When viewing and reading informational text containing some form of graphics, critical reading skills are still required. However, the addition of graphic text to the written word challenges the reader to employ certain strategies differently, since graphs, charts, diagrams, drawings, or photographs convey meaning in a far more subtle or unusually structured way. Be aware that conventional syntax can be dramatically influenced by an accompanying graphic. Word text used in graphic communication has the following unique characteristics:

- fragmented syntax
- irregular word placement
- spatial grouping of text (columns, boxes, bubbles)
- use of different font types and sizes
- application of bold and italicized text
- inferred connections between word and graphic text
- use of white space and framing for effect
- organization by headings, bullets, and lists

Although charts and tables use fragmented syntax and a unique spatial arrangement of text, the reading process remains logical, since information is organized vertically and horizontally and is typically grouped in a recognizable form. However, when the drawing, diagram, or photograph plays a dominant role in graphic communication, the "reading" process becomes far more intuitive, since the language is frequently subordinate to the image. You will find yourself going through fewer steps and applying fewer strategies, but the key steps remain the same.

- establish your purpose for reading
- understand the writer's purpose
- apply any background knowledge
- identify the building blocks: words and image
- construct a whole meaning: interpretation
- apply critical thinking
- reflect and analyze: accept or reject

SKILLS APPLICATION

Taking into consideration the accompanying notes, compare reactions to the political poster and the magazine photograph. Keep in mind the reader/viewer's point of view as well as the writer/illustrator's motivations and intent.

ONE THAT ALMOST GOT AWAY
Final Edit

PUERTO RICO
Why We Pulled the Taffeta

Sample Viewer Notes for "Why We Pulled the Taffeta"

- The featured picture of little dresses hanging on a clothesline was to accompany a magazine article on Puerto Rico's rural heartland.
- The word *rural* is the opposite of *urban*. It suggests country living, farming, or a more rustic life style.
- Taffetta is a kind of stiff silk cloth with a smooth glossy surface used for clothing requiring stiff, decorative features.
- Commercial photographs are chosen to vivify an impression rather than to record reality. This suggests that what is real and what is perceived are often quite different.
- One might fairly conclude that the editor did not wish to confuse her reading/viewing audience with an image that conflicted with the intended theme of her article on the Puerto Rican rural heartland.
- One might also conclude that the details selected by all writers are discriminatory in that they are rejected if they do not contribute to the central purpose of the piece.
- All communication is selective.

Grün bricht durch!
FARBE BEKENNEN

This is a campaign poster for the Green Party, the German environmental political party that currently forms part of the German government. The poster was designed by Holger Matthies. The caption reads "Green breaks through! Show your colours."

Sample Viewer Notes for the Green Party poster

- Posters are forms of promotional text intended to grab the attention of all potential readers.
- Posters typically use few words and striking images to catch the reader's attention.
- The written text tells the viewer this is a political party attempting to gain support for the party.
- The Green Party has an environmentally-friendly platform: conservation and sustainability are key beliefs.
- The poster's building blocks are picture and text, the most dominant feature being a picture of plant shoots breaking through the soil.
- The text conveys two short messages: "Green breaks through!" and "Show your colours."
- There is an obvious relationship between text and picture since both communicate in one form or another a kind of "breaking through." The young plants are breaking through the soil and it is inferred that the Green Party is achieving some sort of political break through.
- The second statement, "Show your colours," infers that the reader/viewer should show his colours or make clear his or her beliefs by supporting the Green Party and its platforms.
- The critical viewer/reader must first decide if the Green Party's message is accurate. Has the party actually acted on its platforms? Are its platforms truly beneficial to the country? Are they practical platforms? Can they be employed? If so, at what cost? Do you support these platforms? Do you think they can be employed by any other party? Does the Green Party have a chance of gaining enough support to be able to enact these policies?
- As you analyze the techniques used to persuade the viewer/reader, ask yourself if these techniques are fair. The use of a large picture filling most of the poster space is a direct appeal to emotion rather than reason. The image of plant shoots breaking through the soil subtly conveys a variety of associations including among other things spring growth, new beginnings, fragile growth, mother nature, the cyclical nature of life, the permanence and strength of nature, and the need to nurture, protect and, support growth.
- As you reflect, you must weigh your response to the image and its inferred message. Are you aware of and moved by the emotional appeal generated by the picture? Does that appeal conform to what you would have reasoned independent of the picture? If there is any conflict between the emotional message suggested by the picture and any factual information you are aware of, how do you reconcile those differences?
- Has the poster confirmed or changed your beliefs, and how will you act in response to it?

NOTES

READING AND VIEWING PRACTICE QUESTIONS

Read the following passage to answer questions 1 to 8.

FOLLOWER

My father worked with a horse-plough,
His shoulders globed like a full sail strung
Between the shafts and the furrow.
The horses strained at his clicking tongue.

An expert. He would set the wing
And fit the bright-steel-pointed sock.
The sod rolled over without breaking.
At the headrig, with a single pluck.

Of reins, the sweating team turned round
And back into the land. His eye
Narrowed and angled at the ground,
Mapping the furrow exactly.

I stumbled in his hob-nailed wake,
Fell sometimes on the polished sod;
Sometimes he rode me on his back
Dipping and rising to his plod.

I wanted to grow up and plough,
To close one eye, stiffen my arm.
All I ever did was follow
In his broad shadow round the farm.

I was a nuisance, tripping, falling,
Yapping always. But today
It is my father who keeps stumbling
Behind me, and will not go away.

—by Seamus Heaney

---

1. The simile "His shoulders globed like a full sail strung" **most strongly** suggests that guiding the plough required

   A. strength

   B. patience

   C. knowledge

   D. concentration

2. That the father is "an expert" is **best** indicated by the quotation

   A. "The horses strained at his clicking tongue"

   B. "And fit the bright-steel-pointed sock"

   C. "Narrowed and angled at the ground"

   D. "Mapping the furrow exactly"

3. The quotation "with a single pluck / Of reins, the sweating team turned round" **most likely** indicates that the father

   A. handled the horses cruelly

   B. drove the horses relentlessly

   C. controlled the horses skillfully

   D. treated the horses considerately

4. In the phrase "hob-nailed wake," the image created by the word "wake" is **most similar** to the image created by the phrase

   A. "a full sail strung"

   B. "his clicking tongue"

   C. "bright-steel-pointed sock"

   D. "single pluck / Of reins"

5. The quotation "All I ever did was follow" **most strongly** suggests that the speaker feels that when he was young, he was

   A. useless to his father

   B. irritated by his father

   C. admired by his father

   D. entertaining to his father

6. The quotation "But today / It is my father who keeps stumbling" **best** conveys the idea that the speaker is

   A. bitter

   B. critical

   C. reflective

   D. apologetic

7. In the last two lines of the poem, the observation can be made that the father

   A. is the son's good friend

   B. has taken the son's role

   C. wants the son to farm

   D. is wiser than the son

8. The **main** idea of this poem is that

   A. feelings should be expressed

   B. attitudes should be optimistic

   C. awareness is often unpredictable

   D. perception changes with maturity

Read the following passage to answer questions 9 to 40.

THE ANSWER IS BLOWIN' IN THE WIND

My knowledge and appreciation of rap music is limited to what escapes from the open
windows and thundering bass speakers of passing cars in downtown Toronto, and the
occasional halt on one of the music channels, where the latest street poet delivers up the
story of hard life in the hood in four basic rhymes, a knot of aggressive hand signals, and
5   a lot of leaning into camera.

Between the bleeps and the high-volume override of music, not many of the words seep through.
Most rap lyrics, I am convinced—though this could be laziness on my part or the thought
that the bullion is not worth the dive—could be in Sanskrit or ancient Coptic. I've tried to
work through a few interviews with visiting rappers on one of the MuchMusic seminars,
10   *Intimate and Inarticulate*, with no notable triumph. I gather, from the all-purpose mantra
of these colloquia, they are "telling it like it is."

Blurring the words for the sake of the sound is nothing new. Bob Dylan, who is the very
Homer of the mumble and the Shakespeare of strangled syllables, built himself a career
that, for some, was very close to godhead, going on in a low whine that would challenge
15   the acoustic skills of a nervous cat. The greatest Dylan anthem of all time, I suppose, and
one of the most recklessly pretentious pop songs of all time—only Simon and Garfunkel's
tumid "Bridge Over Troubled Water" and the great vaporous escapism of John Lennon's
insufferably saccharine "Imagine" offer serious competition—contains the line: "The answer,
my friend, is blowin' in the wind." And, if that wasn't clear enough, the next line offers the
20   terse paraphrase: "The answer is blowin' in the wind."

I guessed the point Dylan was trying to make was that, as most will have gathered, the
answer was blowin' in the wind.

Fatuous platitude and windy sentiment were a speciality of the boomer protest music.
Anti-religious they may have been, but their unction was extreme. How some of them
25   came to be regarded as poets might be put down to the pressure on a education system that
not only tolerated hootenannies but actually, in some cases, encouraged them. The hootenanny
was a horror of my youth, an ersatz festival of acoustic guitars wedded to mush so ripe it
invented seizure.

The innocence of the protest generation, much like its high Eden moment at Woodstock,
30   was always more indulgence than art. I don't know the medical payoffs of marijuana, and
am indifferent to its legalization, but I do know that the cannabis haze of the boomers'
radical period let many brains that were already impressively relaxed go limp altogether.
The songwriters knew this. They were big on blur, and high on treacle. Cf, Peter, Paul
and Mary—"Puff the Magic Dragon."

35   All of it, despite the pieties of that time or the recall of those same pieties now as at the arsonist
reunion of Woodstock 3, was commercial. Be it the Mamas and the Papas or the Rolling
Stones or the Beach Boys, they may have been strumming peace, love, and rebellion, but
their eye was on the charts and their real best friends were always the accountants.

Continued

It takes a pose. Then it was peace, today it's attitude. They are the same. The question
40   ultimately, or solely, is: Does it move the record, the CD, or the video?

Hence the charming career of the latest wildperson of pop music, the delightful Eminem,
a.k.a the Real Slim Shady. Eminem has a turbulent domestic life. His wife very recently
attempted suicide, his mother is suing him, and he himself is up on weapons charges.
Should he falter as a rap hero, this is a one-man *Survivor* series. Eminem is notorious for
45   the rage of his lyrics. I gather he slags just about everyone with great force and with, of
course, the obligatory wild and unzipped language of rap, which is as stylized in its edge
and raunch as the floral cooing of yesteryear's folkies or the hard blast of yesteryear's rock.

Trouble is, for many of the great pop consumers of the previous generation, it's *their* pieties
that are being mocked or trod on this time. And so it has come to pass that the lyrics of this
50   rapper, his homophobia, his disrespect of women, his hate language, are percolating a debate
that calls to mind a hundred school-board meetings a generation ago when the "new culture"
was waving its long hair and psychedelic posturing in the faces of its elders.

They shouldn't worry. He's just moving a product. Same old, same old. Anything for a buck.

The generation that cooked up liberation as an all-purpose philosophy for their gratification
55   doesn't look cool trying to rein in a generation they trained. In the immortal words of a million
forgotten sit-ins, let the circle be unbroken.

Rap on, Mr. Shady. Rap on. You the *real* Slim Shady.

—*by* Rex Murphy

9. The description "the latest street poet delivers up the story of hard life in the hood in four basic rhymes, a knot of aggressive hand signals, and a lot of leaning into the camera" **best** describes the

A. genre's stylistic traits

B. influence of multimedia

C. artist's rebellious attitude

D. current commercial product

10. The phrase "not many of the words seep through" contains an example of

A. figurative imagery

B. personification

C. allusion

D. irony

11. This article can be **best** described as

A. editorial writing

B. objective writing

C. allegorical writing

D. autobiographical writing

12. As it is used in the phrase "the bullion is not worth the dive," the **best** synonym for the word "bullion" is
    A. treasure
    B. adventure
    C. evaluation
    D. consequence

13. The expression "the bullion is not worth the dive" **most likely** means that
    A. the outcome is not worth the interpretation
    B. revelation is not worth the effort
    C. the product is not worth the cost
    D. honesty is not worth the energy

14. The tone that is communicated through Murphy's comparison of rap lyrics to "Sanskrit or ancient Coptic" is
    A. sardonic
    B. sarcastic
    C. reverent
    D. belligerent

15. Murphy's use of the phrase "all-purpose mantra" refers to a
    A. universally disputed doctrine
    B. highly individual viewpoint
    C. widely adopted attitude
    D. falsely emulated proof

16. As it is used in the phrase "the all-purpose mantra of these colloquia," the word "colloquia" can be **best** described as an
    A. informal meeting
    B. awkward encounter
    C. unexpected occurrence
    D. enlightening conversation

17. Rex Murphy's comment "Bob Dylan, who is the very Homer of the mumble and the Shakespeare of strangled syllables" contains an example of
    A. literary allusion
    B. biblical allusion
    C. historical allusion
    D. mythological allusion

18. Both Homer and Shakespeare can **best** be described as

   A. renowned poets

   B. informal musicians

   C. contemporary artists

   D. successful playwrights

19. The phrase "strangled syllables" contains an example of

   A. sound imagery

   B. internal rhyme

   C. alliteration

   D. oxymoron

20. In the phrase "was very close to godhead," the term "godhead" means

   A. divine

   B. superb

   C. respected

   D. unchallenged

21. Murphy's description of Bob Dylan's acoustic skills is humorous because

   A. the image created is completely unfair

   B. a complimentary description is expected

   C. readers know Bob Dylan would take offense

   D. an unexpected comparison is vividly described

22. Murphy describes the Simon and Garfunkel song "Bridge over Troubled Water" as "tumid" which, considering the context, **most likely** means that Murphy finds this song

   A. cryptic and intricate

   B. pompous and inflated

   C. repetitive and imitative

   D. unemotional and predictable

23. The term "vaporous escapism" (line 17) is intended to describe music that is

   A. unsubstantial and idealistic

   B. mediocre and annoying

   C. formulaic and didactic

   D. insipid and typical

24. Rex Murphy's comment about Bob Dylan's lyrics for "Blowin' in the Wind," beginning with "And, if that wasn't clear enough," **most directly** pokes fun at the song's

    A. tone and lack of sincerity

    B. repetition and lack of meaning

    C. commercialism and consumers

    D. pacifists and the protest movement

25. Murphy puts some of the blame for what he describes as "a horror of my youth" on

    A. the education system

    B. lax law reinforcement

    C. lack of political leadership

    D. the influence of pop music

26. According to Murphy, the protest movement of the 1960s was corrupted by

    A. art

    B. music

    C. narcotics

    D. indulgence

27. Considering Murphy's opinion, the word "treacle" (line 33) **most likely** refers to

    A. an antidote to life

    B. a collective energy

    C. an arrogant violence

    D. an immoral philosophy

28. Murphy's choice of the word "hootenannies" to describe the protests shows his

    A. disdain

    B. humour

    C. approval

    D. resentment

29. Murphy believes that the protest artists of the past were fuelled by

    A. rebellion

    B. apprehension

    C. misinformation

    D. commercialism

30. Murphy equates the "peace" marketing of past music with today's marketing of

    A. attitude

    B. terrorism

    C. belligerence

    D. environmentalism

31. Murphy's choice of the words "charming" and "delightful" (line 41) creates a tone that can be **best** described as

    A. reluctant

    B. sarcastic

    C. reverent

    D. formal

32. Murphy's reference to Eminem as a "one-man *Survivor* series" contains an example of

    A. irony

    B. allusion

    C. metaphor

    D. hyperbole

33. As it is used in the phrase "Eminem is notorious for the rage of his lyrics," the word "notorious" can be **best** described as

    A. considered a danger to mainstream society

    B. internationally recognized and supported

    C. well-known for something disreputable

    D. an expression of contemporary culture

34. As it is used in the phrase "I gather he slags just about everyone with great force," the word "slags" **most likely**

    A. has a negative connotation

    B. has a positive connotation

    C. is a current colloquialism

    D. is a past colloquialism

35. The description "the obligatory wild and unzipped language of rap" implies that

    A. the abhorrent content in rap is required

    B. what seems to be freedom is restriction

    C. freedom of expression is always criticized

    D. the shocking elements of rap are marketed

36. Murphy's point that the previous generation's "pieties are being mocked" is **best** described as

    A. inflammatory

    B. prejudicial

    C. comical

    D. ironic

37. The overall tone of the essay "The Answer is Blowin' in the Wind" can be **best** described as

    A. condescending

    B. hypocritical

    C. satirical

    D. neutral

38. The **main** focus of the essay's criticism is one of

    A. hypocrisy

    B. corruption

    C. conformity

    D. commercialism

39. In the last sentence of the essay, the italicized word "real" not only quotes frequently repeated lyrics from one of Eminem's songs but also ridicules him and all pop artists for their apparent lack of

    A. motivation

    B. ingenuity

    C. talent

    D. greed

40. The writer's **main** purpose in writing this essay is to show that

    A. all generations of music consumers have been manipulated by marketing

    B. the rebellious music of each generation pushes the social limits further

    C. it is difficult for musicians to break out of commercial music trends

    D. all musicians from all cultures are corrupted by fame and fortune

Read the following passage to answer questions 41 and 42.

SNOW

Yesterday we had a snowstorm that lasted from early morning right on through the night, and now the world is clothed in white. Snowfall this heavy is rare, here on the lower edge of the Cévennes,[1] where the foothills begin rolling up out of the vineyards. Farther north and into the mountains, there's always enough to ensure winter skiing but in Latourne,[2] if
5   it comes at all, it's only a light teasing tickle, a mere frosting. Today's snow, however, is thick and deep and means to stay. *This* snow would do Ottawa proud.

Shortly before dawn this morning—the sky still dark—the telephone rings, and a gruff male voice informs me that he is the courier service and has a package to deliver, and where is my house. He is calling on his cellphone from the *mairie*[3] on the main road, and
10   he needs directions. I explain—I've memorized this patter in French—and when I get to the bit about his turning the corner around the monastery and continuing over the small bridge, he stops me.

He says he will not be able to come to my house, for not only are the narrow country roads leading to Mas Blanc[4] blocked with snow, but he will not attempt to cross the bridge.
15   He understands now where I am located, and he knows that little bridge: it has no railing. Under the snow, the roads are sheer ice, he says, he could slide off. He will not do it. Don't I know that overnight everything has been freezing? It's too dangerous, *madame*, he says.

My stars, I say to myself, what a wimpy courier. But I do know that he has reason to be
20   fearful, as I was out in the blizzard yesterday and saw for myself that cars were slipping and sliding out of control, several in accidents and even more headfirst in ditches along the highway. Of course, given the unlikelihood of this kind of weather, no one has snow tires, and there are no plows or machines to scatter sand and salt: one simply manages as best one can and waits for the snow to melt and disappear, which, ordinarily, it will do
25   within hours.

Thus I am understanding and polite, and when he asks if I will come over to meet him, if he drives as far as the old church of St-Baudile across the way, I agree. It never occurs to me, I realize later, that I might ask *him* to walk to my house. No, and he wouldn't have done it, either.

30   I throw on clothes over my flannel pyjamas and pull on a pair of old winter boots I smartly brought back last summer from the attic where they'd been stored in Ottawa since I left in 1987. As soon as I step out the door and smell the silvery fragrance of new snow, I realize that this call has been a gift from the gods, for without it I would never have ventured out so early and would have missed this odd sensation of being enveloped in pastel light, as if I am
35   dancing through a dream sequence in an old Hollywood musical. The rising sun, filtered through pearly clouds and reflected by the snow, shines everywhere. The eastern sky is rose grey streaked with lemony gold, and the vineyards glowing blue and apricot. The world has turned, overnight, into an opal.

Continued

---

[1] Mountains in south-central France.
[2] Village in the Cévennes region of France.
[3] Town hall (French).
[4] White farm house (French) where the author lives.

40　The birds are already at their feeder under the *micocoulier* tree, making busy little *"dix-huit, dix-huit"*[5] noises, but as I walk farther down the lane I hear nothing and am struck by the solemn and ponderous nature of snow itself, the grave way it stifles sound. The silence feels like a secret I cannot tell.

As I walk across the narrow bridge and around the monastery, I see that the courier has been right, for the road is really quite icy under the snow, and he would easily have gone off into

45　the stream that still runs merrily, not yet frozen over. I make my way through the vineyard instead of the road to reach the church, where I can see there's a small blue van parked and waiting. Inside sits the courier, a red-faced man about my age, who has been watching me scuff through the snow. I am wearing my old rabbit-fur hat held on by a plaid scarf, and he probably finds me pretty funny, for I see that he is laughing.

50　He gets out to give me the package—I have to sign for it—and we exchange a few pleasantries about the weather. I tell him I am Canadian and this is nothing, *monsieur*, really nothing, compared with what one encounters in Ottawa. If one has the correct tires, one can drive in snow like this with no problem, I say, but of course here … I shrug meaningfully and let the sentence dangle, sharp criticism of France—and all things French—implied.

55　He laughs again and drives off, and I walk home with the sun, now fully up from behind the clouds, making everything ahead of me glitter and gleam. I feel a great ball of joy welling up in my throat, a ball of laughter ready to float out into the bright air. White snow lies luminous everywhere and the package in my hands, I can see from the address, is from a Canadian publisher. Too curious to wait, I stop and tear open the end of the padded

60　envelope and pull out a letter telling me that, at the author's request, I have been sent these galleys of her new novel, *A Student of Weather*.[6] Might I consider providing a comment and if so, could I…

I spin around twice, kicking up snow and laughing out loud, and run then through the drifts onto the road, heading home happy but more than just happy, amazed—and as thrilled as a

65　gambler by patterns of chance and probability. What else in the world but *this* book, so propitiously titled, might have called me out early to walk in the fresh snow? Am I not, this winter's morning, a true student of weather? Nevertheless, far stronger than the book's coincidental pull, is a new friendship that seems, suddenly, enormously powerful.

On the lane to the house, I stop for breath at the olive grove and think how strange the

70　green oval leaves appear, so thickly covered with snow. I pull a branch toward me and stick out my tongue, licking the lovely stuff off in one sweeping mouthful. The instant prickle of melting snow explodes in my mouth—flakes disintegrate like stars—as it transforms itself to a swallow of water. A sweet, chalky taste, and then gone in a gulp. Another mouthful and another, and I stand there for a long time, thinking of you and eating

75　snow … far away in another country but, in my heart, home.

—*by* Isabel Huggan

---

[5] Eighteen (French). Pronounced "deez wheet." *Micocoulier* tree: a Mediterranean nettletree, also known as hackberry.
[6] Elizabeth Hay is the author of *A Student of Weather*. She is also the author of *Crossing the Snowlines* and *The Only Snow in Havana* [Huggan's note].

41. The phrase "the world is clothed in white" contains an example of

    A. simile

    B. metaphor

    C. hyperbole

    D. personification

42. The main purpose of the opening paragraph is to

    A. introduce the topic of snow

    B. compare this snowfall with that of Ottawa

    C. describe the characteristics of the snowfall

    D. grab the reader's attention with shocking information

Read the following passage to answer questions 43 to 50.

from PLATO'S *REPUBLIC*

In this excerpt from one of the dialogues recorded by the Greek philosopher Plato, Socrates (the "I") tells of speaking with Glaucon (the "he") about the human situation. The brief replies made by Glaucon are typical of a Socratic dialogue. The dialectic teaching method of question and answer is called the Socratic method.

THE MYTH OF THE CAVE

And now, I said, let me show in a figure how far our nature is enlightened or unenlightened:— Behold! Human beings living in an underground den, which has a mouth open toward the light and reaching all along the den; here they have been from their childhood, and have their legs and necks chained so that they cannot move, and can only see before them, being
5   prevented by the chains from turning round their heads. Above and behind them a fire is blazing at a distance, and between the fire and the prisoners there is a raised way[7]; and you will see, if you look, a low wall built along the way, like the screen which marionette players have in front of them, over which they show the puppets.

I see.

10   And do you see, I said, men[8] passing along the wall carrying all sorts of vessels, and statues and figures of animals made of wood and stone and various materials, which appear over the wall? Some of them are talking, others silent.

You have shown me a strange image, and they are strange prisoners.

Like ourselves, I replied; and they see only their own shadows, or the shadows of one another,
15   which the fire throws on the opposite wall of the cave?

True, he said; how could they see anything but the shadows if they were never allowed to move their heads?

And of the objects which are being carried in like manner they would only see the shadows?

Yes, he said.

Continued

---

[7] way – road or path.
[8] men – people, human beings.

20 And if they were able to converse with one another, would they not suppose that they were naming what was actually before them?

Very true.

And suppose further that the prison had an echo which came from the other side, would they not be sure to fancy when one of the passers-by spoke that the voice which they heard
25 came from the passing shadow?

No question, he replied.

To them, I said, the truth would be literally nothing but the shadows of the images.

That is certain.

And now look again, and see what will naturally follow if the prisoners are released and
30 disabused of their error. At first, when any of them is liberated and compelled suddenly to stand up and turn his neck round and walk and look toward the light, he will suffer sharp pains; the glare will distress him, and he will be unable to see the realities of which in his former state he had seen the shadows; and then conceive someone saying to him, that what he saw before was an illusion, but that now, when he is approaching nearer to being and his eye is
35 turned toward more real existence, he has a clearer vision—what will be his reply? And you may further imagine that his instructor is pointing to the objects as they pass and requiring him to name them—will he not be perplexed? Will he not fancy that the shadows which he formerly saw are truer than the objects which are now shown to him?

Far truer.

40 And if he is compelled to look straight at the light, will he not have a pain in his eyes which will make him turn away to take refuge in the objects of vision which he can see, and which he will conceive to be in reality clearer than the things which are now being shown to him?

True, he said.

And suppose once more, that he is reluctantly dragged up a steep and rugged ascent, and held
45 fast until he is forced into the presence of the sun himself, is he not likely to be pained and irritated? When he approaches the light his eyes will be dazzled, and he will not be able to see anything at all of what are now called realities.

Not all in a moment, he said.

He will require to grow accustomed to the sight of the upper world. And first he will see the
50 shadows best, next the reflections of men and other objects in the water, and then the objects themselves; then he will gaze upon the light of the moon and the stars and the spangled heaven; and he will see the sky and the stars by night better than the sun or the light of the sun by day?

Certainly.

55 Last of all he will be able to see the sun, and not mere reflections of him in the water, but he will see him in his own proper place, and not in another; and he will contemplate him as he is.

Certainly.

He will then proceed to argue that this is he who gives the season and the years, and is the guardian of all that is in the visible world, and in a certain way the cause of all things which
60 he and his fellows have been accustomed to behold?

Continued

Clearly, he said, he would first see the sun and then reason about him.

And when he remembered his old habitation, and the wisdom of the den and his fellow-prisoners, do you not suppose that he would felicitate himself on the change, and pity them?

Certainly, he would.

65 And if they were in the habit of conferring honours among themselves on those who were quickest to observe the passing shadows and to remark which of them went before, and which followed after, and which were together; and who were therefore best able to draw conclusions as to the future, do you think that he would care for such honours and glories, or envy the possessors of them? Would he not say with Homer,[9]

70 *Better to be the poor servant of a poor master, and to endure anything, rather than think as they do and live after their manner?*

Yes, he said, I think that he would rather suffer anything than entertain these false notions and live in this miserable manner.

Imagine once more, I said, such a one coming suddenly out of the sun to be replaced in his
75 old situation; would he not be certain to have his eyes full of darkness?

To be sure, he said.

And if there were a contest, and he had to compete in measuring the shadows with the prisoners who had never moved out of the den, while his sight was still weak, and before his eyes had become steady (and the time which would be needed to acquire this new habit of sight might
80 be very considerable) would he not be ridiculous? Men would say of him that up he went and down he came without his eyes; and that it was better not even to think of ascending; and if anyone tried to loose another and lead him up to the light, let them only catch the offender, and they would put him to death.

No question, he said.

85 This entire allegory, I said, you may now append[10], dear Glaucon, to the previous argument[11]; the prison-house is the world of sight, the light of the fire is the sun, and you will not misapprehend me if you interpret the journey upwards to be the ascent of the soul into the intellectual world according to my poor belief, which, at your desire, I have expressed whether rightly or wrongly, God knows. But, whether true or false, my opinion is that in the world of
90 knowledge the idea of good appears last of all, and is seen only with an effort; and, when seen, is also inferred to be the universal author of all things beautiful and right, parent of light and of the lord of light in this visible world, and the immediate source of reason and truth in the intellectual; and that this is the power upon which he who would act rationally either in public or private life must have his eye fixed.

Plato (427–347)
Most of what is known about the ideas of
Socrates (469–399) can be found in the writings of Plato

[9] Homer (8th or 9th Century BC) – Greek poet; author of the *Iliad* and the *Odyssey*; allusions to his work were frequent in classical Greece.
[10] append – add to.
[11] previous argument – this extract does not include all of the conversation between Socrates and Glaucon.

43. The theme of limited perception is **most strongly** expressed in which of the following quotations?

    A. "Behold! Human beings living in an underground den, which has a mouth open toward the light and reaching all along the den"

    B. "here they have been from their childhood, and have their legs and necks chained to that they cannot move, and can only see before them, being prevented by the chains from turning round their heads"

    C. "and you will see, if you look, a low wall built along the way like the screen which marionette players have in front of them, over which they show the puppets"

    D. "And do you see, I said, men passing along the wall carrying all sorts of vessels, and statues and figures of animals made of wood and stone and various materials, which appear over the wall?"

44. According to Socrates, the liberated prisoner will paradoxically

    A. regret his liberation

    B. throw caution to the wind

    C. have to be forced to leave the prison

    D. experience more intense levels of pain

45. The meaning of the word "append" (line 85) is

    A. add to

    B. consist of

    C. insert into

    D. include with

46. Quotation marks are **most likely** absent from this Socratic dialogue because

    A. quotation marks were not a form of punctuation in the 5th century

    B. Socrates never used quotation marks in his writings

    C. there is no need for quotation marks in a dialogue

    D. line breaks are used instead of quotation marks

47. In the context of this passage, the **main** function of a "myth" such as the one told by Socrates is to

    A. express a truth about the human condition

    B. make a vivid image, which readers can "see"

    C. state, through images, a thought that is too difficult for ordinary words

    D. briefly summarize a moral principle—the moral that is sometimes stated at the end of a story

48. The function of the dialogue in the telling of this myth is **best** summarized as a way

    A. to simplify a complicated story

    B. for readers to infer the meaning of the argument

    C. of teaching by proceeding one step at a time through question and answer

    D. to provide a "yes-man" that will cause unconscious agreement with the argument

49. The narrator's overall attitude toward human nature is **best** described as

   A. cynical

   B. realistic

   C. optimistic

   D. pessimistic

50. The meaning of the phrase "show in a figure" is **most clearly** explained as

   A. a shadow play

   B. a figure of speech

   C. the result of calculation

   D. an illustration that demonstrates truth

READING AND VIEWING UNIT TEST

Read the following passage to answer questions 1 to 16.

SONNET 116

LET me not to the marriage of true minds
Admit impediments. Love is not love
Which alters when it alteration finds,
Or bends with the remover to remove:
5   O, no! it is an ever-fixed mark,
That looks on tempests and is never shaken;
It is the star to every wandering bark,
Whose worth's unknown, although his height be taken.
Love's not Time's fool, though rosy lips and cheeks
10   Within his bending sickle's compass come;
Love alters not with his brief hours and weeks,
But bears it out even to the edge of doom.
If this be error, and upon me prov'd,
I never writ, nor no man ever lov'd.

—*by* William Shakespeare

---

1. This sonnet is divided into

   A. three quatrains and one couplet

   B. two quatrains and one sestet

   C. one octave and one sestet

   D. one sestet and one octave

2. The second quatrain contains metaphors that refer to

   A. the beauty of nature

   B. navigating the seas

   C. devout religion

   D. mythology

3. The metaphors in the second quatrain emphasize which of the following qualities of love?

   A. Elusiveness

   B. Transience

   C. Constancy

   D. Obsession

4. The second quatrain refers to a "tempest," which is the archetypal symbol for
   A. inner turmoil
   B. corruption
   C. obstacles
   D. passion

5. The third quatrain addresses the
   A. enduring nature of true love
   B. inconsistencies of love
   C. ambiguity of love
   D. value of love

6. In the couplet of the sonnet, the poet asserts his certainty in the form of a
   A. prediction
   B. prayer
   C. wager
   D. plea

7. This poem contains transparent metaphors and a readily recognizable theme. The simplicity of this straightforward technique underscores the speaker's
   A. certainty and conviction
   B. lack of formal education
   C. reluctance to employ complex terminology or figures of speech
   D. attempt to emphasize the purity of true love through uncomplicated speech

8. The "bending sickle" is a reference to
   A. the image of death as the Grim Reaper
   B. the scepter of Queen Elizabeth
   C. a plentiful harvest
   D. melting ice

9. The speaker magnifies the metaphor of a guiding star for love by
   A. situating it almost squarely in the centre of the poem
   B. choosing not to place an adjective before it
   C. using negation liberally through the sonnet
   D. using alliteration

10. Which of the following literary techniques is used to describe the image of a star in the phrase "That looks on tempests and is never shaken" (line 6)?

   A. Personification

   B. Metonymy

   C. Hyperbole

   D. Simile

11. The speaker defines love by

   A. declaring both what love can and cannot be

   B. citing examples of his own experiences

   C. elaborating on the struggles of love

   D. giving advice to young lovers

12. *Volta* is the Italian term for the change or shift in feeling that occurs in some sonnets. Between which of the following lines does the *volta* occur in the poem?

   A. Second and third lines

   B. Fourth and fifth lines

   C. Eighth and ninth lines

   D. Twelfth and thirteenth lines

13. Which of the following quotations suggests that love will continue even if it is unrequited?

   A. "Which alters when it alteration finds"

   B. "Or bends with the remover to remove"

   C. "Love's not Time's fool"

   D. "Love alters not with his brief hours and weeks"

14. Which of the following words in the third quatrain **most strongly** reinforces the metaphor introduced in the second quatrain?

   A. Compass

   B. Hours

   C. Sickle

   D. Edge

15. Which of the following statements **best** explains the speaker's use of consonance in the first quatrain?

   A. It establishes the defining rhythm of the poem.

   B. It draws the reader into the poem rapidly.

   C. It intensifies the tone of his assertion.

   D. It helps to illustrate a festive mood.

16. Which of the following statements **best** describes the theme of the poem?

A. True love endures through its timelessness and immutable nature.

B. Love is easily ravaged and eroded by the effects of time.

C. It is a rare thing to experience true love.

D. Love is easily altered or extinguished.

Read the following passage to answer questions 17 to 43.

---

excerpt from DR. JEKYLL AND MR. HYDE

Two doors from one corner, on the left hand going east, the line was broken by the entry of a court; and just at that point, a certain sinister block of building thrust forward its gable on the street. It was two storeys high; showed no window, nothing but a door on the lower storey and a blind forehead of discoloured wall on the upper; and bore in every feature, the marks
5 of prolonged and sordid negligence. The door, which was equipped with neither bell nor knocker, was blistered and distained. Tramps slouched into the recess and struck matches on the panels; children kept shop upon the steps; the schoolboy had tried his knife on the mouldings; and for close on a generation, no one had appeared to drive away these random visitors or to repair their ravages.

10 Mr. Enfield and the lawyer were on the other side of the by-street; but when they came abreast of the entry, the former lifted up his cane and pointed.

"Did you ever remark that door?" he asked; and when his companion had replied in the affirmative, "It is connected in my mind," added he, "with a very odd story."

"Indeed?" said Mr. Utterson, with a slight change of voice, "and what was that?"

15 "Well, it was this way," returned Mr. Enfield: "I was coming home from some place at the end of the world, about three o'clock of a black winter morning, and my way lay through a part of town where there was literally nothing to be seen but lamps. Street after street, and all the folks asleep—street after street, all lighted up as if for a procession and all as empty as a church—till at last I got into that state of mind when a man listens and listens and begins
20 to long for the sight of a policeman. All at once, I saw two figures: one a little man who was stumping along eastward at a good walk, and the other a girl of maybe eight or ten who was running as hard as she was able down a cross street. Well, sir, the two ran into one another naturally enough at the corner; and then came the horrible part of the thing; for the man trampled calmly over the child's body and left her screaming on the ground. It sounds nothing
25 to hear, but it was hellish to see. It wasn't like a man; it was like some damned Juggernaut. I gave a view halloa, took to my heels, collared my gentleman, and brought him back to where there was already quite a group about the screaming child. He was perfectly cool and made no resistance, but gave me one look, so ugly that it brought out the sweat on me like running. The people who had turned out were the girl's own family; and pretty soon,
30 the doctor, for whom she had been sent, put in his appearance. Well, the child was not much the worse, more frightened, according to the Sawbones; and there you might have supposed would be an end to it. But there was one curious circumstance. I had taken a loathing to my gentleman at first sight. So had the child's family, which was only natural. But the doctor's case was what struck me. He was the usual cut and dry apothecary, of no particular

Continued

---

35 age and colour, with a strong Edinburgh accent, and about as emotional as a bagpipe. Well, sir, he was like the rest of us; every time he looked at my prisoner, I saw that Sawbones turn sick and white with desire to kill him. I knew what was in his mind, just as he knew what was in mine; and killing being out of the question, we did the next best. We told the man we could and would make such a scandal out of this, as should make his name stink from one

40 end of London to the other. If he had any friends or any credit, we undertook that he should lose them. And all the time, as we were pitching it in red hot, we were keeping the women off him as best we could, for they were as wild as harpies. I never saw a circle of such hateful faces; and there was the man in the middle, with a kind of black, sneering coolness—frightened

45 too, I could see that—but carrying it off, sir, really like Satan. 'If you choose to make capital out of this accident,' said he, 'I am naturally helpless. No gentleman but wishes to avoid a scene,' says he. 'Name your figure.' Well, we screwed him up to a hundred pounds for the child's family; he would have clearly liked to stick out; but there was something about the lot of us that meant mischief, and at last he struck. The next thing was to get the money;

50 and where do you think he carried us but to that place with the door?—whipped out a key, went in, and presently came back with the matter of ten pounds in gold and a cheque for the balance on Coutts's, drawn payable to bearer and signed with a name that I can't mention, though it's one of the points of my story, but it was a name at least very well known and often printed. The figure was stiff; but the signature was good for more than that, if it was

55 only genuine. I took the liberty of pointing out to my gentleman that the whole business looked apocryphal, and that a man does not, in real life, walk into a cellar door at four in the morning and come out with another man's cheque for close upon a hundred pounds. But he was quite easy and sneering. 'Set your mind at rest,' says he, 'I will stay with you till the banks open and cash the cheque myself.' So we all set off, the doctor, and the child's father, and our friend

60 and myself, and passed the rest of the night in my chambers; and next day, when we had breakfasted, went in a body to the bank. I gave in the cheque myself, and said I had every reason to believe it was a forgery. Not a bit of it. The cheque was genuine."

"Tut-tut," said Mr. Utterson.

—*by* Robert Louis Stevenson

17. The phrase that refers to the door as being "prolonged and sordid negligence" (line 5) **most likely** means that the door was

A. boarded up

B. seldom used

C. broken open by force

D. vandalized by schoolchildren

18. The quotation "It was two storeys high; showed no window, nothing but a door on the lower storey and a blind forehead of discoloured wall on the upper; and bore in every feature, the marks of prolonged and sordid negligence" contains which of the following figures of speech?

A. Allusion

B. Metaphor

C. Metonymy

D. Alliteration

19. The metaphor in the phrase, "a blind forehead of discoloured wall," which suggests a face devoid of eyes, **most likely** criticizes which of the following characteristics about Victorian society?

    A. A refusal to recognize the disparity between classes

    B. Hypocrisy with respect to issues considered sinful or immoral

    C. An inability to understand the complex issues surrounding poverty

    D. Failure to take advantage of possible improvements afforded by technology

20. As it is used in the phrase "Did you ever remark that door," the word "remark" means to

    A. observe

    B. mention

    C. consider

    D. comment

21. Which of the following literary devices is contained in the sentence "I was coming home from some place at the end of the world, about three o'clock of a black winter morning"?

    A. Simile

    B. Allusion

    C. Metaphor

    D. Hyperbole

22. In the quotation "Street after street, and all the folks asleep—street after street, all lighted up as if for a procession and all as empty as a church—till at last I got into that state of mind when a man listens and listens and begins to long for the sight of a policeman," the **most likely** explanation for the writer's use of parallel structures is to

    A. emphasize the mood of loneliness and desolation

    B. help the reader imagine a grid of long, narrow streets and lanes

    C. create a sense of monotony to exaggerate the effect of a sudden shock

    D. evoke the rigidity of the Victorian morals against which this story is set

23. The collision of the man and the little girl at the corner could **most likely** be interpreted as the writer's intention to

    A. emphasize the narrator's integrity

    B. reveal a deviant segment of society

    C. foreshadow the collapse of his society

    D. underscore the hypocrisy of Victorian values

24. The incident that solidifies Enfield's revulsion of the man that trampled the child is his observation of the

    A. injured child's terror

    B. reaction of the child's family

    C. attending physician's loathing

    D. man's lack of remorse for his deed

25. In the phrase "But the doctor's case was what struck me," the **best** definition of the word "case" is

    A. observation

    B. situation

    C. satchel

    D. patient

26. The description of the doctor as "the usual cut and dry apothecary, of no particular age and colour, with a strong Edinburgh accent, and about as emotional as a bagpipe" contains an example of

    A. juxtaposition

    B. hyperbole

    C. metaphor

    D. simile

27. The description of the doctor as "the usual cut and dry apothecary, of no particular age and colour, with a strong Edinburgh accent, and about as emotional as a bagpipe" suggests that the narrator believes him to be

    A. an unwilling participant at the scene

    B. a stereotypical physician

    C. an inept practitioner

    D. a skilled surgeon

28. The manner in which the doctor and Enfield deal with the man's mistreatment of the child underscores the Victorian emphasis on

    A. reputation

    B. religion

    C. candor

    D. charity

29. Which of the following statements **best** summarizes the course of events described in the sentence "Well, we screwed him up to a hundred pounds for the child's family; he would have clearly liked to stick out; but there was something about the lot of us that meant mischief, and at last he struck"?

   A. We listened as he boasted of how much money he carried with him, but he suspected we wanted to steal it, so he retreated.

   B. We took a sum of money from his pocket, and forced to defend himself, he punched an onlooker.

   C. We demanded a sum of money, which he argued, but seeing our determination, he capitulated.

   D. Although he was not a heavy man, he was confident and aggressive as he attacked.

30. As it is used in the sentence "I took the liberty of pointing out to my gentleman that the whole business looked apocryphal, and that a man does not" the **most likely** definition of the word "apocryphal" is

   A. disjointed

   B. terrifying

   C. alarming

   D. dubious

31. The man's response to Enfield's qualm about his ability to come up with the money is **best** described as

   A. derisive

   B. desperate

   C. deceptive

   D. disruptive

32. The alliteration in the last line of the passage **most likely**

   A. provides finality and punctuation to Enfield's long, fearful narrative and brings the reader back to reality

   B. imitates the sound of an adding machine to emphasize the image of money changing hands

   C. indicates Mr. Utterson's reluctance to believe his companion's account

   D. foreshadows a possible confrontation

33. The first line of the passage foreshadows the occurrence of an act that

   A. breaks with convention

   B. is intended to shock

   C. evokes empathy

   D. remains secret

34. In the context of Enfield's reference to the man who runs over the girl as "some damned Juggernaut," the word "Juggernaut" is a reference to a

A. mythological monster

B. self-propelled vehicle

C. side show freak

D. crushing force

35. Enfield's response after witnessing the collision between the man and the young girl is to

A. assist the girl

B. abscond in fear

C. apprehend the man

D. alert the girl's family

36. The man's collision with the young girl **most likely**

A. hurt both of them

B. injured her severely

C. did not harm her physically

D. caused more harm to him than to her

37. Enfield's description of the women at the scene as "harpies" is an allusion to a

A. monster from Greek mythology

B. ferocious animal

C. female musician

D. feral cat

38. In the quotation "And all the time, as we were pitching it in red hot, we were keeping the women off him as best we could, for they were as wild as harpies. I never saw a circle of such hateful faces; and there was the man in the middle, with a kind of black, sneering coolness—frightened too, I could see that—but carrying it off, sir, really like Satan," the writer continues his comparison of the man with Satan by making references to

A. morality

B. religion

C. colour

D. nature

39. The description of an unwelcoming and neglected doorway that introduced Enfield's narrative **most likely** suggests that his story will touch on a

    A. period of time that has been long forgotten

    B. topic or issue that society refuses to address

    C. time in his life that he considers very private

    D. scientific discovery that will alter his society

40. Which of the following statements is **not** an accurate description of the doorway depicted in the opening paragraph of the passage?

    A. It has not been used for a long time.

    B. No one knows of its existence.

    C. It does not invite use.

    D. It attracts vagrants.

41. The **most likely** reason for Mr. Utterson's "slight change of voice" (line 14) is

    A. consternation

    B. curiosity

    C. disdain

    D. denial

42. The narrator's initial description of the doctor as having an expression as "emotional as a bagpipe" **most likely** serves to

    A. criticize Scottish physicians

    B. indicate his disdain for foreigners

    C. introduce an atmosphere of apathy

    D. emphasize the evil man's effect on his onlookers

ANSWERS AND SOLUTIONS—READING AND VIEWING PRACTICE QUESTIONS

1. A	11. A	21. C	31. B	41. D
2. D	12. A	22. B	32. B	42. C
3. C	13. B	23. A	33. C	43. B
4. A	14. A	24. B	34. A	44. C
5. A	15. C	25. D	35. A	45. A
6. C	16. A	26. D	36. D	46. A
7. B	17. C	27. A	37. C	47. A
8. D	18. A	28. A	38. A	48. C
9. A	19. C	29. D	39. B	49. B
10. A	20. A	30. A	40. A	50. D

1. A

The simile that likens his shoulders to a full sail shows the force that must be exerted to plow the field. A "globed" sail would be rounded because of the powerful winds blowing against it. Just like the wind, resistance is transformed into something useful by moving the boat forward; his father's exertion transforms the land into fields that grow crops of food. While plowing the land in this way would certainly require knowledge and skill, this simile does not refer to these qualities.

2. D

Reference to the father's expertise is indicated by his "mapping the furrow" and doing so "exactly."

3. C

A "sweating team" of horses indicates that they are working hard, but not necessarily that they are being handled cruelly or driven relentlessly. The fact that the father can turn the horses around with only "a single pluck" indicates that he has skill working with them.

4. A

The only quotation that also alludes to water includes the sail reference in "a full sail strung."

5. A

One can imagine that his father's reaction to his unskilled son's presence could include feelings of admiration or entertainment. The son himself might also reasonably feel irritated by his father, who is clearly busy completing his own tasks with little time to focus on his son. However, by focusing on the context of the phrase "All I ever did was follow," it is reasonable to assume that the son was "useless to his father." Instead of leading the way or working alongside him, the speaker's trailing behind his father shows that he was not contributing to his father's work in a meaningful way.

6. C

In this case, the son's attitude toward his father can be identified in his brief description of his father's stumbling in the present time of "today." This stumbling parallels his own as a boy while following his father in the fields. The words *bitter*, *critical*, and *apologetic* do not reflect the attitude described here because they all imply that some wrongdoing harmed their relationship in some way. It is most likely that the son is reflective because he is remembering, or reflecting, on his early days stumbling after his father on the farm.

7. B

If the father is now stumbling behind the son, it is similar to the way the son stumbled behind the father earlier. The father would not have become the son's friend, but he has taken the son's role.

8. D

The best response is that "perception changes with maturity" because the poem portrays a mature son reflecting on his upbringing with his skillful farming father.

9. A

Rap is a genre of music that has a particular style; the description outlines the common elements that characterize rap music and how it is presented. The genre's stylistic elements all contribute to the presentation of an attitude that is not specific to any one particular rap artist. Rap is not the only current music genre that is presently being marketed.

10. A

The word *seep* generally refers to a gas or liquid that slowly passes or escapes through an opening. In the given phrase, words are compared with a fluid through this figurative image.

11. A

Editorial writing expresses the opinion of the writer and is subjective in nature. Rex Murphy makes his opinion about the commercialism and purpose of pop music clearly evident in his essay. Autobiographical writing focuses on one's life. Objective writing focuses on

facts and presents all sides of an issue letting readers form their own opinions. Allegorical writing is characterized by symbolic characters, events, and objects that collectively present a deeper level of meaning illustrating humanity or society as a whole.

12. A

Rex Murphy compares figuring out the words and meaning in rap music with completing a dive in the ocean to obtain some reward. He wonders if the reward of learning the meaning behind the music is really worth the effort. A reward is most similar to a treasure. Bullion is gold or silver in the form of bars or ingots.

13. B

A revelation is an enlightening disclosure that can be compared with a treasure or bullion that can be found by diving to the bottom of the sea. One hopes the effort of the dive will be worth it and that a sizeable bullion will be found.

14. A

To be sardonic means to mock or use disdainful humour. Murphy's comparison is a humorous exaggeration that reveals his disdain for the inaccessibility of rap lyrics; his tone is quite sardonic. Sarcasm can be defined as having bitter or hurtful intent, which is not applicable in this instance. Reverence is awed respect. Belligerence is exhibiting hostility; Murphy's humour is not hostile.

15. C

One's mantra is an expression or idea that is repeated, often without thinking about it. An "all-purpose mantra" is an idea or expression that is commonly believed or expressed. Thus, the "all-purpose mantra" is best described as a widely adopted attitude.

16. A

The word *colloquia* means informal meeting, which would be the nature of an interview to take place on a show that Murphy misnames *Intimate and Inarticulate* (the show's actual title is *Intimate and Interactive*). Though Murphy does seem to indicate in his renaming of the show's title that the personalities interviewed are "inarticulate," he makes no indication that the interviews are awkward. Interviews with celebrities would rarely be unexpected for a taped television show. Murphy's sarcastic remarks about the program, including the renaming of the show's title, intimate that Murphy probably finds the conversation to be less than enlightening.

17. C

Homer is a Greek epic poet who wrote the *Iliad* and the *Odyssey* in the 7th or 8th century B.C. Shakespeare is a playwright and poet who wrote influential works in the 16th and 17th centuries. Both Homer and Shakespeare are historical figures, so reference to them by means of comparison is a historical allusion. A literary allusion is a reference to a specific work of literature. A mythological allusion refers to specific literary myths, such as a Greek or Roman myth. A biblical allusion is a reference to a specific detail from the Bible.

18. A

Both Homer and Shakespeare are celebrated poets who are firmly canonized in Western literature. Neither Homer nor Shakespeare were known as musicians. Homer is not known historically as a playwright, although his narrative poetry has been translated and enacted many times. The word *contemporary* refers to present-time—a time in which neither of these poets exist.

19. C

Alliteration occurs when the first consonant sound is repeated in two or more words in a line or sentence. The *s* sound is repeated twice in this short phrase. Sound imagery allows readers to imagine a sound. Internal rhyme occurs when two words in the same line rhyme. An oxymoron is a contradiction of terms within a phrase.

20. A

The word *divine* means relating to God or a god. Murphy is referring to the worship that Bob Dylan received from many fans. *Godhead* means divine nature or essence, so to call someone a "godhead" means that they are perceived to be divine or god-like.

21. C

Murphy compares Bob Dylan's songs with the "low whine" of a "nervous cat" (line 16), which is an unusual comparison. The image is surprising, vivid, and humorous. It quickly engages readers' imaginations of sound and image. The judgment of musical value is subjective, and some people may see this assessment as quite fair. The writer's intent in writing this article seems to be focused on commenting on broader cultural issues rather than insulting or offending specific individuals. A complimentary description should not be expected following the sentence, "Blurring the words for the sake of sound is nothing new" (line 13). This shows that further criticism is coming.

22. B

The word *tumid* is characterized by a style or language that is trying to sound better than it actually is. Since the song is already described as "recklessly pretentious," Murphy establishes that it pretends or appears to be more than it truly is. The words *pompous* and *inflated* imply an excessive sense of self-importance that is not warranted. The words *cryptic* and *intricate* imply depth and are the opposite of "recklessly pretentious." The lack of meaning or depth in the songs is introduced in the topic sentence of this paragraph. Neither repetition nor lack of originality is specifically identified as criticism for this particular example.

23. A

The word *vaporous* means of a fanciful, ridiculous, or unsubstantial nature. The word *escapism* refers to the departure from reality or truth characteristic of idealism. Idealism is the belief in and pursuit of perfection as an achievable goal. Idealism ignores the unpleasant but truthful limitations of human experience. Overall, the Murphy's criticisms of 1960s culture seem to focus on the vapid, unrealistic nature of the music of this era.

24. B

Murphy points out that "the next line offers the terse paraphrase: 'The answer is blowin' in the wind,'" which makes fun of the simplistic and vague assertion that is only repeated and never explained. He definitely targets the repetition and lack of meaning in his criticism.

25. D

The "horror of my youth" refers to the mass protests and consequences of the 1960s that Murphy refers to as "hootenannies," the existence of which were largely the result of the influence of pop music.

26. D

Murphy identifies the force corrupting the purpose of the protest movement as being indulgence: in his words, "The innocence of the protest generation, much like its high Eden moment at Woodstock, was always more indulgence than art" (line 29).

27. A

The word *treacle* refers to an antidote for poison. The protesters of the 1960s wanted to bring about change because they were highly critical of many social realities of their time. What they believed in was finding an antidote or cure for the problems of their time as well as for the problems of the future.

28. A

A hootenanny is a gathering at which folksingers entertain the audience with audience participation. Informally, it has also been used to describe ridiculous, chaotic, or uncontrolled actions or events. Choosing this word rather than some other more standard choice shows the writer's disdain for how ridiculous these events were to him.

29. D

Commercialism is identified as fuelling the protest music of the 1960s. Murphy points out that they "may have been strumming peace, love, and rebellion, but their eye was on the charts and their real best friends were always the accountants" (lines 37, 38).

30. A

According to Murphy, "then it was peace, today it's attitude" (line 39) that drives the music industry as an image of choice.

31. B

Eminem's history involves suicide, weapons, and court challenges, all of which are anything but charming. Murphy uses verbal irony because he means the opposite of what he says and is critical of the artist's lifestyle. *Reverent* means expressing profound respect or awe. *Reluctant* is defined as unwilling or disinclined. A formal tone involves adherence to social conventions.

32. B

The reference to the television series *Survivor* is an allusion to the self-destructive and attention-seeking nature of the contestants on the popular reality show. Eminem being a "one-man" variation of the show seems to pick at the artist's outlandish behaviour and use of public outrage to garner publicity. Irony involves a discrepancy between what is real and what is perceived. A metaphor is a comparison of two unlike things without the use of *like* or *as*. Hyperbole is an intentional exaggeration.

33. C

Being well-known for violent lyrics expressing rage is considered disreputable, and consequently, notorious is a fitting adjective to use when describing someone who has achieved fame for this reason.

34. A

Slag is a colloquial term that means to insult someone. Obviously, Eminem's seemingly indiscriminate "slagging" of family members and celebrities alike is negative. Since the writer has found little value in the pop music thus far in the essay, it is safe to assume that the term has a negative emotional meaning.

35. A

Obligatory means required or obligated, and *unzipped* refers to content that is considered inappropriate or abhorrent, which means capable of arousing strong feelings of repugnance or disapproval.

36. D

Piety refers to devout religious belief. It is ironic that today's boomer generation is criticizing today's youth for falling for the same marketing for the same reasons as they did in the 1960s. An inflammatory statement is meant to incite outrage. The bite of criticism is lessened by the fact that Rex Murphy is most likely among the boomer generation's ranks. Prejudice involves prejudging or being less accepting of individuals who are part of a particular grouping. Murphy criticizes all generations of the same thing, so he is not singling one group out for criticism. Murphy is making an insightful point and is focused on that purpose rather than on comedy for its own sake.

37. C

Texts that aim to poke fun at, ridicule, or expose human weakness or folly are satirical. Murphy exposes the hypocritical criticism of older generations while criticizing past and present cultures in general for blindly buying into the commercialism of pop music.

38. A

Murphy's essay is emphatically focused on showing that pop music of past generations was just as controversial and driven by greed as pop music is now. The reason that he does this is to show how older generations are hypocritical in their concern about today's youth artists. The essay is devoted to showing the similarities of two musical trends to express that nothing new is happening.

39. B

Ingenuity is defined as cleverness or originality. The suggestion is that Eminem's "real" appeal is an echo of past examples of the marketed rebellion of young adults. The message is that he is not the "real" or the first. Murphy is also poking fun at Eminem by quoting lyrics from one of his songs, "The Real Slim Shady," in which the phrase "real Slim Shady" is repeatedly used.

40. A

The details of the essay relate to the idea that all generations have bought into music that has seemingly rebellious or profound identity or depth, but the purpose is always attached to marketing and profit.

41. D

The phrase contains an example of personification, which is defined as a literary device in which something non-human is given human characteristics. The technique of "clothing" the world with snow gives the world a human characteristic.

42. C

The purpose of the opening paragraph is to describe the characteristics of the snowfall to which the narrator awakens.

43. B

The question is about limited perception. All of the quotations come from Socrates' description of the cave. However, only one makes it clear that, being unable to turn around, the prisoners can only see what is in front of them. Their perception is limited by their chains: "here they have been from their childhood, and have their legs and necks chained so that they cannot move, and can only see before them, being prevented by the chains from turning round their heads."

44. C

The liberated prisoner will be confused and uncertain (lines 31–34), will have to be forced out of the prison (line 40), and will experience pain. In the end, the prisoner will congratulate himself on his release (line 55).

45. A

Append means to add something at the end. For example, you can append one file to another. Append is the root for words such as *appendage* (a thing that has been added to something) and *appendix* (material at the end of a text or a tube at the end of the large intestine).

46. A

Quotation marks were first used to quote directly in speech in the early eighteenth century, so Plato would not have used them in his Socratic dialogue or any of his other writings. Some editors and publishers might choose to rewrite early texts with modern punctuation, but this is not apparent in this excerpt. However, the editors have included other punctuation marks that were not present in Plato's day. This was probably done to help readers understand the dialogue. There is no need for quotation marks in dialogue that is set out in play format, but modern writers would use quotation marks in other dialogues. Line breaks have been used to denote a new speaker, but they do not denote the exact words spoken by either of the characters.

47. A

Myths have more than one purpose, and this myth expresses a truth about the human condition and the limited perception that all humans experience. While the myth does provide a vivid image that readers can "see," the purpose of the image is to express a truth. The image is not invented for its own sake. While the myth presents a thought that is too difficult for ordinary words, the thought is a truth about the human condition. The moral principle is derived from the truth that has been expressed. The myth is designed to lead up to the truth, but it does not summarize the truth.

48. C

The Republic, from which this dialogue is taken, is largely a collection of dialogues because Plato was recording Socrates' teaching method. These dialogues had a definite purpose. They do help to simplify the story, but the story itself is not really complicated. The reader is not left to infer the meaning of the argument, for Socrates himself explains what the images in the story stand for. This is a technique (the Socratic method) of teaching by proceeding one step at a time through question and answer. At each stage, Glaucon is given a chance to respond to what has just been said. One method of persuasion is to arrange for constant agreement by asking a series of questions that will almost certainly be answered affirmatively. Thus, a final agreement is set up without the need for honest argument and clear logic. An inattentive reader could just agree along with Glaucon. However, the questions are simple and the whole argument is laid out carefully, with every step clearly explained. It seems that the purpose is instruction, not persuasion.

49. B

Cynical refers to a distrusting or contemptuous attitude toward other people's motives. Socrates believes that other people are unenlightened because of factors beyond their control. Even the prisoner who escapes has to be helped (forcibly) to make the first steps. The anger of the prisoners who are told about the real world is also seen as inevitable under the circumstances. So Socrates is not cynical. Socrates seems to be realistic about human nature: there are real problems and improvement is hard. Optimism and pessimism can describe certain philosophical viewpoints, but in ordinary speech, they simply mean having positive or negative thoughts about life. Not being given any information about the two philosophies, it is best to use the everyday meanings. Socrates is neither optimistic nor pessimistic; he simply describes the situation and says what ought to be done. He does not say how likely or unlikely he thinks the desirable outcome to be.

50. D

The meaning of the phrase "show in a figure" must be understood by inference. The shadow play is what is seen when objects are carried past the fire. These shadows are part of the story. It is the story, not just one of its parts, that is "showing in a figure." A figure is like a figure of speech that contains some truth, only the figure is larger—this figure is the entire story (myth). This response is related to the answer, but is not the answer. In arithmetic, a figure is the result of calculation, but this meaning has nothing to do with the story. This story is all about explaining a difficult truth. An illustration that demonstrates the truth describes "figure" very well.

ANSWERS AND SOLUTIONS—READING AND VIEWING UNIT TEST

1. A	10. A	19. B	28. A	37. A
2. B	11. A	20. A	29. C	38. C
3. C	12. D	21. D	30. D	39. B
4. A	13. B	22. C	31. A	40. B
5. A	14. A	23. D	32. A	41. B
6. C	15. C	24. C	33. A	42. D
7. A	16. A	25. B	34. D	
8. A	17. B	26. D	35. C	
9. A	18. B	27. B	36. C	

1. A

This is an Elizabethan sonnet, which has the structure of three quatrains and one rhyming couplet at the end.

2. B

The speaker refers to an "ever-fixed mark"—a landmark that sailors use to help chart their course and arrive at their destination. The speaker also mentions a tempest (a storm at sea), and still later, the North Star (a star that never changes its position and is used for navigation). An ever-fixed mark refers to a trustworthy aid for navigation.

3. C

This quatrain suggests that time cannot alter or weaken true love. Each of the metaphors mentioned by the speaker alludes to the manner in which sea-faring navigators chart a safe and certain course. The speaker compares the solidity of true love with trusted constants of navigation.

4. A

The poet suggests that love might be tested by doubts and fears, but that true love is able to conquer these through its steadfast nature.

5. A

The third quatrain suggests that time cannot alter or weaken true love.

6. C

In the final lines of the poem, the poet suggests that by writing down his thoughts, they will endure, even after he is gone, to confound the power of time. In this manner, the poet bets that love will win over time.

7. A

The speaker's assertions about true love are straightforward. The speaker's plain, direct thought reinforces the fact that he believes his assertion to be beyond doubt.

8. A

The image of the Grim Reaper wielding a curved sickle is common. Time is often viewed as an antagonistic force, an ever-encroaching predator that steals time and life away from the individual.

9. A

The North Star is situated in the centre of the night sky. Although the positions of the constellations change throughout the night or the changing of the seasons, the North Star remains constant, like an axis around which the stars revolve. The word *star* is placed almost right in the middle of the sonnet, which emphasizes the image.

10. A

Personification is a literary device in which something non-human is given human characteristics. In this case, Shakespeare endows the star with the human characteristics of sight and courage.

11. A

The speaker explains situations that show what true love is not: if it alters and bends when tested, it is not true. Then, he explains what true love is: steadfast, dependable, and enduring.

12. D

The term *volta* refers to the change in feeling or emotion that occurs between the components of a sonnet. The couplet indicates a shift in the speaker's discussion. First, the poet discusses the nature of love. Then, he places a wager on the certainty of his opinion.

13. B

The quotation "Or bends with the remover to remove" refers to one person "removing" his love. According to the speaker, true love will not bend even if a person were to remove his or her love.

14. A

The nautical metaphors in the second quatrain all refer to methods with which sailors plot their course. The compass mentioned in the third quatrain is also a navigational tool for sailors.

15. C

The repetition of the *t* sound in the first quatrain is defined and noticeable. The nature of the sound emphasizes the confident tone with which the assertion is made. It emulates the sound of a speaker pounding a table or the image of a passionate speaker stabbing the air with his finger.

16. A

The speaker explains what love is and what it is not. The speaker defines the nature of true love, explaining that its purity can endure all hardships.

17. B

To the narrator, the door looked as though it had received little attention and that no one had used it for an extended period of time.

18. B

A metaphor is a literary device in which two unlike things are directly compared. The wall that the narrator describes is compared with a forehead with no eyes. This metaphor suggests that the building was bleak and uninhabited.

19. B

The "blind forehead" alludes to the idiom "turning a blind eye." Turning a blind eye refers to the acknowledgement of a problem coupled with a refusal to deal with or solve the problem. Less fortunate members of society were often ignored in the Victorian era in an effort to uphold the strict moral standards that characterized British society.

20. A

To remark is to observe or notice.

21. D

Mr. Enfield uses hyperbole when he exaggerates the distance from which he was returning home. This exaggeration serves to emphasize the bizarre, other-worldliness of the situation he is about to witness.

22. C

This style of narration helps the reader to imagine the long, monotonous walk home. This structure has the effect of making the tale that the speaker is about to relate even more striking and bizarre and enables the reader to feel the same alarm as Mr. Enfield.

23. D

The collision represents a direct conflict between innocence and evil. Victorian society had such strict moral ideals that it ignored the presence of human fallibility and immorality in favour of simply pretending that it did not exist. By showing an innocent child colliding with an evil person, the writer is suggesting that without recognizing the reality of human immorality, society puts the truly innocent at risk.

24. C

The narrator takes great care to explain to the reader that the physician is not a person prone to strong emotional outbursts. The fact that even a person who is typically rational cannot restrain intense loathing indicates to Enfield that his instinct to punish the man should not be suppressed.

25. B

The description that follows this quotation indicates that the narrator is discussing the situation or circumstance of the doctor; none of the other alternatives are remarked upon in the passage.

26. D

Enfield compares the doctor with a loud, raucous instrument that could hardly be considered tender or emotional. This simile serves to emphasize the doctor's reaction of loathing toward the man who ran down the little girl. If a person who is normally rational and slow to anger feels so strongly, it is likely that there is good reason for being alarmed.

27. B

The idiom "cut and dry" refers to the fact that a thing or person shares characteristics typical of its kind. In this case, the doctor seems to share traits that are typical of most doctors.

28. A

The men are angry enough to kill the man, and they can barely restrain their impulse to do this. The next best punishment that they can imagine is to spread the word throughout society of what has happened. The man's immediate capitulation to their wish for money in order to prevent this publicity indicates that reputation was highly valued in Victorian society.

29. C

This scene describes the onlookers forcing the man into giving the family of the little girl a large sum of money as compensation for his actions.

30. D

The witnesses to the collision have earnest doubts about the truth of the man's claims. In the context of this sentence, the word *apocryphal* means "dubious."

31. A

The man responds with "black, sneering coolness," an emotion that displays his arrogance and sense of power. He seems to mock and scorn the people around him. The man's response is derisive.

32. A

The narrative that Enfield has just related contains bizarre content and long, descriptive sentences. Mr. Utterson's "Tut-tut" is short and alliterative.

33. A

The opening sentence contains an explicit, specific description of the location of a building. This explanation suggests orderliness and rigidity. What happens next—the collision of two very different characters at the intersection of this careful gridwork—indicates the severity of the action.

34. D

The definition of the word *juggernaut* is "a force that is relentlessly destructive, crushing, and insensitive."

35. C

Enfield says he "took to his heels and collared the gentleman," which means that he ran after the man and was successful in catching him.

36. C

The doctor suggests that the little girl was "not much the worse, more frightened." What appalls the witnesses to the incident is not the fact that the child was hurt, but rather that a grown person could be capable of committing such an act at all.

37. A

A harpy is a mythological creature defined as "one of several loathsome, voracious monsters with the head and trunk of a woman and the tail, wings, and talons of a bird."

38. C

The colours black and red allude to images of the devil.

39. B

The door suggests that there is indeed access to the space behind it, but that no one has opened it to go inside. This represents a criticism of a society that can recognize an issue, but will not take the necessary steps to deal with it.

40. B

Since the narrator is describing the doorway, and since the area around the doorway seems to be populated, the evidence in the passage does not indicate that no one is aware the door exists.

41. B

When his companion points to a filthy, neglected doorway, it arouses the curiosity of Mr. Utterson.

42. D

The fact that the man's actions could arouse intense emotions in a person not usually given to them only exaggerates how loathsome the incident must have seemed to the onlookers.

NOTES

TABLE OF CORRELATIONS			
General Outcome	**Specific Outcome**	**Practice Questions**	**Unit Test**
C Purposes	C1 write meaningful personal texts that elaborate on ideas and information	Writing Prompt	Writing Prompt
	C2 write purposeful information texts that express ideas and information	Writing Prompt	Writing Prompt
	C3 write effective imaginative texts to develop ideas and information	Writing Prompt	Writing Prompt
	C4 create thoughtful representations that communicate ideas and information	Writing Prompt	Writing Prompt
	C5 select, adapt, and apply a range of strategies to generate, develop, and organize ideas for writing and representing	5	
	C6 select, adapt, and apply a range of drafting and composing strategies while writing and representing	Writing Prompt	Writing Prompt
	C7 select, adapt, and apply a range of strategies to revise, edit, and publish writing and representing	1, 3, 4, 6, 7, 8, 9, 10, 11, 12, 13, 14, 15, 16, 17, 18, 19	1, 2, 3, 4, 7, 8, 9, 10, 11, 12, 13, 14, 15, 16, 17, 18, 19, 20, 21, 22, 23, 24, 25, 26
C Thinking	C8 write and represent to explain and support personal responses to texts	Writing Prompt	Writing Prompt
	C9 write and represent to interpret, analyse, and evaluate ideas and information from texts	Writing Prompt	Writing Prompt
	C10 write and represent to synthesize and extend thinking	Writing Prompt	Writing Prompt
	C11 use metacognitive strategies to reflect on and assess their writing and representing		
	C12 use and experiment with elements of style in writing and representing, appropriate to purpose and audience, to enhance meaning and artistry	2	5, 6
	C13 use and experiment with elements of form in writing and representing, appropriate to purpose and audience, to enhance meaning and artistry	Writing Prompt	Writing Prompt

C2　*create thoughtful representations that communicate ideas and information*

C5　*select, adapt, and apply a range of strategies to generate, develop, and organize ideas for writing and representing*

C6　*select, adapt, and apply a range of drafting and composing strategies while writing and representing*

C7　*select, adapt, and apply a range of strategies to revise, edit, and publish writing and representing*

C12　*use and experiment with elements of style in writing and representing, appropriate to purpose and audience, to enhance meaning and artistry*

C13　*use and experiment with elements of form in writing and representing, appropriate to purpose and audience, to enhance meaning and artistry*

PURPOSE, PROCESS, AND FORM

The goal of writing, as with any other forms of communication, is to express ideas. Although the forms of expression are many and varied, in this portion of the KEY, the types of writing assignments studied will be those required for the provincial examination and those most commonly used in your senior English classes: the expository essay, the analytical essay, and the personal essay. While studying these writing forms, you will review the basic steps necessary for creating thoughtful, purposeful, and lucid compositions: prewriting, drafting, revising, and editing. However, before discussing multi-paragraph compositions, it is appropriate that you understand the basic building block of any essay—the paragraph.

The Paragraph

Although paragraphs can be organized in several ways, many students use the familiar "hamburger format" with its introduction and conclusion that frame the "meat" or body of the paragraph. You can use this structure to write a clearly organized paragraph, and by extension, a well-organized multi-paragraph essay, as long as you remember a few additional points.

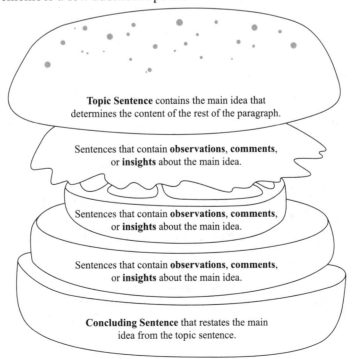

Topic Sentence contains the main idea that determines the content of the rest of the paragraph.

Sentences that contain **observations**, **comments**, or **insights** about the main idea.

Sentences that contain **observations**, **comments**, or **insights** about the main idea.

Sentences that contain **observations**, **comments**, or **insights** about the main idea.

Concluding Sentence that restates the main idea from the topic sentence.

- The number of sentences in each paragraph will vary.
- Every sentence must relate to the topic sentence.
- Each sentence and paragraph must relate to the controlling idea, theme, or essay topic.
- The sentences and paragraphs must be written in logical order.
- Logical order is advanced by transitional devices linking key ideas.

The three essential steps framing the single paragraph are basic to all forms of communication. For example, can you imagine walking up to a total stranger without some form of introduction, regaling him with your thoughts on yoga, and then walking away without saying another word?

Likely not. Both an introduction and a parting goodbye are expected. Without them, your thoughts have no context and appear meaningless.

The Introduction

Just as a salesman needs to introduce himself to a prospective customer and ask which product that customer might wish to learn about, the introduction to a paragraph needs to accomplish two things: capture the interest of the reader and state a clear purpose for writing.

The attention-getter comes in a variety of forms. For example, you can gain a reader's attention by using any of the following methods:

- ask a question
- provide an interesting statistic
- use a thought-provoking quotation
- begin with a mini "story" called an anecdote

Communicating your controlling idea or thesis statement is the more important of these initial steps, for without it, your work lacks the focal point it needs to anchor the ideas that will follow. Keep in mind there must be a logical relationship between the attention-getter and the thesis statement. Otherwise, your attempt to gain the reader's attention will appear not only meaningless, but foolish. Although the thesis statement follows your attempt to gain the reader's attention, it is wise to decide on your thesis first and then ask yourself what provocative and relevant question or statement can best be used to introduce your topic. Also keep in mind that your choice to use an open or closed thesis statement will depend on how much information you wish to reveal before getting into the body of the paragraph/essay. Both have advantages: the open thesis creates curiosity while the closed thesis provides both the writer and the reader with clarity and order.

Consider the following examples of the two-step introduction.

Question	What is a hero? This question can be answered by looking at two modern heroes, John F. Kennedy and Sir Edmund Hillary.
Statistic	Rogue waves can tower more than 40 metres and can bury cargo ships beneath the sea. A project known as WaveAtlas has led to a better understanding of this phenomenon.
Quotation	"It is not the mountain we conquer, but ourselves"—Sir Edmund Hillary, the first person to reach the summit of Mount Everest, in 1953. The story of Sir Edmund Hillary is the tale of a shy man who set out to conquer not just a mountain, but his own fears.
Anecdote	"It seemed like I would never see my loved ones again. I was the last person left in the school by the end of the day."
	*Avoid using personal pronouns in your introduction (except if you are using an anecdote). Do not say things like "I will be talking about…" or "My report is on the topic of…"

The Body

Now that you have introduced your topic effectively, try to develop the topic with interesting supporting details and precise verbs, nouns, and adjectives that paint a visual image in the mind of the reader. The logical order in a paragraph is also a consideration that can be achieved in different ways.

• Narratives (stories) are often told in chronological order (from first event to the last).

• Arguments may be structured in order of importance, from the least to the most important point or from the most to the least important point.

• A physical description can proceed from side to side, near to far, or up to down.

The content of the sentences containing the supporting details will vary according to the topic. Remember that the controlling idea not only controls the choice of supporting details, it also controls the organization and such things as the choice of suitable words and phrases depending on whether the sentences.

• explain

• argue

• list evidence

• list examples

• tell a story

• discuss plot, setting, or characterization

Diction

The words you choose should be precise and specific rather than general and vague. Consider the comparison chart below.

General Words	Precise Words
hit sounded slide	slam, grind, bump roared, crashed slip, skid, glide
General Nouns	**Precise Nouns**
person storm noise	athlete, principal, electrician blizzard, tornado, monsoon crash, snap, swish
General Adjectives	**Precise Adjectives**
large strong strange	gigantic, monstrous powerful, fierce, intense freak, inexplicable

The Conclusion

Like the introduction, the conclusion can take several forms, each signalling the wrapping up of the passage. For example, you can summarize the key points or ideas from the body of the composition or draw a conclusion by reaching a decision, judgment, or opinion that evolves from the information in the body of the paragraph/essay. For example, the following statements could be used to effectively end the passages on rogue waves or heroes.

Examples
- **Rogue Waves**   Perhaps in the future, we will understand why freak waves occur so that fishermen and sailors will have one less unknown to fear.
- **Heroes**   Like Sir Edmund Hillary, we too can be heroes, if we remember his words: "I have modest abilities; I combine these with a good deal of determination, I rather like to succeed."

THE WRITING PROCESS AND EXPOSITION

Depending on your topic and the clarity of your thesis statement, ideas may come quickly or they may need "hatching time." Anything you can do to generate ideas is helpful, for it is imperative that you have a plan of attack before you begin writing. Regardless of whether you are writing a single paragraph or a multi-paragraph composition, the issue of number plays a role in the organization of ideas. How many examples, arguments, pieces of evidence, character traits, or setting details are you going to use? Your decision will help determine how many paragraphs you will need to fully develop your argument. Determining the number of paragraphs can be an effective organizational tool.

Brainstorming is your first step toward clarifying what you know, what you do not know, and what you need to find out. A common error is trying to think up ideas and begin writing prematurely. Take the time to engage in discussions with your teacher, peers, or anyone who may shed additional light on your topic. Gather information from whatever sources are available (the library, the Internet, texts, or prior personal knowledge). Use graphic organizers, charts, mind maps, or webs to record relevant information. Once you have collected the information you feel you need, begin the grouping process. How does the information you have gathered relate to your thesis? Is there an order of development apparent in the information you have gathered?

Drafting or composing a preliminary text is your next step and the one some students find the most difficult. If you hit the writing wall, that point where your mind freezes and you do not know how you are going to phrase your first sentence, push through the wall by putting pen to paper in that wonderfully disorganized activity called free writing. Many interesting ideas can come from simply spending a short period of time writing on a topic without spending too much time thinking about it. With this technique, rules governing grammar, spelling, punctuation, and capitalization are irrelevant. The focus of free writing is to stimulate thinking in order to generate ideas. Put down on paper everything you can think of that relates to your topic. Once this is done, go back and organize what is relevant to your thesis statement. Remember to keep your basic outline in mind: thesis statement, content sentences, and conclusion. As you order your ideas, keep asking yourself these questions:

- How does this point help to develop my thesis?
- Where does this sentence belong?
- Is this idea clearly phrased?
- Are these sentences logically connected to each other?
- Have I used appropriate transitional devises?

When you have re-worked your initial ideas into a **rough draft** that you are comfortable with, share your work with peers and consider their feedback. Often others will see what you have overlooked and suggest ways to improve your composition.

Sample Text

The following exemplar models the first few stages of the writing process. The topic for this essay is less specific than many, but the organizational steps taken to arrive at a clean draft are effective. Consider how both the mind map and the initial questions posed before writing direct the development of this draft.

Topic: "Making a Difference"

Pre-writing

- The student should make a plan, perhaps on a mind map like this:

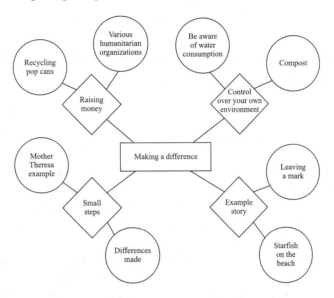

Looking at the plan, the student needs to ask some questions and answer them.

- What is my focus? Making the choice to make a difference
- How can I organize my writing? With some facts and details of examples that can make a difference, some chronological (time ordered) ideas, maybe some cause-and-effect sentences. I will write a paragraph of introduction, two main paragraphs, and a concluding paragraph, each with a clear topic sentence
- What is my purpose for writing? Persuade others to make a difference
- Who is my audience? My classmates
- What is my point of view? I strongly believe that the choices we make create a difference
- How long will my composition be? Four or five paragraphs
- What does format mean? I need to have straight margins and indent each paragraph

Drafting

You are now ready to write or type on the computer a first draft of the composition.

To listen to the news and watch daily images on TV, you would think that the world is on a collision course with disaster. The environment seems to be out of control, supplies of fresh water seem to be dangerously diminished, and extreme poverty is limiting many lives to the bare essentials.

Posing a question
What can I do about these overwhelming problems? What can we do together? What can you do?

Thesis statement—central idea
I strongly believe that the choices we all make can make a difference.

Main idea
You may not be able to control the world's environment, but you can exercise control over your
Supporting detail
own environment. At home, try keeping a pail under the sink for vegetable peelings and other biodegradable matter. Left in a covered bin outside, they will reduce to mulch, which can be dug into
Supporting detail
flowerbeds or gardens. Try cutting five minutes off your daily shower. Do not run water until it is cold for a drink. Instead, just fill a glass and top it with ice. If you do not drink the whole glass, use what's left to water a nearby plant. Plant a tree to commemorate your graduation—each tree planted contributes oxygen to the atmosphere.

Posing a question
Would you like to be living in a Third World country, locked in a never-ending cycle of poverty?
Main idea
You would not. You are a well-fed citizen in Canada, one of the most privileged countries on the planet.
Supporting detail
A simple fundraiser, such as recycling pop cans and bottles, if a small group of friends collect together, can easily yield about $35.00 a month in cash. That is approximately what it takes to support one child in the Third World through a humanitarian observation like UNICEF, World Vision, or Save the Children.
Supporting detail
The money is used to bring healthcare, school supplies, and clean drinking water to that child and often to that child's whole village.

You and I can make a difference if we are willing to take some small steps. Mother Theresa, a winner of the Nobel Peace Prize, was one poor but purposeful individual who tried to make a difference, one
Supporting detail
person at a time. A small story illustrates this final point:

A young boy watched an old man walking along the beach. At low tide, the beach was strewn with starfish, and the old man was stooping to pick them up, one at a time, before flinging them far out over the water.

"Why do you do that?" inquired the boy, his curiosity aroused. "There are too many to help; it can't possibly make much difference."

The man turned to look in the boy's direction. With a half-smile, he answered, as he threw another starfish into the sea, "It just made a difference to that one!"

Summarizing statement
Like the man in the story, you too can make a difference in the world. What "mark" will you leave?

Certain parts of the composition are underlined and labelled so you can see how main ideas are set up and how ideas are supported by details. In the first paragraph, "What can I do about these overwhelming problems" poses a question that is answered in the rest of the composition.

Revising and Editing

After considering peer feedback, revise your rough draft to enhance and clarify any vagaries. At this point of the writing process, you need to carefully edit your work before writing the **final draft**. It is at this stage that all errors in grammar, usage, spelling, punctuation, and capitalization should be corrected.

Transitional Expressions

With expository writing, you will notice that the vocabulary needs to be clear and straightforward. Logical or chronological (time) order needs to be shown by using transitional expressions like the examples on the chart below.

Purpose	Transition Words and Phrases
To show differences	On the other hand In contrast In opposition to this Instead Unlike However In comparison
To show similarity	Just as important Not very different from this In much the same manner Similarly Hence Alike Also
To show preference	In preference to this Preferred by more people However Nevertheless
To indicate time	At the same time A few days prior Following the completion of Next Soon In subsequent months
To indicate more	In addition to that To add to On top of this Furthermore Therefore Moreover It is also true that In the same way Another example of this is

A Review of Parts of Speech

Any discussion of language requires an understanding of the parts of speech. The following brief review is not exhaustive nor does it take account of exceptions, but it does include important information to prepare you for this section of the exam.

A **noun** (derived from the Latin word meaning "name") designates or names a person, place, or thing; a quality, idea, or action; an event or point in time.

- Common nouns are names given to all members of a class: *dozen, child, farm*. Common nouns do not begin with a capital letter.
- Proper nouns name a particular member of a class. They begin with capital letters: *George, Lyndsay, Vancouver, Pacific, Atlantic*.
- Abstract nouns name a quality or general idea that cannot be felt by the senses: *faith, intelligence, fear*.
- Countable nouns like *marbles, trees*, and *stars* can be counted and may be singular or plural.
- Uncountable nouns like *maturity, intelligence*, and *courage* cannot be counted and are singular. Nouns like *water, sand*, and *grain* are countable or uncountable depending on their usage.
- Collective nouns like *committee, staff, family, crowd*, and *class* are singular unless there is a particular reason to treat them as plural.
- Nominals are words or phrases used as nouns. *Skiing, watching paint dry*, and *long distance running* are not nouns, but they could be used as nouns in some sentences.
- Appositives are words or phrases that rename a noun: My friend, *Jack*, will be there. The appositive, *Jack*, renames friend.

Pronouns (from Latin, meaning "in place of a name") take the place of nouns.

- The antecedent of a pronoun is the noun that the pronoun stands for: *Goneril* demanded that *she* be first. The antecedent of *she* is *Goneril*.
- Indefinite pronouns like *all, another, anybody, somebody, nobody*, and *none* are generally singular.
- Interrogative pronouns introduce a question: *who, whom, which, what*.
- Demonstrative pronouns point out and identify nouns or other pronouns: *this, that, these, those, such*.

Adjectives modify or describe nouns and pronouns.

- Most adjectives have endings that mark them as adjectives: *-able* (workable), *-ful* (dutiful), *-ous* (marvellous), *-y* (funny), *-some* (lonesome).
- Adjectivals are any word or group of words that act as adjectives.
- The articles, *a, an*, and *the* are considered adjectives.

Verbs usually name actions: *laugh, sleep, think*.

- Most English verbs are regular; that is, their past tense and past participle forms end in *-ed*. There are about three hundred irregular verbs, but not all are in common use.
- Transitive verbs have a direct object. They do something to the object: The ball *struck* the batter. In the example, the *batter* is the direct object of *struck*.
- Intransitive verbs do not have direct objects. The verbs *lie* (to tell a lie) and *arrive* are intransitive. (You cannot *arrive* anything or *lie* anything.)
- Most verbs can be transitive or intransitive, depending on how they are used: He *produced* a sheaf of papers. The land *produced* abundantly.
- Linking verbs like *be, taste, look*, and *sound* describe states of being. Other linking verbs like *turn, become*, and *grow* describe changes in state. Linking verbs show the relationship between the subject and the noun that follows it: A cheese-doodle *is* a taste explosion. Red skies at dusk *became* the signal for a beach party.

- Remember that linking verbs are usually followed by nouns or adjectives—that is, nominals or adjectivals: She *is* a doctor. She *is* clever. She *sounds* educated. She *turned* pale. My uncle *was* a pilot. He *grew* old. He *turned* eighty yesterday. He *seems* bored.

Adverbs modify or describe a verb, an adjective, or another adverb: She ran *quickly*. His *closely reasoned* argument was brilliant. They worked *very hard*.

- Adverbs are often adjectives that end with *–ly*: The sheriff pursued the outlaws *relentlessly*.
- Frontier language, like that spoken in some Western books and movies, uses *-like* to change adjectives into adverbs. Never use this language on an exam, but it is useful to note the structure: "The cattle-rustlers travelled real *quick-like*."
- Adverbials are any word or group of words that act as an adverb: *After the long, hard day*, we went fishing.
- Adverbs and adverbials describe when, where, how, why, and how much: You can rest *later*. She went somewhere *over the rainbow*. They shuffled their feet *nervously*. Because he was sick, he fell down. I can't believe you ate *all of it*.

Prepositions are linking words used before a noun or pronoun to show its relationship to some other word in the sentence. Note the literal meaning of the word: *pre* (before) plus *position*. For example, for a cause, by the way.

- Together with the noun or pronoun, they modify, or describe, some other word in the sentence: They *worked for a cause*. *For a cause* is an adverbial prepositional phrase modifying *worked*. The *child by them* shouted. *By them* is an adjectival prepositional phrase modifying *child*.
- Prepositional phrases are usually adjectivals or adverbials.

Conjunctions join words, phrases, clauses, and sentences. They also show the relationship between the things that are joined. They show whether the things joined are equal or unequal.

- Conjunctions connect both sentences and sentence parts.
- Coordinating conjunctions like *and*, *so*, and *or* join equal things: Sir Toby likes cakes *and* ale. You must lead *or* follow. Chopping firewood *and* painting the trim are next. We went to the wedding *and* we went to the reception.
- Correlative conjunctions like *either-or* and *neither-nor* join equal parts: Malvolio likes *neither* cakes *nor* ale. You must *either* lead *or* follow. *Either* you must chop firewood, *or* you must paint the trim.
- Subordinating conjunctions like *whenever* and *however* join unequal parts: *Whenever* I hear that song, I want to laugh. You must be careful *whenever* you cross the street. *However* you arrange it, be sure that you are back by Tuesday.

Interjections express some form of emotion: Ouch! That hurts! Oh, I don't know.

SENTENCE STRUCTURE

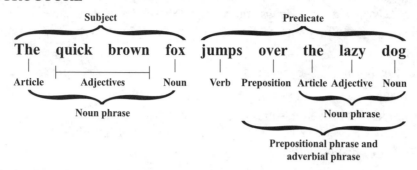

An understanding of sentence structure makes it easier to write and punctuate clear sentences. No matter how long or short it is, a complete sentence requires at least a *subject* (the minimum subject is a noun) and a **predicate** (the minimum predicate is a verb).

> *Dogs* **bark**.

Phrases are groups of words that have meaning and form parts of sentences.

> over the hill
> a long, sad story
> was not ready to go

Clauses are phrases that contain a subject and a predicate; they may form a complete sentence.

Subordinate clauses do not form sentences. They express incomplete thoughts.

> while you were sleeping
> because they had received a large raise

Independent clauses contain a subject and a predicate and can form complete sentences.

> You were sleeping.
> They had received a large raise.

Phrases and clauses are used to build different kinds of sentences. Here is a summary of the different types of sentences.

Simple Sentences

A simple sentence contains one independent clause.

> A boy stood beneath the flag.

Sentence order can be altered for variety or to emphasize one part of the sentence. The part to be emphasized usually comes first.

> Beneath the flag stood a boy.

Compound Sentences

Two independent clauses joined together make a compound sentence. There are four ways to join independent clauses.

1. Independent clauses can be joined by one of the coordinating conjunctions: *for*, *and*, *nor*, *but*, *or*, *yet*, and *so*. (Think FANBOYS to remember the coordinating conjunctions.) Notice that the independent clauses are separated by a comma.

> The boy leapt over the fence, *for* his situation was perilous.
> You cannot win, *but* you can lose gracefully.

2. Independent clauses can be joined by correlative conjunctions such as *either-or*, *neither-nor*, *both-and*, or *whether-or*. No comma is necessary to separate clauses joined by these conjunctions.

> You will *either* work *or* you will fail.
> She had to choose *whether* to hire a locksmith to change all the locks *or* to adopt a large and savage dog.

3. Independent clauses can be joined by a semicolon and a conjunctive adverb, such as *nevertheless, as a result, therefore,* and *however* followed by a comma.

> We have received your application; *therefore*, you are on our list.
> You cannot win; *nevertheless*, you can lose gracefully.

4. Independent clauses can be joined by a semicolon only.

> Winter was long and hard; I hope summer will come soon.
> You finish packing; I'll load the car.

Complex Sentences

Two clauses joined by a subordinating conjunction make a complex sentence. One clause must be independent and one clause must be dependent (*subordinate*).

> *Although the boy stood on the wall*, no one noticed him.
> No one noticed the boy *although he stood on the wall*.
> *While the fire fighters were distracted by brush fires*, three houses burned to the ground.
> Three houses burned to the ground *while the fire fighters were distracted by brush fires*.

Notice that a subordinate clause is followed by a comma when it begins a sentence. When an independent clause is followed by a subordinate clause, as a general rule, no comma is needed to separate them.

Compound-Complex Sentences

A compound-complex sentence contains at least **two independent clauses** and *one dependent clause*.

> *While I slept*, **the sun rose**, and **the birds began to sing**.
> *Although she didn't win a medal*, **Janine competed at the Olympics**, and **she has never forgotten the experience**.

Obviously, this information is as useful for writing as it is for editing and proofreading. When editing, be aware of different kinds of sentences and their structure. When writing, consider varying sentence structure, length, and order both for variety and for emphasis.

ERRORS IN SENTENCE STRUCTURE

Fragments

The long day finally ended can stand alone as a sentence. It is an independent clause that contains both a subject and a predicate.

After the long day finally ended cannot stand alone as a sentence because the word *after* places it in relation to something else. It is now a subordinate clause and would be a sentence fragment if it was written with a period at the end.

Although sentence fragments can be used for emphasis, it is safe to assume that any sentence fragment in the Proofreading and Editing Skills section of the Provincial Examination is an error. When completing the written responses on the examination, it might be best to use sentence fragments only in recorded speech.

> "Not a hope," she said between gritted teeth.

Sentence fragments contain too little; the opposite error is a sentence that contains too much.

Comma Splices and Fused Sentences

The comma splice joins two sentences (two independent clauses) with only a comma.

> She ran to the corner, she saw the train leave the station.

A fused sentence compounds the error by not even using a comma.

> She ran to the corner she saw the train leave the station.

There are several ways to correct these errors. You can rewrite the sentence by using a semicolon, a coordinating conjunction, a subordinate conjunction, or by writing two sentences. Notice that each method presents the same information in a different style.

> She ran to the corner; she saw the train leave.
> She ran to the corner, and she saw the train leave.
> As she ran to the corner, she saw the train leave.
> She saw the train leave as she ran to the corner.
> She ran to the corner. She saw the train leave.

PARALLEL STRUCTURE

Parallel structure is the repetition of words, phrases, clauses, or even entire sentences. The repeated parts must have the same grammatical structure and the same relationship between each part and the whole sentence, as in this example:

> Intoxicated by the excitement of the moment, *he promised his support, he promised his money, he promised his future, he promised his life.*

Notice how the structure of the sentence allows four independent clauses to be connected with only commas; in addition, no *and* is needed before the last list item.

The parallel structure could be started after the word *promised.*

> Intoxicated by the excitement of the moment, *he promised his support, his money, his future, and his life.*

A lack of grammatical agreement is an error in parallel structure.

> Intoxicated by the excitement of the moment, *he promised his support, he promised his money, his future, his life.* (This is incorrect.)

In the previous example, two independent clauses are followed by two noun phrases. There is no longer grammatical agreement between the repeated parts: there is an error in parallel structure.

Although parallel structure can be used for effect, as in the previous examples, most parallel structure and associated errors appear in ordinary writing.

> You will need to bring *your backpack, your tent, sleeping bag, spare clothes, food, and waterproof matches.* (This is incorrect.)

This sentence could be rewritten in two ways:

> You will need to bring *your backpack, tent, sleeping bag, spare clothes, food, and waterproof matches.*
> You will need to bring *your backpack, your tent, your sleeping bag, your spare clothes, your food, and your waterproof matches.*

Both sentences are correct, but notice how the extra repetition in the last sentence produces a rhetorical effect that is out of place in a list of camping supplies. That degree of parallelism is more effective in speeches.

Here is another example. Notice that the faulty structure is not that obvious.

> *In spring, summer, autumn, and in winter*, our weather is unpredictable.

This sentence could be corrected two ways.

> *In spring, in summer, in autumn, and in winter*, our weather is unpredictable.
> *In spring, summer, autumn, and winter*, our weather is unpredictable.

You are free to alter structure for emphasis.

> *In autumn, in winter, in spring, and even in summer*, our weather is unpredictable.

SUBJECT AND VERB AGREEMENT

When writing or editing, do not forget to check that all your subjects and verbs agree in number (they may be singular or plural) and person (they may be first, second, and third person).

	Singular	**Plural**
First Person	I	we
Second Person	you	you
Third Person	he/she/it/one	they

Agreement can be confusing if you only look at the noun nearest the verb. Remember that appositives, prepositional phrases, and adjectival phrases are sometimes placed between the subject and the verb.

> Our *team*, the Lions, *has won* first place.
> That *child* carrying the newspapers *is* hurt.
> And now the two *directors*, flushed with triumph at their latest victory, *step* forward to receive their Oscars.
> The *box* near the exit doors *is* ready.
> The *planes* on runway twelve *are taxiing* for takeoff.
> *Hard work* and *good luck are* necessary for success.

Collective nouns may be singular.

> The *class is* nearly finished its work.

However, collective nouns may be plural if there is some reason to consider the members of the collective as individuals.

> The *class are* arguing over their different plans for the field trip.

Indefinite pronouns are generally singular.

> *Everyone wins* at this game.
> *Each* of the students *has* been warned.

Some of the indefinite pronouns, such as *some*, *any*, and *all* can be singular or plural, depending on the noun that they refer to.

> *Some* of you *are* tired.
> *Some* of the bridge deck *is* damaged.
> *All* of you *are* equally guilty.
> *All* of the lake *is* out of bounds.

Remember that a very common mistake is to make the verb agree with the nearest noun. Certain nouns ending in –s, like *statistics*, *mathematics*, and *politics*, are singular, not plural.

> *Politics is* an important part of national life.

Book titles are also singular although they may seem to be plural. For example, *The Furies* names one book and is therefore singular.

> *The Furies contains* a fascinating story.

AGREEMENT OF PRONOUNS AND ANTECEDENTS

In most writing, most pronouns refer to an earlier noun, the antecedent of the pronoun. There must be no mistaking the noun that the pronoun refers to.

> Both girls agreed that their projects had been prepared thoroughly. They were ready for the science fair. (What or who was ready? The *girls*? The *projects*?)
> When I got to the tax office, they told me they were closing for the day. (In standard written English, *a tax office* cannot be *they*.)
> When the state governor and the provincial premier met, he argued his case vigorously. (Which of the leaders is *he*? Or is *he* someone else present at the meeting?)

In writing and editing, check each pronoun for its antecedent.

CASE OF PRONOUNS

Pronouns present special problems in agreement with other parts of the sentence because pronouns have three cases, as shown in the following chart.

Subjective case used for the subject of a sentence or clause and for the complement of a linking verb	Objective case used for the object of a verb or a preposition	Possessive case used to show ownership	
		Used as an adjective	Used as a subject or as the complement of a linking verb
I	me	my	mine
you	you	your	yours
he/she/it	him/her/it	his/her/its	his/hers/its
we	us	our	ours
they	them	their	theirs
who	whom	whose	whose

Notice that the possessive pronoun *its* follows exactly the same pattern as *his*, *hers*, *yours*, and *theirs*. The possessive form of a pronoun is never formed with an apostrophe.

Also remember that possessive pronouns can be used as adjectives: *my car, your house.*

Whenever you use pronouns, be aware of pronoun case and check for the correct ending.

One common error is using the objective case instead of the subjective.

> *Him and her ran away.*

Another common error is mixing cases.

> *He and her ran away.*

When the pronoun is the subject, use the subjective case.

> *You* have been elected.
> Despite the weather, *we* are certainly going.
> *He* and *she* ran the marathon.
> Even after a late start, *they* still won the marathon.

If the pronoun is the subject and also a possessive, use the second form of the possessive case.

> *Mine* is nearly ready.
> *Yours* is already finished, but *theirs* is not ready.

If the pronoun is the object, direct or indirect, use the objective case.

> Give it to *her*.
> The government mailed *me* a letter.
> When the paper is ready, give it to *her* and *me*.

A pronoun following a linking verb is a noun complement (sometimes called a predicate nominative), and it is in the subjective case.

> It is *he*.
> Yes, I've seen Mrs. Jones. It was *she* that walked past just now.

Sometimes the pronoun agreements cause trouble. Here is a useful rule of thumb: whenever you have more than one pronoun, try the sentence with one of the pronouns at a time.

> *He* did it + *I* did it = *He* and *I* did it.
> *She* is the one + *He* is the one = *She* and *he* are the ones.

When the pronoun after a linking verb is a possessive, use the form of the possessive case that would be used for the subject of a sentence.

> The red one is *mine*. Did you hear me? *Mine* is the red one.
> This car is *hers*—or is it *theirs*? No, *theirs* is the car on the right.

Note the difference when a pronoun is used as an adjective and when it is used as a predicate complement.

> *Their* win was amazing.
> The win was *theirs*.

And what about the pronouns *who* and *whom*? Although the distinction between these two pronouns may be disappearing, you should be able to use both of them in formal writing.

Who is an interrogative subjective pronoun (a pronoun in the subjective case that asks a question). Use it whenever the pronoun is the subject of a sentence or a clause.

> *Who* are you?
> *Who* is going?
> The candidate *who* should be elected is Jesse.

Whom is an interrogative objective pronoun (a pronoun in the objective case that asks a question). Use it whenever the pronoun is the object of a predicate or a preposition.

> The prize will be given to *whom*?
> *Whom* did you tell?
> To *whom* did they refer?

A simple mnemonic (memory technique) based on similarities of sound can be used to remember when to use *whom*. Think "he/she/who" and "him/her/whom." If the sentence could use *he* or *she*, then use *who*; if the sentence could use *him* or *her*, then use *whom*.

> *He* will win. *Who* will win?
> Give it to *her*. Give it to *whom*?
> The crowd followed after *him*. The crowd followed after *whom*?
> For *her*, we would do anything. For *whom* would we do anything?
> Yes, *he* is the person that won. *Who* was it that won?

USE OF PREPOSITIONS

There is one basic rule for prepositions: a noun always follows a preposition. Prepositions show the relationship between the noun and another part of the sentence. The preposition, the noun, and any related words form a prepositional phrase.

> *over the hill*
> *before your exam*

The noun may have articles and adjectives in front of it, of course, and the noun can be a nominal, a word or phrase that functions as a noun.

The noun is the object of the preposition; the preposition is said to govern the noun.

> The boy stood *on the wall*.
> Their yelling and shouting echoed *down the street*.
> *Over the hill* flew the swans.
> You should go *down the street* and *around the corner*.
> *After the concert*, we will meet *in the foyer*.

These examples contain concrete prepositions of time and place.

The difficulty with the more abstract prepositions is that they are used idiomatically; that is, they are used in ways that can confuse or obscure the meanings of the individual words.

> We are angry *at* an insult; we are angry *with* someone who is insulting.
> We feel anger *at* an insult; we feel anger *toward* someone who is insulting.
> We are apprehensive *of* danger; we are apprehensive *for* someone in danger.
> This is an abridgement *of* a book; this book has been abridged *from* the original.

If you do not know the correct preposition to use, the only thing to do is to look it up. You will have to rely on your overall knowledge of English. Check the prepositions and decide whether or not they "sound" right.

Also watch for sentences like this:

> We are not responsible or even connected *to* that part of the project.

While the preposition *to* was correctly used with *connected*, it was incorrectly used with *responsible*. The sentence should read like this:

> We are not responsible *for*, or even connected *to*, that part of the project

USE OF HOMONYMS AND OTHER EASILY CONFUSED WORDS

Words can be confused because they sound exactly the same (its, it's) or almost the same (insure, ensure) or because their meanings are related (lie down, lay down).

Certain contractions (written with apostrophes) and pronouns are very easily confused.

> *Your* list is complete.
> *You're* almost ready.
> *Their* supper is ready.
> *They're* about to sit down.
> *Its* collar came off.
> *It's* a great pity.

Remember that no possessive pronoun is ever written with an apostrophe.

Because possessives written with apostrophes and plurals sound the same, they are often confused.

> The *quarter's* shape is distinctive.
> I have four *quarters* in my pocket.

The list of homonyms, near-homonyms, and easily confused words is long.

SEQUENCE OF VERB TENSES

The sequence of verb tenses means that time relationships must be properly expressed. Often the verbs in a sentence have the same tense.

> After she *moved* to the coast she *discovered* that she liked the rain; she *forgot* her earlier dislike of wet pavement and often *went* for long walks on rainy days.

However, tense can vary in a sentence. Time relationships are expressed by the careful use of verb tenses.

> Yes, he *decided* to stay, but the news we *are* hearing *will change* his mind.

Statements about universal truths require special attention. What is always true is stated in the present tense.

> The ancient Greeks discovered that *Earth is round.*
> After she moved to the coast, she discovered that *the ocean is endlessly fascinating.*

Writing about literature is a special case. It is customary to write in the present tense.

> Shakespeare's Hamlet *is* a complex character.

Of course, other tenses are used to express time relationships within the literature.

> Hamlet *is* caught between his duty to avenge his father's murder and his doubts about the murder itself. He *cannot be* sure if Claudius actually *murdered* the old king. In the end, Hamlet *decides* that he *will test* Claudius in order *to be* sure of his guilt.

Be careful to observe the time relationships between all the verbs in each sentence. In your own written responses, check the time relationships in each paragraph or sequence of paragraphs.

PLACEMENT OF MODIFIERS

Modifiers include adjectives, adverbs, and all phrases and clauses that act like adjectives or adverbs. The placement of adjectivals (all the forms of adjective) is fairly limited. They are usually found before, but they can also be found after the word or phrase they modify.

> A *rubber* ball bounces high.
> The child *hiding behind the door* should be asked in.
> A tall man *at the front of the room* began to sing.

In the last example, the words *at the front of the room* could be moved to the beginning or the end of the sentence, but doing so would alter the meaning of the sentence. Also, the adjectival prepositional phrase would become an adverbial prepositional phrase.

The placement of adverbials (all the forms of adverbs) is much less limited. The extra freedom means that they can be misplaced more easily.

> She whistled *cheerfully.*
> *Cheerfully* she whistled.
> She *cheerfully* whistled.
> He rose and went walking *before dawn.*
> *Before dawn*, he rose and went walking.
> He rose *before dawn* and went walking.

The previous examples are all correct. This example is not.

> She walked her dog *in a bright orange flounced skirt*.

Who or what was dressed in bright orange? In this case, unless the dog was really wearing the skirt, the adverbial phrase must be placed at the beginning of the sentence, or it must be altered in some other way.

> *In a bright orange flounced skirt*, she walked her dog.
> She walked her dog *while wearing a bright orange flounced skirt*.

Otherwise, the modifier is misplaced. Misplaced modifiers (also called dangling modifiers) make sentences unclear at best and ridiculous at worst.

Such errors can look so absurd that it might seem that they are rare, but modifiers are often misplaced. Here is a sentence from a real news report: *She was taken from the room she had shared with her sister for ten years **at gunpoint**.* The misplaced modifier, which actually belongs after the word *taken*, makes nonsense of the entire sentence. The mistake would be amusing if the real circumstances had not been so tragic.

CAPITALIZATION

The basic rule for capitalization is to use capital letters for proper names.

> Alicia, Arthur, Angola, Aristotle, Eastern Hemisphere, Mississippi River

Common nouns are not capitalized.

> girl, boy, country, philosopher, hemisphere, river

Proper adjectives (adjectives formed from proper nouns) are capitalized. However, long use has made some proper adjectives into common adjectives.

> Canadian, Victorian, Manitoban, Haligonian, Roman, Italian, Moroccan
> roman numerals, italic script, moroccan leather

The titles of written works should have the first, last, and all the important words (nouns, pronouns, verbs, adjectives, and adverbs) capitalized.

> The Rule of Law
> Over the Blue Horizon
> Learning How to Capitalize Is Easy and Fun

All titles of people are lower case unless they are used as part of a name or instead of a name.

> the premier of the province, Premier Smith, Good morning, Premier
> the president of the country, President Smith, Good morning, Mr. President
> my aunt, Aunt Abigail, Good morning, Aunt

All common nouns are lower case unless they are part of a name or are being used as a name.

> Fraser River, the Fraser and Columbia rivers
> the North (a region), north (a direction)
> St. Andrew's Cathedral (a name), cathedral (a building)
> Winston Churchill High School (a school), high school (a school building or a level of schooling)

All sentences and sentence fragments begin with a capital letter. Direct quotations are capitalized according to their structure as sentences. No matter where it appears, the beginning of a sentence is capitalized.

> Alfred said, "Are we ready?"
> "I'm finished the job," said Alfred. "We can go now."

A sentence that continues after a speech tag (such as *he said*, *she replied*, or *Alfred said*) is not capitalized.

> "When we are ready," said Alfred, "we will go."

PUNCTUATION

Periods

The period is used at the end of most sentences and after fragments used as sentences.

> I walked to the end of the world. And stopped.

Do not use a period after a complete sentence that is contained by brackets or quotation marks within another sentence.

> The company then sent him a registered letter (he was not answering e-mails or telephone messages) to explain the situation.
> That's my friend Sonja (we call her the Matchmaker).
> When she said, "Class dismissed," chaos erupted.

Notice that the bracketed sentences in the first and second examples do not begin with a capital letter, but the quotation in the third example does. The quotation is also set off with both quotation marks and commas.

Punctuating Possessives

Most possessives are formed by adding an apostrophe and an -*s*.

> a girl's smile
> one country's history
> a coat's buttons

The possessive of nouns that end in -*s* is generally formed with an apostrophe and an -*s*.

> the boss's car
> the countess's speech
> James's, Charles's, Alex's

Watch for the possessive of plurals. The rule is to add an apostrophe after the -*s* of the plural.

> five girls' smiles
> three countries' histories
> the actresses' Oscars
> the girls' car

Commas with Conjunctions

The coordinating conjunctions (*for, and, nor, but, or, yet, so*—think FANBOYS) are usually used with a comma.

> He will be late, *for* he must complete the game.
> Go to the edge of the cliff, *and* tell me what you see there.
> She will not learn from her failures, *nor* will she learn from her successes.

However, when a coordinate conjunction joins two short independent clauses, a comma may not be necessary.

> She's late *and* she's tired.

When subordinating conjunctions (which include *after, because, although, if, before, since, though,* and *unless*) are used in an introductory clause, a comma follows the clause.

> *Because you have been elected*, you must serve.
> *Before she leaves*, she plans to write a note of farewell.

Do not use a semicolon to follow an introductory clause.

> *Because you have been elected; you must serve.* (This is incorrect.)

When the subordinate clause follows the independent clause, a comma is usually not used.

She plans to write a note of farewell *before she leaves.*
You must serve *because you have been elected.*

However, a comma should be used when it is necessary to avoid confusion.

Unclear: He has done all his work since his failure last term threatened his final grade.
Clear: He has done all his work, since his failure last term threatened his final grade.

Until near the end, the original sentence seems to mean that he has done all his work from the time that his failure threatened his final grade. A comma after *work* makes it clear that *since* is a subordinating conjunction and not a preposition.

Colons in Sentences

When used in sentences, a colon must follow an independent clause. It introduces a list, an explanation, or an appositive (a word or phrase that restates a noun).

You should bring the following items: a sleeping bag, a change of clothes, and matches.
There is only one honest thing to do: admit you made a mistake and apologize.
Everything about him was summed up in his nickname: Old Ornery.

The list may be set up in point form. The same rule applies.

The introductory course will cover three topics:
1. algebra
2. geometry
3. trigonometry

If a list does not follow an independent clause (a complete sentence) no colon is used.

You must bring a sleeping bag, a change of clothes, and matches.
The introductory course will cover
1. algebra
2. geometry
3. trigonometry

A simple way of checking colon use is to cover up all the words after the colon. Can the first part of the sentence now stand alone as a sentence? If it does, use a colon. If not, then do not use the colon.

Quotation Marks

Use quotation marks at the beginning and end of all words in a direct quotation (someone's exact words). Watch for the use of quotes before and after a speech tag. Also notice the use of the comma after the speech tag (*Alfred said*) in the first example.

Alfred said, "We are ready."
"I'm finished the job," said Alfred. "We can go now."
"When we are ready," said Alfred, "we will go."

Also notice that the closing quotation mark is placed after a comma or a period.

Closing quotation marks are also used with exclamation marks and question marks. When these punctuation marks belong to the sentence, they are placed outside the closing quotation marks.

Didn't you hear him say, "I'm in trouble"?

If the quotation marks belong to the quotation, they are placed inside the quotation marks.

He said sadly, "Why is it always me?"

The same rules apply to closing quotation marks used for other purposes. Periods and commas belong inside the quotation marks.

You could say that her acting was "over the top."

Exclamation marks and question marks belong either outside or inside, depending on whether they belong to the sentence as a whole or to the words inside the quotation marks.

> She asked, "Are these seats taken?"
> I can't believe you call that dilapidated wreck a "car"!

Indirect quotations never require quotation marks.

> Alfred asked if we were ready.
> Alfred said that he had finished the job and that we could go.
> Alfred said that, when we were ready, we could go.

Quotation marks are also used for such things as the titles of short stories and poems. (See the following section on Italics and Underlining.)

Quotation marks are also used to indicate a word used in an unusual sense.

> "Housekeeping" on the space station is challenging.

Quotation marks can also show that a word is used ironically.

> The "suicide" of Jan Masaryk marked the end of democracy in Czechoslovakia.
> It seems that their "help" has put this project three weeks behind.

SPELLING

When proofreading for spelling, expect to see words that are almost correct. Look for mistakes like *vallies* (for valleys), *recieve* (for receive), or *resent* (for recent). Examples like these just miss being correct, and they can be hard to catch. Any reader who automatically corrects for small errors may find it helpful to read sentences backward. This allows each word to be seen as an individual item and not as part of a sentence. With the pattern of meaning removed, it may be easier to find errors. The same method may help you to proofread your own work in the written-response questions.

ITALICS AND UNDERLINING

Certain names are printed in *italic script*. When handwriting or when submitting a printed manuscript to a publisher, *underline* words that should be printed in italics.

Italicize or underline the titles of all major works, such as books, long poems, symphonies, newspapers, magazines, movies, and television series.

> *A Tale of Two Cities*
> *Time* magazine
> *The Times*
> Beethoven's *Ninth Symphony*
> *The Wizard of Oz*
> *Star Trek*

Use quotation marks to set off shorter works or parts of works, such as chapters, short stories, short poems, songs, articles, and episodes in a television series.

Italics are also used to indicate words and sometimes letters that are considered as objects in themselves, not as structural parts of a sentence.

> The word *since* can be a subordinate conjunction or a preposition.
> Add *-s* or *-es* to form the plural of a noun.

Italics can be used *occasionally* for emphasis, as in this sentence.

A Closing Thought

Regardless of which writing form you are asked to use, keep in mind each requires clarity of purpose, focused planning, and fastidious execution. Put time and effort into your work so that you can be proud of what you have created.

C8   write and represent to explain and support personal responses to texts

C9   write and represent to interpret, analyze and evaluate ideas, information, and understanding from texts

C10   write and represent to synthesize and extend thinking

C11   use metacognitive strategies to reflect on and assess their writing and representing

Applying the Process—Analysis

Having reviewed the essay elements and the writing process, you should feel comfortable in applying what you have learned. The most common type of writing called for in senior English classes is a form of exposition requiring you to analyze and interpret poetry, prose, and movie selections. It is expected that you should demonstrate the strategies and reading comprehension skills at the literal, inferential, and critical levels. When interpreting any selection, you should be able to demonstrate and understand the terms, devices, and techniques relevant to the discussion of the work and be able to support a position, interpretation, or response by citing specific details, features, and information from the piece studied. This section contains examples of analytical responses to a variety of forms of creative expression.

Sample 1—*American Beauty*—Analysis of a Movie

The sample that follows contains the elements necessary for organizing an effective response (introduction, controlling idea, developing paragraphs, topic sentences, concluding sentences, supporting evidence, and concluding paragraph) but uses a different method of development. It was written in response to the following topic:

> Consider how the pursuit of self-fulfillment has been reflected and developed in literary text or texts you have studied. Discuss the idea(s) developed by the text creator(s) about an individual's attempt to secure the satisfaction of self-fulfillment.

Example

In her poem "The Swimmer's Moment," Margaret Avison compares the attempt to secure the satisfaction of self-fulfillment to diving into a whirlpool, suggesting that we need to take a risk and do something, anything, that will jar us out of the rut we find ourselves in. While we may end up in the "black pit" or washed up on the "deadly rapids," taking that risk is the necessary first step if we are ever to find our destiny and reason for being.

Lester Burnham, in the movie *American Beauty*, finds himself in just such a rut. He is living an empty life, working at a job he hates, and married to a real estate agent, Carolyn, whose pursuit of riches and material objects consumes her life. We see him sitting in at the dining table in their sterile home with Carolyn and their daughter Jane, listening to sanitized music and sniping at each other over trivial matters. They do not even communicate with each other well enough to have a real fight. Lester finds even less fulfillment in his job in advertising, which seems to consist mostly of attempting to contact customers who do not bother returning his calls.

He is jarred out of his sedated existence however, when he sees Angela, his daughter's friend. His desire for her jolts him out of the "coma he has been in for the last twenty years." In an attempt to impress her, he tries to recapture his youth. He begins to work out, not because he is concerned about his health and fitness, but because he "wants to look good naked." The other catalyst in Lester's resurrection is his drug dealing teenage neighbour, Ricky, who becomes his new hero because he sees him standing up to his boss. At this point, Lester rebels completely. He quits his job and blackmails his boss for a year's salary, refuses to go along with his wife's pursuit of the middle-class dream, and starts using drugs. When he buys a 1970 Firebird, the car that he had wanted when he was a teenager, he thinks he now has everything he needs in his life to recapture the simple happiness he knew as an adolescent.

Continued

Annotations (right margin):

- Use the idea from one of texts provided for personal response
- Use of metaphor to develop controlling idea
- Transition from poem to literary text chosen to develop idea
- Development/support of idea that character is in a rut
- Character goal
- Development of idea of taking a risk, making an attempt to get out of rut

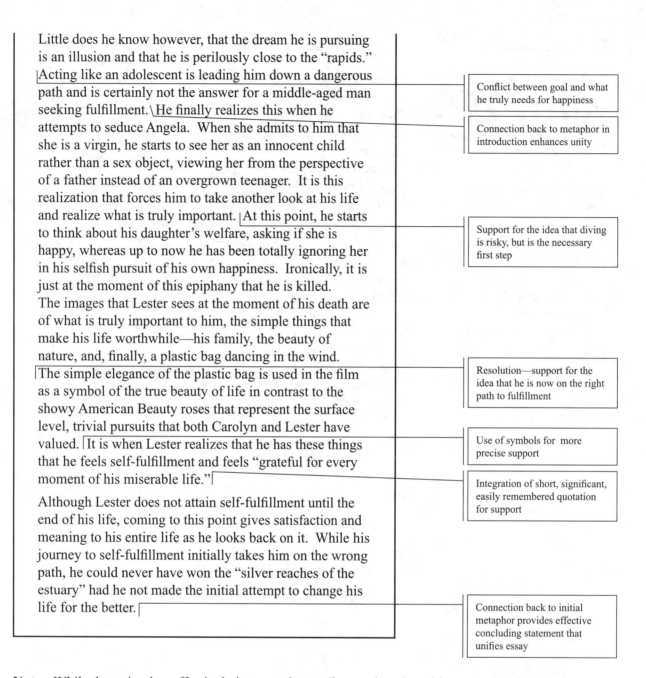

Little does he know however, that the dream he is pursuing is an illusion and that he is perilously close to the "rapids." Acting like an adolescent is leading him down a dangerous path and is certainly not the answer for a middle-aged man seeking fulfillment. He finally realizes this when he attempts to seduce Angela. When she admits to him that she is a virgin, he starts to see her as an innocent child rather than a sex object, viewing her from the perspective of a father instead of an overgrown teenager. It is this realization that forces him to take another look at his life and realize what is truly important. At this point, he starts to think about his daughter's welfare, asking if she is happy, whereas up to now he has been totally ignoring her in his selfish pursuit of his own happiness. Ironically, it is just at the moment of this epiphany that he is killed. The images that Lester sees at the moment of his death are of what is truly important to him, the simple things that make his life worthwhile—his family, the beauty of nature, and, finally, a plastic bag dancing in the wind. The simple elegance of the plastic bag is used in the film as a symbol of the true beauty of life in contrast to the showy American Beauty roses that represent the surface level, trivial pursuits that both Carolyn and Lester have valued. It is when Lester realizes that he has these things that he feels self-fulfillment and feels "grateful for every moment of his miserable life."

Although Lester does not attain self-fulfillment until the end of his life, coming to this point gives satisfaction and meaning to his entire life as he looks back on it. While his journey to self-fulfillment initially takes him on the wrong path, he could never have won the "silver reaches of the estuary" had he not made the initial attempt to change his life for the better.

Callout boxes (right side):

- Conflict between goal and what he truly needs for happiness
- Connection back to metaphor in introduction enhances unity
- Support for the idea that diving is risky, but is the necessary first step
- Resolution—support for the idea that he is now on the right path to fulfillment
- Use of symbols for more precise support
- Integration of short, significant, easily remembered quotation for support
- Connection back to initial metaphor provides effective concluding statement that unifies essay

Note: While the writer has effectively integrated several quotations into this essay, the unnecessary use of quotations should be avoided. For example, if an indirect reference to text or paraphrasing provides the reader with the necessary information, there is nothing gained by following up an assertion with a quotation that makes the same point. Use a quotation only when the writer's word choice provides a significant detail about which you wish to comment. Furthermore, when quoting text, ensure that the information is integrated properly into your own sentence structure rather than "dumped" awkwardly into your discussion.

Example

> Lester eventually realizes that his life, although partially squandered on trivial pursuits is worthwhile after all, and he is <u>grateful</u> for all he has experienced even though at times it has been <u>miserable</u>. He says, "***grateful for every moment of is miserable life.***"

> This inadequate version of the original text unnecessarily repeats in the quotation what has already been established in the first sentence. In addition, the quoted sentence fragment does not blend well into the writer's statement, which remains a sentence fragment.

Sample 2—"Girl at a Crossroads"—Analysis of a Poem

Unlike the multi-paragraph responses to lengthier works such as movies, novels, and short stories, a well-developed single paragraph can be used to analyze a poem. Regardless of its shorter length, the same steps of introducing the subject (fostering reader interest), establishing a controlling idea (thesis statement), developing the central argument (supporting details), and signalling a conclusion (summary or insightful thought) should be evident. Note how the sample that follows incorporates each of these key elements in response to the following topic.

In paragraph form and with reference to the poem, explain how the poet suggests a harsh environment through the use of sound imagery.

Nature has a way of echoing man's world. Milton Acorn plays with this type of pathetic fallacy in his poem "Girl at a Crossroads." Sound imagery is used to echo a young teen's emotional turmoil. The environment that is created around this young lady whose anger is announced in the phrase "whole insides at a slow burn" is equally hostile. For example, the girl's rage is duplicated in the power and noise of the rain, which falls "like hammers rata-tata-tating at sheet-metal." Anyone who has worked with this type of thin metal would easily conjure up a loud, harsh sound and appreciate the noise that surrounded the young girl. The noises are not all foreign, however, for the rain personified takes on an aggressive, human-like quality as the poet writes, "'Go on! Travel!' the whip-tongues of the rain speak…." This phrase contributes to the harshness of the environment, for the "whip-tongues" bring to mind not only the crack of a whip but also its sting and in so doing is threatening and hostile. Lastly, the poet describes the girl as an instrument being played; however, "The clapper clanging her fell of a body" is not a gentle image but rather an unpleasant one. The "clanging" suggests dissonance, internal turmoil that leads to utterances, "words harshly glad." Perhaps she is sobbing or gasping in response to the roll of thunder or the "rip of lightening." Regardless of the cause, it is clear that this human being and her natural environment share a rage, a confusion, a dissonance that must be expressed and violently.

- Introduction begins with an assertion that provokes curiosity
- Title and writer identified, as well as thesis statement identifying sound imagery as the central focus
- Three images are cited and explained
- Quotations are effectively integrated into text
- Transitional devices link the three examples
- A conclusion is provided with a return to the beginning in the form of a rephrasing of the central assertion

C1   *write meaningful personal texts that elaborate on ideas, information, and understandings*

C2   *write purposeful information texts that express ideas and information*

C3   *write effective imaginative texts to develop ideas, information, and understandings*

MODIFYING THE PROCESS

Personal writing comes in many forms and each modifies the rules so clearly set out for the academic essay. The fundamental difference between the two lies in the fact that personal writing is an activity undertaken to express your own ideas and feelings, while much of the expository writing you are required to do is used to comment on what others have written. While personal writing frees your voice, it also allows you to experiment with various forms of writing.

After selecting a significant moment from your own experiences (or a scene from a novel, movie, or play) that you found especially memorable, write a description of that setting in such a way that your description conveys a recognizable feeling (delight, revulsion, nostalgia, disappointment, etc.) more through the use of concrete and specific details than by direct statement of attitude.

Note: Any composition is improved by a variety in sentence structure. The basic subject/verb pattern that forms the primary English sentence pattern can be varied in a number of ways at the beginning of a sentence.

- Basic pattern: The young customer stormed out of the car dealership.
- Begin with a participle [verbal adjective]: Frustrated and dejected, the young customer stormed out of the car dealership.
- Begin with an adjective: Young and inexperienced, the customer stormed out of the car dealership.
- Begin with an adverb: Indignantly, the young customer stormed out of the car dealership.
- Begin with a participial phrase: Feeling patronized, the young customer stormed out of the car dealership.
- Begin with a prepositional phrase: Out of the car dealership stormed the offended young customer.
- Begin with a subordinate clause: Because the salesman appeared to be avoiding him, the young customer stormed out of the car dealership.

Boys & Girls Clubs
of Greater Vancouver

A good place to be

Boys and Girls Clubs of Greater Vancouver founded in 1936, is a leading provider of programs and services all over the Lower Mainland, that support the healthy, educational and social development of 4,000 young people and their families in the community every year.

Dedicated trained staff and volunteers offer professional services in physical, educational, leadership and social recreation programs as well as a summer wilderness camp experience, substance abuse services and parent support programs.

Boys and Girls Clubs of Greater Vancouver
CENTRAL OFFICE
Tel:604-879 6554

2875 St George St, Vancouver BC V5T 3R8
Fax:604-879 6525 Email:info@bgc-gv.bc.ca www.bgc-gv.bc.ca

INTERESTED IN VOLUNTEERING – CALL 604-324 3210

Donate on-line at <u>www.bgc-gv.bc.ca</u> or call 604-879 6554

any **PACE**
any **PLACE**
any **TIME**

Grade 10

Applications of Math 10
Bible 10
English 10
Essentials of Math 10
French 10
Physical Education 10
Planning 10
Principles of Math 10
Science 10
Social Studies 10

Grade 11

Accounting 11
Applications of Math 11
Biology 11
Business Applications 11
Chemistry 11
Christian Studies 11
Communications 11
English 11
Essentials of Math 11
Marketing 11
Physics 11
Principles of Math 11
Science & Technology 11
French 11
Social Studies 11
Studio Arts 11/12

Grade 12

Applications of Math 12
Biology 12
Chemistry 12
Christian Studies 12
Communications 12
Comparitive Civ. 12
English 12
Entrepreneurship 12
Family Studies 12
Geography 12
Grad Transitions 12
History 12
Journalism 12
Law 12
Physics 12
Principles of Math 12

Advanced Placement

(receive High School and
University credit)

AP Biology
AP Calculus
AP Chemistry
AP Computer Science
AP English Literature

Sign up for fall, spring or summer term High School online courses written from a Christian worldview that meet BC graduation requirements.

Work with experienced certified teachers in an interactive, communicative online setting.

No cost for current Grade 10-12 students.

Quality Educational Choices with Christian Values

To sign up today, or for course descriptions and more information go to our website:

BC ONLINESCHOOL.CA

BC Online School is a division of Heritage Christian Online School and a ministry of Kelowna Christian Center

The CKNW Orphans' Fund is dedicated to promoting the health and welfare of disadvantaged children. It assists by allocating funds generously donated by dedicated CKNW listeners, local businesses, and through sound investments and thoughtful bequests.

The CKNW Orphan's Fund has a long history of compassion and assistance to disadvantaged children in the Lower Mainland. Through the Partners in Education program sponsored by Castle Rock Research, B.C., the Orphan's Fund has made a generous contribution of The Key Study Guides to these children.

For more information on the Orphans' Fund please go to

www.cknw.com

WE'RE ALL TALK. AND ALL ACTION.

AT BCIT, there's a lot of talk—which you'd expect as part of a well-rounded education. But there's also a lot of building, designing, presenting, experimenting, playing, researching, programming, laughing, collaborating and innovating.

Now that's something to talk about.

bcit.ca

TECHNOLOGY
CHANGES
EVERYTHING

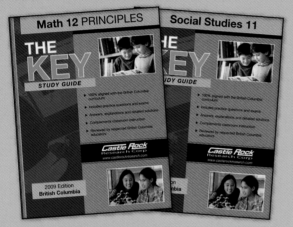
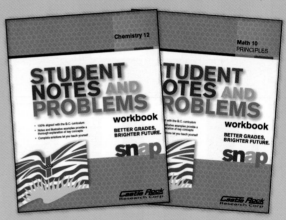

Sample 3—"Music to my Ears—Creative Writing (student sample)

The following excerpt from a personal essay is the beginning of a response to a descriptive writing assignment. Students were encouraged to experiment with a variety of writing techniques in an attempt to convey the details of a significant experience. Although not a professional, note the writer's effective use of descriptive language, in particular personification.

The lights above waiver scoldingly, and all present fall quiet. Abruptly but with softness unfound elsewhere, the huge theatre is plunged into a darkness that envelops everyone—a lightless wave of anticipation. A single light comes up on a man, small, frail, but smiling benevolently at the masses just beyond his circle of light. He nods and turns his back, an impossible blur of white hair above a starched collar and black tails. A hand is raised signalling, hovering, as the light widens to include the orchestra. They remain silent, restless—waiting. Polished wood and flashing metal remain mute. The hand bobs, and with a formal "breathy" sound the whole orchestra is brought up, poised but still silent. Soon they will speak but wait respectfully.

Then the hand drops, gracefully but with practiced precision, and releases a single note, and it has begun. This note, a high, piercing oboe is joined by a bassoon that melds with the first: harmony. A third note enriches the sound, filling it out, and invites the rest to attempt improvment. They all join in, and individual instruments united pour notes like liquid as they mix and change, filling the whole place. The audience breathes it in, intoxicating draughts of purity and sweetness.

And it comes in blasts and in murmurs, exactly as it should. High notes emerge, flying up free followed by a single bass tone, which snatches control. Melodies overlap, layered like a fine veneer inlaid with bright, harmonious patterns. The solid foundation maintains its dignity, while the piece as a whole takes on texture.

NOTES

WRITING PRACTICE QUESTIONS

1. Which of the following sentences contains an adverb clause?
   A. People will not get ahead if they do not study.
   B. Doctor Smith, who was once our family doctor, retired to Arizona.
   C. Because of my defensive driving lessons, I am probably a better driver today.
   D. At the edge of the woods, I encountered an older farmer pushing a wheelbarrow.

2. Which of the following sentences lacks parallel structure?
   A. She thought dancing was more fun than playing the piano.
   B. Most people would rather attend a hockey game than watch it on TV.
   C. The students wanted not only less work but also a shorter school day.
   D. The teacher will help you to understand the assignment better and achieve higher grades.

3. In which of the following sentences does the verb **not** agree with its subject?
   A. Each of your assignments is late.
   B. The windows on this house need cleaning.
   C. Neither Paul nor Peter have made the team.
   D. Some of the stolen coins have bean recovered.

4. In which of the following sentences has the **incorrect** form of the verb been used?
   A. Prices are expected to rise next year.
   B. Whatever he done, I will forgive him.
   C. Before lunch, we swam over to the beach.
   D. When we came home, we found the door locked.

Read the following paragraph to answer the question that follows.

A girl can observe whether her boyfriend treats his family with the same thoughtfulness that she would like to receive from a husband. _For instance_, she should notice how he treats his mother. A man who is kind and considerate _toward_ his mother will act the same way toward his wife. A girl should notice, _too_, how helpful and thoughtful the boy is in the home. Men often say that they will be more interested in doing things around the house when they have a home of their own. _However_, it does not often work out that way.

5. Which of the underlined words from the passage is **not** a transition?

   A. For instance

   B. However

   C. Toward

   D. Too

6. In which of the following sentences has a subjective pronoun been used **incorrectly**?

   A. That was him in the library.

   B. Neither Carl nor he is a good student.

   C. If you and we are late, we'll be unpopular.

   D. The children and I went to the swimming pool.

7. In which of the following sentences has an objective pronoun been used **incorrectly**?

   A. Do you think Kim looks like her or me?

   B. Paul was looking for you and them.

   C. The captains will be Dan and him.

   D. Will you take Susy and her?

8. Which of the following sentences has the **incorrect** use of *who/whom*?

   A. Who were you talking to?

   B. Who is your partner?

   C. Whom shall we call?

   D. Whom did you see?

9. In which of the following groups of words are all the words spelled correctly?

   A. cashier, heifer, reciept

   B. seize, thievery, conceit

   C. handkerchief, forfiet, leisure

   D. mischeivous, ceiling, freight

10. In which of the following groups of words are all the words spelled correctly?

    A. pleasent, exellent, writing

    B. believe, committee, occured

    C. seperate, privelege, immediately

    D. acquaintance, cafeteria, necessary

11. In which of the following groups of words are all the words spelled correctly?
    A. inflamable, definate, describe
    B. privilege, recommend, business
    C. disappoint, ocassionally, noticing
    D. pronounciation, receive, judgment

12. In which of the following groups of words are all the words spelled correctly?
    A. applause, apearance, agravate
    B. misspeak, disarrange, mislead
    C. disapproval, diservice, distrust
    D. acelerate, acquaintance, acquire

13. In which of the following groups of words are all the words spelled correctly?
    A. ilfated, uncertain, inopportune
    B. inoperable, immense, unecessary
    C. unconscious, illiterate, impregnable
    D. inpratical, unfaithful, misbehaviour

14. In which of the following groups of words are all the scientific words spelled correctly?
    A. relitivity, cadmium, galaxy
    B. anemometer, osmosis, inertia
    C. aparatus, gravety, electrolysis
    D. dynamo, chlorophyl, phosforus

15. In which of the following sentences have the commas been used or omitted correctly?
    A. Paul is a courteous, industrious, popular student.
    B. Your work should be written in ink, correctly titled, and, handed in on time.
    C. On April 1st 2007 we moved to our new house at 2000 Greystone Road, Oshawa, Ontario.
    D. Scattered across his desk were science textbooks boxes of coloured pencils and sheets of loose leaf paper.

16. In which of the following sentences has the end mark been used correctly?
    A. Oh, what a disaster!
    B. What a lucky break you had?
    C. Stunt flying requires altitude and speed!
    D. Will you please forward your newsletter to me.

17. In which of the following sentences has the apostrophe been used or not used correctly?

   A. You have been taught to mind your Ps and Qs.

   B. I know your right regarding the children's toys.

   C. *Oliver Twist* is possibly the most famous of Dickens' books.

   D. The chameleon has the ability to change it's skin colour to suit the background.

18. In which of the following sentences have the quotation marks been used correctly?

   A. "How far do you have to travel to school"? she asked me.

   B. "When you arrive," she advised me go straight into the office."

   C. Paul said, "If only you had said, "Marie is visiting from France," I would have come straight over."

   D. David said, "You must read my new book *The Wreck of the Strathnavar*, which has just been published."

19. In which of the following sentences has the colon or semi-colon been used correctly?

   A. Caesar was dead: Rome was in confusion.

   B. A pronoun is used in place of a noun; for example, she, who, they.

   C. A first aid kit should contain the following articles; bandages, gauze, soap, antiseptic, plasters, and lotion.

   D. *A Tale of Two Cities*: written by Charles Dickens, begins as follows, "It was the best of times; it was the worst of times."

Writing Prompt A (Biographical Narrative)

Throughout your life, several people have no doubt influenced your development in positive ways. Think about someone who has been a particularly significant role model for you. What caused you to look up to this individual?

Write an essay in which you discuss a person who has been your positive role model. Explain what has made this person such a meaningful influence. Use details and examples to support your ideas.

_____

_____

_____

_____

_____

_____

_____

_____

_____

_____

_____

_____

_____

_____

_____

_____

_____

_____

_____

_____

_____

_____

_____

_____

_____

_____

_____

_____

_____

_____

_____

_____

_____

_____

Writing Prompt B (Persuasive Writing)

It is not hard to think of a list of problems in the world. It has been said that if each person cared about making just one small difference in the world that many world problems could be solved.

Imagine that you have approached your school administration with some suggestions on the topic of "Making a Difference." You have been asked to share your vision in a student assembly. Write a persuasive essay for the occasion that explains, with precise examples, some areas where students as individuals could make small differences to help solve world problems.

WRITING UNIT TEST

1. Which of the following who/whom clauses is **incorrect**?

    A. She is a student whom everyone likes.

    B. He did not tell me whom he was looking for.

    C. She is one of the students who I want to meet.

    D. We were seen by two teachers who would recognize us.

2. In which of the following sentences is the word usage **incorrect**?

    A. Nick runs faster than he.

    B. Are you as funny as she?

    C. We can do as well as them.

    D. You gave Bob more than me.

3. Which of the following sentences has been written in the active voice?

    A. The children were taken home.

    B. The game was won by our team.

    C. Phillip enjoyed a game of tennis last night.

    D. Jeremy's homework was finished before supper.

4. Which of the following sentences has been written in the passive voice?

    A. Nancy did not believe she could do it.

    B. Lake Tahoe was visited by our family.

    C. New Zealand is a land of many wonders.

    D. David's assignment was to research soccer.

5. Which of the following words **best** describes the mood of the phrase "a long grey journey"?

    A. Fearful

    B. Tedious

    C. Unhappy

    D. Desperate

Read the following passage to answer the question that follows.

> After that the nap of surface resettled.
> Mites danced on both sides of it.
> Coming up, my face seemed beautiful.
> The sun broke on my back.

6. Which of the following words **best** describes the mood portrayed by the given stanza?
   A. Joyful
   B. Warm
   C. Nostalgic
   D. Thoughtful

7. Which of the following groups of technical terms is spelled correctly?
   A. intranet, jarva, netizen
   B. cyberspace, Ethernet, gigabyte
   C. satelites, atmospheric, equivalents
   D. trajectory, constellatians, nevergational

8. Which of the following groups of historical words is spelled correctly?
   A. anarchy, consentration, tsar
   B. prohibition, sufferage, yeoman
   C. pacifism, reperations, resteration
   D. abolitionist, Napoleonic, seigniorial

9. Which of the following groups of business-related terms is spelled correctly?
   A. apparel, architectural, engineering
   B. advertisment, textiles, occupational
   C. accounting, terminology, packeging
   D. management, maintanance, meckanical

10. Which of the following groups of mathematical terms is spelled correctly?
    A. paralell, circumference, theorem
    B. binary, equalateral, permutation
    C. Pythagorus, geometric, multiplicand
    D. polynomials, concurrent, logarithmic

11. Which of the following groups of literary terms is spelled correctly?
    A. euphamism, parody, tragedy
    B. alliteration, rhetoric, soliloquy
    C. asonance, figurative, synecdoche
    D. didactic, onomatapoeia, aphorism

12. Which of the following groups of geographic terms is spelled correctly?
    A. antartic, fjord, meridian
    B. antipodes, chanell, topographic
    C. archipelago, peninsula, tributary
    D. cartographer, equater, Capricorn

13. In which of the following sentences has the verb *lie/lay* been used **incorrectly**?
    A. Ed enjoys lying there and reading his book.
    B. Please lay your book on the table over there.
    C. Debris from the flood was laying all over Main Street.
    D. If you lie down for a while, you will begin to feel better.

14. In which of the following sentences has the verb tense been used **incorrectly**?
    A. On our return, we learned that you called.
    B. If Stephen waits longer, we would have met him.
    C. John was able to win the game because he had practised rigorously.
    D. Several small vessels, which had been securely anchored, were washed ashore.

15. In which of the following sentences has the irregular verb been used **incorrectly**?
    A. When we came home, we found the door locked.
    B. The dog was killed as he ran in front of the truck.
    C. The doctor thought Fred had tore a ligament in his leg.
    D. He won the race because his opponent fell just before the finish line.

16. Which of the following sentences is a fragment?
    A. The bus finally rolled into view.
    B. Just as we had almost given up hope.
    C. Your test results should have been signed by your parents.
    D. All our friends gathered around to help us pack up our belongings.

17. In which of the following sentences has the word *who/whom* been used **incorrectly**?

    A. Whom do you believe?

    B. Whom have you talked to?

    C. Whom do you think this is?

    D. Whom shall we turn to for help?

18. Which of the following words is spelled **incorrectly**?

    A. Tournament

    B. Interpretted

    C. Laboratory

    D. Parliament

19. Which of the following words is spelled **incorrectly**?

    A. Rehearse

    B. Guarantee

    C. Optomistic

    D. Immediately

20. Which of the following words is spelled **incorrectly**?

    A. Leisure

    B. Movable

    C. Disatisfied

    D. Candidates

21. Which of the following words is spelled **incorrectly**?

    A. Parallel

    B. Morgage

    C. Colossal

    D. Exhausted

22. Which of the following words is spelled **incorrectly**?

    A. Definitely

    B. Municipal

    C. Priviledge

    D. Recommend

23. Which of the following sentences contains a comma splice?
    A. John, my older brother, and I are the same height.

    B. At the end of the day, there was a severe thunderstorm.

    C. After years of hard work, Hugh achieved his law degree.

    D. Dan will be glad to help us, his experience is very valuable.

24. Which of the following sentences is a run-on?
    A. We will take the express bus it has a fantastic service.

    B. For two days, gale force winds drove heavy rain against our tent.

    C. Mark did not try out for the team because he could not afford the time.

    D. We decided it was a good idea to wait until summer for our family picnic.

25. In which of the following sentences has the comma been used or omitted **incorrectly**?
    A. "I have finished my test," she declared.

    B. Mrs Grey said, "Omit the first exercise."

    C. Father called out "When did you get here?"

    D. "All you need," the teacher said, "is a little self-confidence."

26. Which of the following sentences lacks agreement between its verb and its subject?
    A. Each of his ideas has merit.

    B. Neither of your arguments make sense.

    C. Every car, van, and truck was used in the rescue.

    D. The criminal responsible for these crimes has not been caught.

WRITING PROMPTS

Writing Prompt A: Expository Composition

Internet networking programs such as MSN, MySpace, and Facebook are becoming more and more common, as are interactive computer games like *The Sims*. These programs allow young people to experience virtual worlds within their real worlds. While most people use these experiences for fun, creative expression, and entertainment, some may risk replacing reality with virtual experiences almost exclusively.

Write an essay discussing the advantages and pitfalls of both virtual and real experiences. Provide examples or details to illustrate your points. Develop and support your ideas clearly so that a reader will be able to understand both the strengths and weaknesses of virtual experiences.

Writing Prompt B: Business Letter

Imagine that a school alumnus, Dr. Roland Balfour, has tentatively agreed by phone to give the commencement address to the graduating class. He has requested a formal letter of invitation that will provide essential details of the request and event.

Write a business letter to Dr. Balfour in which you invite him to speak on the topic "Mountain High." Be sure to observe the appropriate business letter format and to include the type of information he would require for the speaking engagement.

_____

_____

_____

_____

_____

_____

_____

_____

_____

_____

_____

_____

_____

_____

_____

_____

_____

_____

_____

_____

_____

_____

_____

_____

_____

_____

_____

_____

ANSWERS AND SOLUTIONS—WRITING PRACTICE QUESTIONS

1. A	6. A	11. B	16. A
2. D	7. C	12. B	17. C
3. C	8. A	13. C	18. D
4. B	9. B	14. B	19. B
5. C	10. D	15. A	

1. A

The adverb clause, *if they do not study*, modifies the verb phrase *will get* by answering the question "why" with a reason that addresses the verb phrase.

2. D

Parallel structure pairs an infinitive with an infinitive: "The teacher will help you *to understand* the assignment better and *to achieve* higher grades.

3. C

Singular subjects joined by *either/or* or *neither/nor* must be used with a singular verb: "Neither Peter nor Paul has made the team."

4. B

The correct form of the verb should be *did*: "Whatever he did, I will forgive him".

5. C

The word *toward* is not a transition. Rather, it is a preposition that introduces the prepositional adverb phrase *toward his mother*.

6. A

"That was *he* in the library" is the correct form of the pronoun, which must be subjective to agree with the linking verb *was*.

7. C

The linking verb *will be* must be followed by the subjective form of the pronoun, which is *he*: "The captains will be Dan and he."

8. A

In the sentence "Who were you talking to?" the first word is actually the object of the preposition *to*, so the objective form *whom* must be used: "Whom were you talking to?"

9. B

The words *receipt*, *forfeit*, and *mischievous* are misspelled in the other groups of words.

10. D

The words *pleasant*, *excellent*, *occurred*, *separate*, and *privilege* are misspelled in the other groups of words.

11. B

The words *inflammable*, *definite*, *occasionally*, and *pronunciation* are misspelled in the other groups of words.

12. B

The words *appearance*, *aggravate*, *disservice*, and *accelerate* are misspelled in the other groups of words.

13. C

The words *ill-fated*, *unnecessary*, and *impractical* are misspelled in the other groups of words.

14. B

The words *relativity*, *apparatus*, *gravity*, *chlorophyll*, and *phosphorus* are misspelled in the other groups of words.

15. A

In the second sentence, the comma after *and* should be omitted. Commas should be used after the date and year: "April 1st, 2007". Commas should be used in the series: "science textbooks, boxes of coloured pencils, and sheets of loose leaf paper."

16. A

The exclamation mark is used to show excitement.

17. C

Apostrophes should be used in *P's and Q's*. The word *your* should be the contraction *you're*, with an apostrophe where the letter *a* has been omitted. The possessive form of the pronoun *it* does not require an apostrophe; the word that has been used incorrectly is the contraction for *it is*.

18. D

Quotation marks should be after, not before, the question mark. There should be quotation marks before the word *go*. Single quotes should be used around *Marie is visiting from France*.

19. B

A semicolon should be used to separate two independent clauses. A colon should be used to introduce a list. A comma should be used instead of the colon, and a colon should be used after the word *follows* instead of a comma.

WRITING PRACTICE

Throughout the year, you will most likely be given writing prompts and will be expected to fulfill the task by demonstrating

- a knowledge of content
- an understanding of content
- the use of planning skills
- the use of processing skills
- the use of critical/creative thinking processes
- the expression and organization of ideas and information
- communication for different audiences and purposes
- the use of conventions
- an application of knowledge and skills
- a transfer of knowledge and skills
- the ability to make connections within and between various contexts

The following section of the practice test will provide you with writing prompts to practise your writing and example responses.

WRITING PROMPT EXEMPLARS

Writing Prompt A

STUDENT RESPONSE—FULLY MEETS EXPECTATIONS

The most significant role model in my life has been my mother's older sister, Aunt Ena. Aunt Ena was consistently fashionable, a stylish person who taught me that you don't have to be a celebrity to look your best for your audience. With her globe trotting confidence, she inspired me to be a world traveller. Aunt Ena was a family leader in cultural sophistication. To her dying day, though, my Aunt's greatest gift was the importance she placed on family.

As a grade one teacher for more than 40 years, Aunt Ena once told me that she dressed up for her students. "The children are just learning their primary colorus. When I dress in bold red and black, with shiny red earrings and matching beads, they just stare! Then we talk about all the red things in the classroom, at home, and the red apples in their lunch kits. They love it!" Even when she was finally in a wheelchair, Aunt Ena and I were still shopping for a yellow blouse to wear with her wide-brimmed yellow hat and navy suit.

Aunt Ena also inspired me to become a seasoned world traveller, to explore those magic kingdoms and exotic places she first saw in her *National Geographic* magazine. Every summer brought a new trip—by air, by land, by sea. Walking along the Great Wall of China, relaxing in a gondola on the canals of Venice, marveling at the treasures of the Louvre, or lingering in the factory that produced her favourite English bone china, Aunt Ena was a lifelong learner who brought home pictures, experiences, and mementoes we could share through the winter at one of her lively dinner parties. When I finger the sparkling stones of an Austrian Crystal necklace she left me, or walk past a small Japanese print on my guest bedroom wall, I remember those times.

Continued

Probably because she had travelled so extensively, Aunt Ena loved culture. Whether it was attending Agatha Christie's *The Mousetrap* in London, or a performance by our hometown symphony orchestra, my aunt basked in the riches of art, music, literature, and theatre. If a show came to town, Aunt Ena bought tickets. Well into her eighties, she could join in a knowledgeable discussion of cultural experiences and trends.

Lastly, and most importantly, Aunt Ena taught me to celebrate family. She kept in touch, by letter and phone, across the country, with loved ones near and far. Aunt Ena was the driving force behind her father's 100th birthday party. In a well-guarded journal, she kept birthdays, marriages, births, deaths, and milestones. We were a large and extended family, and postage kept going up, but, as well as I can remember, there were always cards in the mail for those special occasions. Single by choice all her life, she hosted grand games nights at Christmas, where we shouted at boisterous games of Rook, and devoured abundant plates of Christmas goodies.

A wonderful fashion sense, love of the world's unexplored corners, passion for culture, and devotion to family, live on in my memories of Aunt Ena. To be seen as "a bit like your Aunt Ena" is the ultimate compliment, for me. The giant atlas she once used lies open on a table in my home, to a map in Italy … where my travels will take me, this fall. Where I would take her, if only I could.

Rationale for Score

In this response, the writer responds to the writing task meaningfully with a thesis that directly addresses the prompt to write about a significant role model.

The thesis is supported by four main ideas: the aunt is a role model in fashion, in travelling, in appreciating travel, and in making family a priority. These ideas are elaborated throughout the essay with specific examples and details from the writer's memory.

The organization is purposefully controlled by following the order established in the opening paragraph. The focus on the "role model" is maintained throughout by using a personal tone ("Aunt Ena once told me") that reminds the reader that this role model was an important part of the writer's life. The writer seems to have a clear sense of a comfortable, accepting audience that is receptive to the writer's ideas and memories.

There are a variety of sentence types: "The most significant…," "As a grade one teacher…," "They love it!" The writer tries to use precise, descriptive language. Examples of this are "Shiny red earrings," "wide-brimmed yellow hat," and "gondola on the canals of Venice."

The essay shows some signs of being a first draft piece of writing. Some of the wording, for instance, could be rearranged or tightened but is essentially error-free.

STUDENT RESPONSE—MEETS EXPECTATIONS

Throughout your life, several people will have influenced you as a positive role model. My Aunt Ena was one of those people. She influenced me in her role as an educator and also as a person.

As an educator, my aunt was quite remarkable. She taught children their primary colours by modelling bright clothing with colour-matching jewellery. She designed picture flashcards at home and made learning numbers into a game. She brought a friend who was a writer to class to inspire her students to read good books.

I absorbed my aunt's love of reading, but she was more than an educator. Aunt Ena was also an amazing human being. She loved departing on trips, but after all the sightseeing was done, arrive home beat out the Eiffel Tower. Her love of family was legendary. Here was a woman who never forgot a birthday or special occasion.

I miss her, & I miss her extraordinary influence in my life, I hope & pray that I may be more like her as I grow older. Role models are great!

Rationale for Score

In this response, the writer adequately responds to the prompt—to write about a role model with a thesis paragraph that introduces the aunt's two main roles that influenced the writer's life: her role as an educator and as a fine human being.

The writer is able to support the main ideas introduced with somewhat general details and examples such as "modelled bright clothing" and "loved departing on trips."

The focus on the aunt as a role model is consistent throughout the essay, as is the tone of summarizing for the reader the key influences in the writer's life. There is a general sense of writing for an unknown audience, although it lapses somewhat in the impulsive-sounding outburst at the end: "Role models are great!"

The writer does endeavour to provide some variety in sentence types: "Throughout your life," and "I absorbed." The essay also includes some descriptive language, such as "my aunt was quite remarkable" and "her extraordinary influence."

The essay contains a few errors in conventions (such as using the symbol & in the last paragraph), but the errors do not interfere with the reader's understanding of the essay.

STUDENT RESPONSE—BELOW EXPECTATIONS

In my life I have had a lot of role models and I learnt a lot from them, but my best role model was probally by aunt, I learnt a lot from her.

My aunt was a great person. When I saw the question I knew she would be the one, cause her role is more clear than anyone els. I did love her, I realy did, cuz she always sent us kids gifts & cards, rain or shine. She was a great teacher too, the little kids loved her bright cloths.

Well anyway, that's about all there is to say on this topic. I think we shuld all have a role model. All's well that ends well, as they say. Thanks for the Canct to write about my aunt. She was a great lady.

Rationale for Score

This response does provide a thesis that is related to the writing task: "my best role model was probally my aunt, I learnt a lot from her." The somewhat brief response includes some limited details and examples, such as "always sent us kids gifts & cards" and "kids loved her bright cloths."

The focus on the aunt is inconsistent with unrelated statements such as "All's well that ends well." This also makes the tone inconsistent—at times, the writer is enthusiastic about the subject ("I did love her"), and at other times, vague and dismissive ("Well anyway, that's about all there is to say on this topic"). The inconsistent focus and tone contribute to a rambling style that demonstrates little or no sense of audience. There are few types of sentences—most are simple subject/verb patterns or run-ons. The language is basic and predictable: "learnt a lot," "us kids," "great teacher," "great lady." The writer makes fairly frequent errors in conventions. The spelling errors in particular may interfere with the reader's understanding of the response.

Writing Prompt B

STUDENT RESPONSE—FULLY MEETS EXPECTATIONS

To listen to the news and watch daily images on TV, you would think that the world is on a collision course with disaster. The environment seems to be out of control, supplies of fresh water seem to be dangerously diminished, and extreme poverty is limiting many lives to the bare essentials. What can I do about these overwhelming problems? What can we do together? What can you do? I strongly believe that the choices we all make can make a difference.

You may not be able to control the world's environment, but you can exercise control over your own environment. At home, try keeping a pail under the sink for vegetable peelings and other biodegradable matter. Left in a covered bin outside, they will reduce to mulch, which can be dug into flowerbeds or gardens. Try cutting five minutes off your daily shower. Do not run water until it is cold for a drink. Instead, just fill a glass and top it with ice. If you do not drink the whole glass, use what's left to water a nearby plant. Plant a tree to commemorate your graduation—each tree planted contributes oxygen to the atmosphere.

Would you like to be living in a Third World Country, locked in a never-ending cycle of poverty? You are not. You are a well-fed citizen in Canada, one of the most privileged countries on the planet. A simple fundraiser, such as recycling pop cans and bottles, if a small group of friends collect together, can easily yield about $35.00 a month in cash. That is approximately what it takes to support one child in the Third World through a humanitarian organization like UNICEF, World Vision, or Save the Children. The money is used to bring healthcare, school supplies, and clean drinking water to that child, and often to that child's whole village.

In conclusion, you and I can make a difference if we are willing to take some small steps. Mother Theresa, a winner of the Nobel Peace Prize, was one poor but purposeful individual who tried to make a difference, one person at a time. A small story illustrates this final point:

A young boy watched an old man walking along the beach. At low tide, the beach was strewn with starfish, and the old man was stooping to pick them up, one at a time, before flinging them far out over the water.

Continued

"Why do you do that?" inquired the boy, his curiosity aroused. "There are too many to help; it can't possibly make much difference."

The man turned to look in the boy's direction. With a half-smile, he answered, as he threw another starfish into the sea, "It just made a difference to *that* one!"

Like the man in the story, you too can make a difference in the world. What "mark" will you leave?

Rationale for Score

In this response, the writer states and maintains a position ("I strongly believe that the choices you make can make a difference"), authoritatively defends that position with precise and relevant evidence, and convincingly addresses reader concerns and biases.

The writer provides precise evidence for affecting the environment, such as mulching and water conservation suggestions, and for improving conditions for the poor, such as by supporting one child in a Third World Country. Possible reader bias about the futility of affecting change is addressed in the starfish parable at the end of the essay.

The focus and tone are consistent and persuasive, even for a possibly cynical audience. Organization is purposeful with the use of rhetorical questions to introduce the thesis and a final rhetorical question following the closing parable.

The writer uses a variety of sentence types, such as "To listen to," "What can I do," and "You are a well-fed citizen" and employs precise, descriptive language, such as "dangerously diminished," "cut five minutes off," and "contributes oxygen to the atmosphere." Any errors present are negligible.

STUDENT RESPONSE—MEETS EXPECTATIONS

People can make a difference if you just look for opportunities. One opportunity that not too many people know about is writing letters of encouragement to soldiers.

An organization called Forgotten Soldiers Outreach, Inc. can coordinate a letter-writing project for students with the school's permission.

Your letters should be uplifting and encouraging, not about death or negative political opinions. It would help if you researched the country, like Iraq or Afghanistan, where the soldiers are stationed. When you write, just be yourself and share things they might like to hear about, like new movies, new music, or concerts you attended.

When you write, you don't want to ask personal questions, but it would be encouraging for them to hear about "normal" life back at home, like how you are finding school, sports events, and the latest trends. Remember, some of our soldiers are just a few years older then you!

In conclusion, you never know how much you might benefit as a person simply by making a difference in a stranger's life. Let them know that you care and that you do appreciate the daily sacrifices they are making. You can find out more about this project at www.forgottensoldiers.org.

Rationale for Score

In this response to the writing prompt, the writer states a position ("People can make a difference if they just look for opportunities") that is generally defended throughout the rest of the paper through the example of an organization that encourages soldiers who are posted overseas. Reader concerns are indirectly addressed near the end with the sentence, "you might benefit as a person."

The writer is generally able to defend a position with precise and relevant evidence about the outreach to soldiers, even though the reader might need more explicit information to participate, such as whether young people can participate independently or only as part of a sponsored group.

The tone and focus are quite consistent, addressing the audience on the subject of the writer's proposal in the second person.

The essay contains a variety of sentence types ("People can make" and "When you write") and some descriptive language ("uplifting and encouraging" and "personal questions"). Occasional errors in conventions, such as a spelling error and grammatical mistakes, do not interfere with the reader's understanding of the essay.

STUDENT RESPONSE—BELOW EXPECTATIONS

How to make a difference can be a problem. One problem lead to more problems. One problem is to know what to do. But you can always reduce, reuse, and recycling. Something we have learnt that since Grade 2.

I think this is a good subject to write on because the worlds problems are big, and getting bigger all the time. If we reduce, re-use, and recycle, it might not help much, but it help some and we must all do are best to help the sitiation. Thank you for reading my opinion on the subject.

Rationale for Score

The position stated at the beginning of the response is somewhat vague ("How to make a difference can be a problem"), but it does demonstrate reasonable comprehension of the writing task. The writer provides minimal evidence ("If we reduce, re-use, and recycle") and vaguely addresses possible reader concerns ("we must all do are best to help the sitiation"). As the reader states, the response is more of an expressed "opinion" than the persuasive essay that is requested in the prompt.

The tone and focus are vague and inconsistent with no discernible organization. The response seems to circle the topic with generic and trivial observations and clichés. The writer does not demonstrate awareness of any particular audience. Rather, the writer simply addresses the need to get a few sentences written. The sentences are simplistic and lacking in variety, and the vocabulary is basic and predictable, such as the repetition of the words "problem" and "reduce, re-use, and recycling." The writer demonstrates weak control of conventions.

ANSWERS AND SOLUTIONS—WRITING UNIT TEST

1. C	8. D	15. C	22. C
2. C	9. A	16. B	23. D
3. C	10. D	17. C	24. A
4. B	11. B	18. B	25. C
5. B	12. C	19. C	26. B
6. A	13. C	20. C	
7. B	14. B	21. B	

1. C

"She is one of the students *whom* I want to meet." The objective form of the pronoun must be used because *whom* is the object of the infinitive phrase *to meet*.

2. C

"We can do as well as *they*" is correct. The comparison implied by the phrase *as well as* is parallel (*we can/they can*) even though the second *can* is not included.

3. C

Philip enjoyed is in the active voice. The other three alternatives are written in the passive voice. When the passive voice is used, *by* is either stated or implied.

4. B

The phrase *by our family* is the indicator that the verb phrase *was visited* is in the passive voice.

5. B

A "long grey journey" could be defined as tedious, which can mean long, slow, dull, or boring.

6. A

While the sun does warm the speaker's back, the overall mood of the entire poem is one of peace and joy.

7. B

The words *Java, satellites, constellations,* and *navigational* are misspelled in the other groups of words.

8. D

The words *concentration, suffrage, reparations,* and *restoration* are misspelled in the other groups of words.

9. A

The words *advertisement, packaging, maintenance,* and *mechanical* are misspelled in the other groups of words.

10. D

The words *equilateral, Pythagoras,* and *parallel* are misspelled in the other groups of words.

11. B

The words *assonance, onomatopoeia,* and *euphemism* are misspelled in the other groups of words.

12. C

The words *Antarctic*, *channel*, and *equator* are misspelled in the other groups of words.

13. C

"Debris from the flood was *lying* all over Main Street" is correct. This form of the verb implies that the debris was stationary on the road where it had landed during the flood.

14. B

The verb phrase *would have met* is a conditional tense that requires the preceding verb to be a past tense, such as *waited* or *had waited*. In other words, if the condition of Stephen waiting longer had occurred in the past, *we would have met him*.

15. C

The correct form of the irregular verb as used in this sentence is *torn*. *Torn* is the past participle of the verb *to tear* and is used in past tenses using auxiliary verbs like *had*.

16. B

The fragment is a relative clause, and the required main clause is missing. The relative clause could be made into a main clause by deleting *Just as* or by providing a main clause to go with the relative clause: *Just as we had almost given up hope*, the rescue helicopter appeared overhead.

17. C

The linking verb *is* requires the subjective form of the pronoun, *who*.

18. B

The word *interpreted* is spelled incorrectly.

19. C

The word *optimistic* is spelled incorrectly.

20. C

The word *dissatisfied* is spelled incorrectly.

21. B

The word *mortgage* is spelled incorrectly.

22. C

The word *privilege* is spelled incorrectly.

23. D

To correct the comma splice, the comma should be a semicolon. *Dan will be glad to help us* and *his experience is very valuable* are both main clauses, making this a compound sentence. Each clause could stand on its own as an independent sentence.

24. A

The phrases "We will take the express bus" and "it has a fantastic service" are both main clauses that can stand alone as separate sentences. The run-on could be corrected by inserting a semicolon after *bus*.

25. C

A comma is required after *out*.

26. B

Neither implies a single choice between two arguments (neither this one nor that one); therefore, the verb must also be the singular form *makes* in order to agree with the subject.

Writing Prompt A: Expository Composition

STUDENT RESPONSE—FULLY MEETS EXPECTATIONS

Knowing that virtual experiences are here to stay and that they are important to teenagers, both for communication and entertainment, it is important to be aware of the benefits and the faults of these experiences. Knowledge can hopefully lead users to make wise choices that will enrich and benefit their lives without hurting anyone.

First of all, young people today have grown up with the "reality" of virtual experiences, and they take them for granted as both necessary and enriching. Doing research for school projects using the Internet has almost made libraries obsolete. It's all there—from electronic encyclopedias to topic links.

Research a famous person, like Terry Fox. Or lookup Elvis Presley, and listen to him sing one of his many hits. Subscribing to MSN, MySpace, and Facebook allows young people to develop both real and virtual friendships. They only share what they want to share, which is not unlike old-fashioned pen pals but allows for the ability to share pictures and music. This is especially valuable to young people who live in remote areas. They do not have to depend on real people to develop their social skills.

However, nothing in this world is perfect. Virtual experiences can be too superficial, false, or misleading. In research, for instance, not all sites contain reliable information. Users are able to "edit" Wikipedia (the free online encyclopedia) entries, so you have to be careful. It does not hurt to double check information using some library resources, just to be sure. Also, you should exchange personal information on friendship and chat sites with caution. Remember that anyone can register and anyone can post fake pictures or wrong information. It is a little bit like "Buyer Beware" in advertising. You have to use common sense—never let a stranger dictate your choices.

All in all, virtual experiences can be both educational and entertaining. Enjoy and benefit from all that the computer has to offer, but do not let it rule your real life, take the place of your real friendships, or overrule your basic intuitions and your common sense.

Rationale for Score

This paper presents a meaningful thesis in the opening paragraph that is clearly related to the writing task: because virtual experiences are here to stay, it is important to be aware of both benefits and faults. Knowledge of these should lead the user to make wise choices (with respect to virtual experiences).

The body of the paper is purposefully organized into two parts—a paragraph dealing with benefits and a paragraph dealing with faults. Each subtopic of the thesis is thoroughly supported with specific examples and details—the ease with which research can be developed, for instance, versus a caution about checking the reliability of research information from electronic sources like Wikipedia.

The tone is consistently fair and non-judgmental, providing balanced information on both sides of the analysis. The focus consistently addresses the thesis in two purposefully organized paragraphs.

The implied audience appears to be both the writer's peers and adults, inviting them to think in two opposing dimensions in order to be knowledgeable enough to make wise choices.

The essay contains a variety of well-controlled sentence types, such as "Knowing that," "Knowledge hopefully can," and "However, nothing in this world is perfect." The writer has made a commendable effort, for first draft writing, to use precise and descriptive language, such as "enriching" and "obsolete." Other than an infrequent sentence error, such as "Or lookup," errors in conventions are almost non-existent.

STUDENT RESPONSE—MEETS EXPECTATIONS

A good example of a virtual experience is *The Sims*. Many young people like to play this game because it simulates real life. You can create your own virtual family and walk the members through the activities and choices of daily life in the suburban household that you create for them near Sim City. The player has a lot of virtual power, but some drawbacks need to be considered as well.

The main value of *The Sims* is pure entertainment. There are so many permutations, especially if you have the most recent version of the game or have purchased extension packs. You can build your own model family, design their house, pick their pets, and plan their careers. You have to work through their choices and consequences, such as disappointment and illness if you do not make good choices. Thus, the user can learn about the consequences of their choices in real life while being entertained. *The Sims* is a great learning game with many creative opportunities.

However, it is only fair to consider some drawbacks. One is time with real family and friends. Especially for a shy person, the game can become an escape from interacting with family or developing actual friendships. Remember, your Sims family can never be "there for you" when you need advice or help because it is a one-way-street—you control your Sims family like puppets. Most importantly, there are unrealistic flaws in earlier versions of the game, like characters who never age or die.

Although *The Sims* can be a great entertainment experience, they are no substitute for the real people in your life. The game cannot harm you as long as you keep the real and the unreal in proper perspective.

Rationale for Score

In this response, the writer responds to the writing task with a thesis that analyses a well-known computer game, *The Sims*. Both positive features of the game and some drawbacks of overuse are presented, which allows readers to reach their own conclusion about the value of this "virtual experience."

Appropriate details and examples are used to support and develop the thesis. The writer first shows how the entertainment value of the game is enhanced by user interaction and by purchasing extension packs and then balances the features by stating some drawbacks, such as using the game as a substitute for real social interaction.

The tone is consistent with an objective reporting style that is focused on the game, while the content is organized in a controlled fashion, moving from entertainment value to social problems.

There is a general sense of third person audience with some switching to second person. The essay includes a reasonable variety of sentence types ("The main value" and "While being entertained") and some descriptive language ("simulate real life" and "many creative opportunities"). Any errors that are present do not interfere with the reader's understanding of the essay.

STUDENT RESPONSE—BELOW EXPECTATIONS

We can use computers for information and such, plus we can have many experiences on a computer. But it is not as good as real life. And there is the danger of predaters. Should you talk to someone you don't know online? I don't think so.

In the end, there are the pros and cons. You can do a search to learn a lot of stuff, you can meet friends, but there you have to be careful on what you say and what you get yourself into. Remember your parents warn you don't talk to strangers.

You have to think about both the pros and the cons before you make a decishun, sometimes it might be better if computers were never invented.

Be aware of the risks then using it wisely. Mabey try to spend more time away from the computer. That way you can get a life, and just use it when neccessary.

Rationale for Score

The writer seems to provide a thesis that is partially related to the writing task in the opening paragraph: "But it is not as good a real life." This suggests that the writer is adopting a position rather then presenting both the strengths and weaknesses as requested by the writing task. Rather than develop the position, the writer presents the pros and cons in the second paragraph. This change, along with limited examples, contributes to an inconsistent tone and focus, leaving the reader to fill in missing information. The response is too undeveloped to appear organized—it is more like a restatement of the thesis with scant support.

The sentences that begin "You have to think about" and "Sometimes it might be better if" demonstrate a stream of consciousness that ignores the notion of audience.

The writer uses a few different sentence types, such as "We can use" and "Be aware of," along with a rambling run-on sentence that begins with, "You have to think." The language is general, basic, and predictable: "learn a lot of stuff" and "Don't talk to strangers."

Writing Prompt B: Business Letter

STUDENT RESPONSE—FULLY MEETS EXPECTATIONS

Dear Dr. Balfour:

I am writing on behalf of this year's graduating class at Parkview Composite High School. We would like to invite you to deliver the commencement address at our formal ceremonies on May 26, 2008. As a highly respected alumnus of our school, you have been an important role model, particularly to our basketball players. They see the provincial award from 1988 hanging in the gym, see your team photo on the wall, and are reminded that academic plus athletic excellence can walk hand in hand.

The graduation theme chosen by this year's class is "Mountain High." With your recent mountain-climbing experience in Nepal, the students are sure you will find challenges to share that fit the theme.

Continued

The ceremonies are scheduled as follows:

> 2:00 p.m.
>
> Friday, May 26, 2008
>
> > Parkview Composite Auditorium
> >
> > 3210 Riverbend Parkway
> >
> > Vancouver, British Columbia

The platform party is asked to meet in the school office at 1:45 p.m. to proceed to the auditorium stage. We are allowing 20–25 minutes for your address. You are cordially invited to attend the reception that follows the ceremonies. It is being held in the school gymnasium.

I ask that you respond to this invitation by Friday, Feb. 20, so that the Grad Committee can finalize the program details. Be assured that we would be highly honoured to have you return to your school as the guest speaker.

Sincerely yours,

Randy Holmes
Class President
Class of 2008

Rationale for Score

This response consistently provides clear and purposeful information and addresses the intended audience appropriately. The writer immediately identifies a specific purpose (to invite a speaker to deliver the commencement address), acknowledges the suitability of the recipient as "a highly respected alumnus," and proceeds to provide clear and precise details that the prospective speaker would need, including the theme, date, location, and length of speech. The letter stays focused and to the point with the central ideas clearly stated.

The vocabulary, tone, and style are consistently appropriate and take into account the knowledge and interests of the recipient, such as his history as a basketball player for the school and his recent mountain-climbing experience. Words and phrases like "you have been an important role model" and "the students are sure that you would find challenges" maintain the clear but respectful tone established by the writer.

The writer consistently follows a conventional (block form) style. The salutation and the closing are correctly formatted.

STUDENT RESPONSE—MEETS EXPECTATIONS

Dear Dr. Balfour:

I have been asked by my class to invite you to be our Commencement Speaker on May 26, 2008 at the School Auditorium. This year's theme is "Mountain High." We chose it with you and your example in mind. Not only have you recently returned from a mountain-climbing adventure in Nepal, but you also managed to keep a high grade point average while acting as captain of the basketball team during your senior year here at the school in 1987–88.

We would love to hear some of your stories! We are allowing about 20–25 minutes for the address and ask that you arrive at the school office at 1:45 p.m. to be escorted to the stage before the graduates enter the auditorium at 2:00 p.m.

We hope you are willing and able to help us out. Since you attended Parkview Composite High School as a student, you know where to contact us as soon as possible. The school phone number is 938-7295, so you can leave a message for me with the secretary.

Thank you,

Randy Holmes
Class of 2008

Rationale for Score

This response provides clear and purposeful information and addresses the intended audience appropriately. The writer immediately introduces the purpose of the letter and the commencement theme before offering flattering reasons that Dr. Balfour is being invited to speak (theme chosen with Dr. Balfour's mountain-climbing experience and his academic and athletic record in mind). The next two paragraphs provide sufficient information for the recipient to make a decision and contact the school. It is inferred that more specific information will be provided if and when Dr. Balfour accepts the invitation.

The vocabulary, tone, and style are respectful and take into consideration the recipient's relationship with school ("during your senior year here" and "since you attended").

The writer stays focused on the task and appropriately to the point. The letter is presented in a conventional style (block form), with correct formatting of the salutation and the closing.

STUDENT RESPONSE—BELOW EXPECTATIONS

Dear Roland Balfour,

Hi, I'm the Class President, and our class decided to ask you to speak at our Commencement. You being an alumnus and all. We hear you did some great stuff for the school way back then, and held your marks up too. We think you are cool and hope you will agree to speak to us.

The theme is Mountain High but if you don't like that then any topic will do. Don't make it too long, cause you know how figety we will be in those long robes.

The ceremony start at 2 on May 26 here at the School. Try to be a couple minutes early so I can take you to the stage first and get back in line. Please let me know at 938-7295. If you cant make it, that ok, but it would sure put us in a bind to get someone.

Your truly,

Randy Homes

Rationale for Score

This response provides adequate information and sometimes addresses the intended audience appropriately. The writer states that "our class decided to ask you to speak," "the theme is Mountain High," and the time, date, and location of the event. The writer also provides a contact phone number. The purpose of the letter is weakened by informal comments, such as "We think you are cool," and a dismissive attitude toward the stated theme, such as "if you don't like that then any topic will do."

The vocabulary is very basic and any respectful tone frequently lapses through the use of slang jargon such as "cool" and inappropriate comments like "Don't make it too long cause you know how figety we will be." Spelling errors and grammatical mistakes interfere with its readability.

The writer attempts to follow a conventional (block) format, but the salutation is incorrectly punctuated and "Your" should be "Yours" in the closing.

NOTES

METACOGNITION

B11   use metacognitive strategies to reflect on and assess their reading and viewing

B12   recognize and explain how structures and features of text shape readers' and viewers' construction of meaning and appreciation of author's craft

B13   demonstrate increasing work skills and vocabulary knowledge

The word *metacognition* refers to thinking about how you think; this process includes thinking about how you learn. As you discover and think about strategies that work best with your individual learning style, you will become a more confident and productive learner. It is important to think about your learning and to ask yourself questions about how it works for you. Do you work better in groups or on your own? Do you memorize things visually? What kind of reading do you like to do best? The more time you spend analysing how you think, the better able you will be to pinpoint areas you excel at as well as areas you have trouble with.

The following section of your *KEY* gives you many examples and guidelines on metacognition. The examples are designed to show how an individual student performs metacognition activities. Keep in mind that the way you think and learn is unique, so different methods may appeal to you more than others. Learning what appeals to you is also a part of metacognition.

SETTING GOALS

One of the keys to improving your English skills is to set personal goals for language growth. You may wish to use the following rubric that identifies some of the major English skills in order to identify your strengths and areas for growth. Reviewing assignments and assessment rubrics from your current or past English courses will help you to assess your strengths and areas that need improvement.

Skill	Yes	Needs Improvement
Read regularly		
Predict and ask questions while reading, discuss unfamiliar concepts with others		
Take note of words I am not sure of and use context or references to find meanings		
Go back to re-read passages to clarify meaning		
Use visualizing and graphic organizers as aids to analyzing text and planning for communicating ideas		
Connect what I am reading to what I know about and to other texts I have read		
Understand symbols, archetypes, and literary devices and use them to enhance understanding of texts		
Use ideas in texts to better understand and communicate understandings of self and the world around		

Skill	Yes	Needs Improvement
Know how to effectively introduce and conclude topics in writing or oral presentations		
Connect all ideas to a controlling idea		
Fully support ideas with explanations and examples		
Identify when ideas are not communicated clearly		
Use a variety of sentences and precise diction for effect		
Find and correct errors in spelling, usage, and punctuation		
Understand oral instructions		
Listen carefully, build on the ideas of others, ask questions to help others clarify ideas		
Feel comfortable making formal presentations		
Use voice effectively—volume, rate, tone, and pacing to communicate effectively and convey emotion		
Use eye contact and gestures for emphasis		
Use charts, graphs, and visual aids to contribute to presentations		
Know how to find resources, effectively record information, and correctly reference sources		

READING METACOGNITION CHECKLIST

The following questions are examples of what you can ask while using metacognition to examine your learning.

- What is the best way to approach this learning task?
- At this point, how well do I understand information, concepts, characters, etc.?
- How can I maintain my motivation to complete what I have started?
- Am I using the best tools for this learning task?

The following checklist shows different strategies that you can use to get the most out of your reading. More importantly, it helps you think about how you approach various reading tasks. You could use this checklist several times during the school year to help you understand or change your approach.

USING THE CHECKLIST

Put check marks in the "Most Effective for Me" column next to each of five strategies in the checklist that work best for you.

- Write a number beside each check mark showing how effective the strategy is for you (1 is most effective, 5 is least effective).
- Think of logical reasons for the order you have chosen.
- Discuss and compare your top five most effective strategies with a peer.
- Collaborate to identify the top five strategies from both of you and describe the best uses for each strategy.
- List five ways that you and your peers can become better readers.

Reading Metacognition Checklist

Thinking About My Reading Strategies	Most Effective for Me	Use Most Often	Use Sometimes	Should Try
Before Reading I *preview* (look over exams, texts, stories, articles, and assignments) to determine • What is involved in this text? • What is my purpose for reading? • How should I approach this? • How should I read (speed, etc.)?				
I think about my *prior knowledge*—what I already know that might be relevant to the topic or task in front of me.				
I *visualize* or try to picture the characters, setting, what I hope to find out, etc.				
While Reading I *check back* to verify a definition, information about a character, etc.				
I use *vocabulary strategies* like context clues, root words, prefixes, and suffixes to understand unfamiliar words and phrases.				
I make point form notes or *graphic organizers* when I need to remember plots, key ideas, etc.				
I pause while reading and *predict* what I think will happen next in the story.				
I *tag text* with sticky notes or mark parts I find confusing so I can ask about it later.				
I use a *highlighter*—when I am allowed—to mark the text (notes, handouts, etc.) for key phrases and important ideas.				
I write *notes*, *questions*, and *comments* in margins if I am allowed. Sometimes, I use these later on to clarify information.				

Thinking About My Reading Strategies	Most Effective for Me	Use Most Often	Use Sometimes	Should Try
I ask questions such as the following to *monitor my understanding* of what I read: • Does this make sense to me? • What exactly is the writer saying? • What is the narrator's point of view? • Do I agree? Why or why not?				
When the text does not state something directly, I make *inferences* and draw *conclusions* from my reading.				
I deliberately use *skimming* and *scanning* skills when appropriate, such as to locate a specific answer or idea in the text.				
I *adjust my reading rate* as needed, slowing down for detailed information, etc.				
I *pay attention* to diagrams, pictures, charts, and graphs—anything that may help me make more sense of the text.				
After Reading I *summarize*, using notes or a graphic organizer.				
I write my thoughts, questions, and reactions in a *personal response journal*.				
I *share with a peer* in the following ways: • In written form, like a double response journal, in which we write back and forth • by discussing informally within a share-pair or small group • by explaining a newly-learned concept I try to *support my own opinions* and to *show respect* for the opinions of others.				

Thinking About My Reading Strategies	Most Effective for Me	Use Most Often	Use Sometimes	Should Try
I write *critical responses* to text when invited to do so. I try to include comments on the form, purpose, writer's viewpoint, historical context, mood, imagery, etc. When possible, I point out comparisons to other texts or draw from my personal experiences to deepen my response.				

SAMPLE APPLICATIONS OF METACOGNITION

The following section shows you some strategies that involve metacognition. Journals, visual charts, and literature circles/book clubs are all great methods of making yourself more aware of how you read. Some of these may be more useful to you than others. Figuring out which methods work best for you will give you insight into your learning style.

PERSONAL RESPONSE JOURNAL

A personal response journal can be a great record of what you read. A journal can also be a good starting point to get ideas for homework assignments. A journal entry should include the date, title, and name of the work that you describe. The entry should express your connections with the text. How does the work connect to your experiences? How does it relate to your opinions?

The following example shows a poem and one student's personal response journal entry regarding that poem. The personal response describes that student's individual experience with the poem. To practise metacognition, try writing your own response to this poem.

Example

DRAGON NIGHT

Little flame mouths,
Cool your tongues.
Dreamtime starts,
My furnace-lungs.

Rest your wings now,
Little flappers,
Cave mouth calls
To dragon nappers.

Night is coming,
Bank your fire.
Time for dragons
To retire.

Hiss.
Hush.
Sleep.

—*by* Jane Yolen

Personal Response Journal Entry: "Dragon Night" by Jane Yolen

February 27, 2008

Although this poem seems to be written as a lullaby for baby dragons, it means something different and very personal to me. Of all the poems we studied in our September poetry unit, this is my absolute favourite. It brought back lots of memories of the summer, sitting with my family on the deck of our cottage at Muskoka Lake, relaxing and looking at the lake. As I read the poem, I thought of tiny flashes of light down by the lakeshore—fireflies flicking their mini-lanterns on and off. The poem has lots of summer/evening imagery. I felt quiet and relaxed by the end of the poem.

The great thing about journal entries is that you do not have to worry that you are being too casual with your language. Even though the entry may be casual and talk about your own life experience, the information about your opinions can be used to write something more formal later on. Keeping a journal about what you read is a great tool for keeping track of your learning.

LITERATURE CIRCLES AND BOOK CLUBS

A literature circle or a book club may help you better understand a novel. It can also be a fun way to talk with classmates about literature in a more casual way than in the classroom. Everyone interprets literary works a little differently. By talking to others freely about your impressions of a text, you can learn about different ways of looking at it. You also gain a better understanding of your own opinions by having to express them to others.

SKILLS THAT AID READING

Now that you are in Grade 12, you have developed a variety of communication skills that both help you as a reader and improve as you read more. As your reading improves, for example, your ability to state your opinions aloud also improves. Honing your skills in presenting ideas in different media, such as plays or poster art, can improve your skills in summarizing or understanding concepts as you read.

COMMUNICATION TOOLS

Being able to communicate using one tool will boost your ability to communicate using another. The following examples show different communication tools and how improving them will improve your reading overall.

LISTENING AND READING

When good readers read out loud, they use several tools to make their reading effective: for example, clear articulation, appropriate tone and expression, pacing, rate of reading, and pauses. As you acquire these skills through listening, you can use them when you read out loud.

When you listen to peers in a small group setting, take the following actions:

- clarify things you missed or misunderstood
- hear a description of an experience that you might not have known or thought about
- discuss views and opinions arising from the same text, and learn to use text to support your own viewpoint
- consider the viewpoint of a peer, which could be just as well supported in the text as your own opinion

SPEAKING AND READING

As you share your insights and viewpoints from your reading, you will

- improve your reading comprehension
- learn to support your viewpoint using text statements and inferences
- improve your oral reading skills as you read aloud

In a pair or a small group, comfortably express your ideas from your reading. In a peer group there is no pressure to use precise or formal language. You can feel free to explain your ideas in a more casual setting. Discussion is used to shape your ideas, so they do not have to be perfectly formed at this time.

WRITING AND READING

When you write a response to your reading, you can craft a thoughtful response that uses words you take time to decide upon. Written responses are also an efficient way for you to answer questions from a text and to reread parts of it—both are strategies used by effective readers.

VIEWING AND READING

Viewing material can enrich your reading experience. When characterization, costumes, and settings in a film enhance the descriptions in a book that it is based on, the stories can come to life in a new way. Viewing a film version of a book may help you associate better with the characters in the book. Sometimes you might find that the film version is not how you imagined it as you read it. Perhaps the actors do not look the way you imagined the characters to look, or the setting is different than you pictured it. Readers can become resentful if a movie does not seem true to a novel.

It is important to keep in mind that the film version of a novel is based on how the people who made the film interpreted the novel. One of the best things about reading is that you, in a sense, have the power to create the same visuals in your mind that a director does when making a movie. You direct the movement and appearance of a book in the same way that a director might. In order to understand your interpretation of a novel better, you could adapt portions of a story to a dramatic form. This will enhance your effectiveness as a reader as you review the story for accurate dialogue and consistent character portrayal.

PRESENTING IDEAS USING DIFFERENT MEDIA

Taking ideas from a text and using them in a different medium can aid your understanding of the text. After reading a book, taking ideas from it and addressing them in a play or on a poster can give you a better understanding of the book's focus and themes. Presenting a text in a new way can highlight aspects of a book's theme, mood, character qualities, or symbolism that you might not have thought about otherwise. For example, a poster or a collage could be used to show the dominant theme in a novel using nothing but pictures cut from magazines.

APPLYING YOUR SKILLS

The following section provides a few examples to demonstrate more specific learning situations in which interconnected skills are used to understand text more effectively. A single work is shown to be presented in different media. This can give you ideas as to how you can do a similar project with texts that you have read.

APPLYING SKILLS: USING RESEARCH IN PROJECTS

Research is a vital part of writing formal papers. Metacognition can be applied to your research in order to see where you can improve your researching techniques. In the following fictional account, two students were given a news article about a local issue and were asked to use research to clarify and extend their understanding of the article and the issues it presents. As you read about their assignment, try and think about how you might go about researching this issue if it were your own assignment. How might the techniques you would use be different from the ones used by the fictional students in the following example?

The students are given two weeks to work on a project about current events. They are asked to identify an issue raised in a news article that they are given, track the issue for two weeks, consider perspectives and possible outcomes, and afterwards, engage their classmates in the issue.

The article is about an airport safety issue arising from a recent crash landing at Pearson International Airport in Toronto that could have resulted in a tragic loss of lives. According to the news item, an Air France jet carrying 309 passengers and crew had landed halfway down the runway during a summer rainstorm. Overshooting the 90-metre buffer zone at the end of the runway, the plane careened over a bank and finally came to a stop. Fortunately, before the damaged aircraft burst into flames, everyone on board was safely evacuated and removed from danger. The accident was caused by human error, but the issue arising from this incident involved passenger safety and accident prevention. After reading the information, the students felt that the runway buffer zone should be extended to 300 metres, the required length at most major European airports.

The students decide to use a kind of tracking log to record what they did to clarify or extend their understanding of this story and the issues it raised. This is what they recorded over their two-week assignment:

Example

Class Project: The Pearson Airport

1. We collected stories on the topic from the newspaper, television, and Internet for about two weeks. We ended up with a total of 21 news items.
2. We recorded facts or messages common to all of the stories, such as
   * the Pearson runway has a 90-metre buffer zone
   * the weather conditions were severe
   * the pilot landed halfway down the runway
   * incidents such as this happen more frequently than is commonly believed
3. We looked for public reactions on the newspaper and television websites and on the editorial page of the newspaper. We recorded repeated responses, such as
   * safety is of major concern
   * the expense of extending the runway is worth possibly saving lives
   * Pearson airport should have the same standards as the rest of the world
4. We watched for different opinions on the issue and found opinion articles from
   * the Airline Pilots' Association
   * the Ontario Department of Tourism
   * city and provincial governments (about who would bear the cost of the runway upgrade)
5. Based on all that we found, we tried to predict an outcome:
   * the runway extension would be built over the next two years, funded by the province
6. We watched to see if the issue was resolved in two weeks. It wasn't, but the matter was under review by a transportation committee.
7. We summarized our findings and prepared our class presentation.

8. After our presentation, we will allow a brief time for discussion on our issue. We will then ask Miss Fergusen to review business letter format and take us to the computer lab to write letters to the Transportation Safety Board of Canada to be forwarded to the Honourable Lawrence Cannon, Minister of Transport, Ottawa. The purpose of the letters will be to request mandatory lengthened buffer zones for major Canadian airport runways by 2010.

> Our concluding comments:
> Through reading, research, and discussion, we clarified and extended our understanding of an important and newsworthy safety issue. We came to have a strong personal interest in the outcome of this issue because, like most Canadians, we will use air travel throughout our lives. If a short-sighted decision is made, we ourselves could someday be victims.

Research is critical to writing non-fiction text. The more you learn about an issue, the better able you will be to form an opinion that is informed and balanced. Finding information that is accurate and that does not have a bias can be difficult. As you become a better researcher, understanding information and how to find good information will become easier.

Use metacognition the next time you are researching for a project. Think about areas of research you may have missed and how you could use the research you have found effectively.

EVALUATING YOUR PROCESS

Metacognition consists of two processes occurring at the same time: monitoring your progress as you learn, and changing and adapting your strategies if necessary. In writing, this involves identifying what strategies you found most helpful before, during, and after writing and what steps you can take to improve as a writer. After you have finished a writing project, think back to how you developed your ideas for writing, the research you did, and how you sorted and organized it. This will help you to identify the strategies you used. Next time you do similar writing, use the strategies that worked the best for you and reconsider the others.

For example, a Grade 12 student came up with the following examples of strategies he had used during the first half of the year. Here is his list of strategies.

Example

MY WRITING STRATEGIES

Before Writing

- Went online to find information about topics when I could, like the natural disaster topic we read about in the short story "The Worst Day Ever."
- Jotted down books, TV shows, and music titles related to topic
- Talked with mom about topic choice
- Wrote down purpose, audience
- Made a web plan or outline

During Writing

- Spread out notes and outlines by computer
- Tried to follow outlines
- Checked with assignment criteria
- Tried to write correctly
- Tried to use good transitions
- Tried to include things teacher was emphasizing, like different sentence openers, "said is dead" replacements, etc.

After Writing

- Labelled my revisions to make sure I was intentionally including teacher suggestions
- Read drafts aloud from computer screen while revising and editing
- Paid attention to my peer partner so we could help each other improve

Next, the student explained the strategy he found the most helpful. The strategy he chose was the idea of labelling revisions to require thinking specifically about what he was changing and why. Since the students were sharing their metacognition activities with the teacher, he submitted the following paragraph:

Example

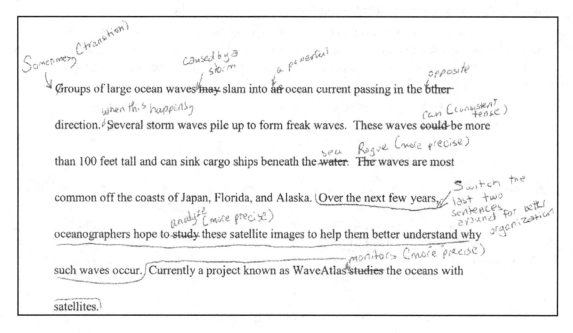

Finally, the student identified several steps he could take to improve as a writer. His list included the following ideas:

1. Keep a writing log, with sections: Spelling Errors, Writing Errors, Story Ideas
2. Start a list of words I want to use in my writing
3. Look online for sites where I can share some of my writing

After collecting the class's reflections, Ms. Harmon gave the students two 4 3 6 cards to tape inside their writing logs. The cards contained reminders to help the students think about each piece of writing.

This Piece

- What is best?
- What could I improve?
- What stage was smoothest?
- What ideas could I use for new writing?

Learning from this Piece

- Have I learned any new techniques?
- Did I try something new?
- Have I eliminated personal errors that I have commonly made in the past, like sentence fragments.

WRITER'S REFLECTION

Reflecting on your writing is something you probably have to do in class. The following example shows you examples of answers a fictional student has written in response to metacognition questions from his or her class. You may have to answer questions similar to these in class about your own writing and language skills. See if you can answer the following questions yourself.

Example

Before Grade 12, what did you know or understand to be your strengths as a writer? Has this changed?

I always thought that my greatest strength was writing humour. It was because I found it easy to remember the punch line of a good joke, and I could always seem to make my friends laugh—sometimes at the wrong time, like in the middle of your class on sentence fragments! When you asked us to think hard about our strengths in September and to think of ways to branch out from those strengths, I realized that one reason I can describe things in a humorous way is that I am a people watcher. I am always watching what people do, how they react, and what they say in certain situations. I used that strength to branch out when I wrote my one act play on peer pressure. With realistic sounding dialogue and characters based on what I had really seen around me, I think I was able to get some serious points across using humour. During your comments after my group presented my play, you said our dialogue was convincing and real.

What did you learn about yourself as a writer as a result of the group writing experience?

You mean the short story project. The truth is, I wasn't too happy at first. I actually like writing independent stories from my own head, so it was annoying to have to stop and pay attention to the other two guys in my group. One hated writing, period, and the other didn't want to write anything but fantasy, which I have never read. We wasted a bit of time in the beginning, but when you started posting deadlines on the board we had to think of something. We had just learned about parodies, so we decided to write a modernized parody of a well known fairy tale. The partner who hated writing didn't mind working from a basic plot we all knew—"Little Red Riding Hood". He even started to contribute a few ideas. My other partner added some twists, I added some ideas for humor, and we all liked the result, because it turned out like a bit of a fantasy. What I learned about myself as a writer was that

- I am more creative than I realized
- sometimes other points of view can improve writing
- I can motivate a peer who thinks writing is an unpleasant chore

How do you determine whether the peer feedback you receive is valid or not?

I pay the closest attention to revision ideas. I figure if my ideas are boring or confusing to any reader, especially a peer, I need to fix that. Sometimes it's just the organization that is confusing, so I make it more chronological, or use better transitions. When a peer suggests different spelling or punctuation, I look at it but not as hard unless the peer is a classmate I know to be a strong speller or one who makes very few errors in their own writing. Even when I don't agree with the peer feedback, it does force me to take another look at my writing before publishing the final draft.

How you learn matters. Keeping track of what has affected your language skills is important. How easy was it to answer the three questions in the example? Could you think of any other questions that might be good to ask about your learning?

Metacognition means thinking about your learning while you are learning. The more you ask yourself questions like the ones in the given example, the more aware you will become of your learning.

INTERCONNECTED SKILLS

Learning to be a good writer does not happen in isolation. What you hear, speak, and see influences what you write. Many of the skills you practise every day help you develop as a writer. In fact, everything you do and experience can become part of your writing experience if you take time to reflect on it. To start thinking about how language skills are connected, consider the following questions.

- What do you know about different media texts that might help when you are writing? Media texts are found in newspapers and magazines as well as in advertising, posters, and leaflets.
- In what way do you think the reading you do helps you as a writer? Can you give an example?
- What do you listen to that might help you as a writer?
- Have you ever seen a picture or a movie that made you think of a story? Or, have you ever written a story based on something you saw?

The following chart shows how different communication skills overlap and interconnect to help you write more effectively.

Connecting Related Skills to Better Writing	
Listening	• Provides inspiration for writing (speaker who is a role model) • Helps writer listen to peer suggestions for revision, editing, and evaluating writing • Allows listening to a taped interview for research • Allows detection of bias and stereotyping
Reading	• Provides ideas from magazines, newspapers, and books • Provides models of correct sentence patterns, spelling, and dialogue • Correct spelling • Gives basic ideas for settings, plots, and characters • Provides research information • Broadens understanding of a writing topic • Allows writer to see work to revise and edit
Viewing	• Films, documentaries, or advertisements can provide ideas for critical writing, summarizing, expressing or analysing a viewpoint, and interpreting • Pictures can provide ideas for creative writing • Develops higher level critical thinking skills in writing (compare short story to video version of same)
Speaking	• Turning written composition into speech forces writer to fine tune writing for larger audience • Allows peers to communicate ideas for revision to fellow writers • Reading work aloud is a good strategy for revision and editing • Speaking for a purpose (inform, entertain, persuade) improves awareness of writer's purpose • Group discussion is good for brainstorming ideas, discussing how to improve writing, and practicing clear expression
Representing	• Helps connect writer with other ways to communicate message (theme poster) • Helps clarify main ideas and details (character web, plot graph)

To understand more about how different skills interact, read the following fictional experience of Timothy, a Grade 12 student. His experiences retold here describe how interconnected skills played a part in helping him write more effectively. As you read, think about how your own experiences in English class can be improved upon by using a variety of skills.

Listening

Timothy is sitting with his friends in a Grade 12 assembly. He doesn't know what to expect as his English teacher, Mr. Kennedy, introduces the guest speaker.

"Ladies and gentlemen, our guest today was once a teacher like myself. Like me, he too wracked his brains on a daily basis, trying to think of ways to encourage his students to write, to get them excited about writing. He came up with the idea of writing a novel for them. The novel, *Stand Your Ground*, was set in the school where he worked. The setting was his community. Many of the characters had the same names as his students. That novel came out in 1993. It was a big hit, especially with the students who found their names in the book.

Since 1993, our guest has given up his teaching career to become a full time writer of at least 45 novels with more on the way. He has won more than 30 awards, including the Ontario Library Association Silver Birch Award, three times. The selection panel was made up of over 750,000 young people like yourselves, country-wide, who voted for Mr. Eric Walters. It is my honour to present him to you today. Eric Walters is a man who loves a great story, and who knows how to turn young people into fans of his books."

As the writer approaches the podium, Timothy starts to pay attention, especially when Mr. Walters launches into the dramatic reading of a chapter from his novel called *Shattered*. The chapter is about a 15-year-old boy, Ian, starting to work as a volunteer in a soup kitchen as part of a social studies project. After a near mugging, in which Ian is saved by a homeless man, Ian later spots the man at the soup kitchen. It turns out he is a returned member of the Canadian Armed Forces, whose last tour had involved peacekeeping duties in Rwanda.

Mr. Walters also reads a foreword from the novel composed by Canadian General Romeo Dallaire, Force Commander for the United Nations Mission to Rwanda. The rest of the presentation is a blur. Mr. Walters calls a couple of students up who have prepared some interview questions. He is both entertaining and serious, and he talks about writing, and about researching historical events in Canada to get ideas for writing. All Timothy can think about is getting his hands on that first novel. Timothy is not from Rwanda, but his parents did come to Canada from Zaire before it was renamed Congo. He was too young to remember, but he wants to find out about why his parents ended up in a refugee camp for a year before they emigrated.

Reading and Viewing

Timothy signs out the novel *Shattered* from the school library. The librarian suggests that he might also like to watch the movie *Hotel Rwanda*, which is about a courageous hotel manager who saved people from being caught in a tribal massacre during the Rwandan crisis. Timothy rents the movie after he finishes the book.

Writing

The teacher, Mr. Kennedy, has encouraged his students to try writing some form of historical fiction using suggestions from Eric Walters. Timothy decides to create five journal entries written by a fictional character, Akunda, who lives with his parents in a refugee camp in Congo, from where they are hoping to emigrate to Canada.

Speaking

Timothy tapes his journal entries to play for his writing group. He uses his older brother to be the voice of Akunda, and he reads the part of the narrator. As a writer, Timothy is supposed to use the group's suggestions to help him revise his writing.

Reflection

Mr. Kennedy poses the following two questions to his student writers, which they are to attach to the final draft of their writing before handing it in. You can read Timothy's answers to both questions.

How did listening to the taped reading of your writing help you to revise it?

One of my peer listeners suggested that I write two more entries to show the contrast when Akunda started his new life in Canada. He said the journal ended too abruptly. I thought that was a good idea, so I added those to my assignment. They also thought I could make the African entries a bit more realistic if I used actual places, so I looked up a map of the Congo on the Internet when I went home and changed a couple of location names.

What did you discover from reading Young Adult fiction that you could apply to your own story?

After Mr. Walters spoke to us a month ago, I read his novel *Shattered*. I tried to make my character, Akunda, seem as real as Ian seemed to me when I read the book. I also did some research on the Congo and talked to my parents about their experiences, to make the journal entries as authentic as I could. I went on Eric Walters' website for more ideas, but what I learned from that one novel was

- Use real places and events
- Make your main character have the same worries and concerns as young people all over the world—with dreams of a better life, a successful future, and solid friendships.

The great thing about all your language skills being connected is that you can tailor your learning to how you learn best. If you learn better by talking to others or by speaking out loud about your ideas, do that. Your writing will improve if your ideas come to you more easily through verbal communication. Or maybe you need to write out what you think before you prepare a formal essay. Some people learn better by reading, and some learn better by listening to others speak or by watching others demonstrate something visually.

It is important to remember that related skills in listening, speaking, reading, viewing, and representing contribute to improving your proficiency as a writer. The more you are able to recognize these connections, the better your writing will become.

Portfolios

A portfolio is a collection of your writing pieces, usually representing a time period of at least one school year. Keeping your writing together allows you to

- see your growth as a writer
- review topics and writing forms that you have tried
- evaluate your writing skills
- set writing goals for improving or refining your skills

A portfolio may also contain a writer's log or journal, personal spelling lists, personal error record, or reflections about your writing. In this section, you will find some examples of ways you could use your portfolio as a resource to help you improve your writing skills.

In the following example, a student compares a first draft to a final draft, both of which she has found in her writing portfolio. Look at the first draft of a paragraph on rogue waves that appears earlier in this section. Next, read the revised final draft from the student's portfolio. By comparing the two drafts, the student was able to not only pinpoint the improvements she made, but also to explain what she learned from the redrafting process.

Example

Revised Final Draft of Rogue Waves Paragraph

Sometimes, groups of large ocean waves caused by a storm slam into a powerful ocean current passing in the opposite direction. When this happens, several storm waves pile up to form rogue waves. These waves can be more than 100 feet high and can bury cargo ships beneath the sea. Rogue waves are most common off the coasts of Japan, Florida, and Alaska. Currently, a project known as WaveAtlas monitors the oceans with satellites. Over the next few years, oceanographers hope to analyse these satellite images to help them better understand why freak waves, or "rogue waves" as they are known to scientists, occur so that scientific warnings can prevent unnecessary tragedies at sea.

Improvements Made

- Used better transitions
- Used more precise and consistent vocabulary
- Used consistent verb tenses throughout paragraph
- Created a more logical order in last section of paragraph
- Added a safety reason for scientific studies to round out paragraph

What I Learned from the Redrafting Process

- Read out loud to make sure writing flows smoothly
- When you use consistent verb tenses throughout a piece of writing, the ideas are clearer to the reader
- Your writing can sound better if you take the time to think about changes for improvement
- It is more satisfying to hand in redrafted work because you are sure that it is clear and says what you want it to

In the following example from a fictional student writing portfolio, the student had been given the following information from a local television news broadcast during a week of bitter cold in the city:

- Only 826 of 1200 available overnight Shelter Spots are being used.
- City council fears that homeless people are not using the shelters.
- The hotline number to call for information about the shelters is 416-SHELTER.
- Citizens are urged to cooperate to prevent homeless people from freezing.
- The city spokesperson is Ellen McCall.

The assignment involved writing a poem and a news report based on the information the student was given. He was asked to include a reflection with his writing, comparing the processes used for each form, and identifying challenges he had to overcome.

The following section includes the student's two writing pieces, followed by the reflection that accompanied the pieces in the portfolio.

DEEP FREEZE INCREASES RISK TO HOMELESS

Fears Grow for Unsheltered

Toronto—While most of us struggle with getting the car to start and risking a fender-bender on the way to work, the homeless of our city struggle with survival in the frigid temperatures that have gripped the region this past week.

Ellen McCall, spokesperson for city shelter co-ordination, reports that 1200 beds prepared for weather emergencies are being filled nightly.

While no one is being turned away from shelter facilities, it is feared that some people needing shelter may not be finding it for a variety of reasons, including voluntary choices to spend the night in makeshift temporary shelters outside.

Bus drivers and police have been cautioned to be on the alert for anyone needing assistance or shelter.

Commuters and other citizens are asked to report possible shelter-related emergencies to the shelter hotline at 250-SHELTER (743-5837). All calls will be treated as urgent.

So far, there have been no reported deaths as a result of freezing. However, each period of severe cold in the past has generated at least one fatality in the city. It is hoped that 2008 will remain fatality-free.

—*by* E. Meyer, Vancouver Sun City Desk

BALLAD OF A COLD MAN

The winds they chill me to the bone,
A man who calls Vancouver home,
My cardboard walls are way too thin
I wish I could go home again.

Chorus

Home again, yes home again,
I wish I could go home again,
To Mother's stew without the pain,
I wish I could go home again.

The streets they mock me with their ice,
The cops assume I act with vice,
My cardboard walls no shelter give,
Must move if I expect to live.

Continued

Chorus

How did I reach this point so low?
How did my dreams descend below?
The ice outside, that's not so bad,
It's ice within, that makes me sad.

And so if winter's got you down,
And risky drivers make you frown,
Just pause while at that traffic light,
And say a prayer for someone's plight.

I, too, was once a man like you,
The 101 my trial too,
But life can change and paths can turn,
So don't complain, be still, and learn.

My Challenges for this Writing Assignment

The news story was not too difficult to write because of the notes we had from class on the inverted pyramid format for news reporting. Most of the key facts were provided in the points listed on the board, so I tried to be as factual as possible. To create the byline and dateline correctly, I checked a newspaper at home and tried to make it look similar with my computer using special fonts and the column feature. I sometimes make spelling mistakes on words like *frigid*, so I used spellcheck and had my older sister proofread my draft for spelling. I remembered that newspaper reporting should always be correct English, so I used sentence patterns I could use with confidence and did not try anything fancy.

I was able to be more creative with the poem. I chose the ballad form because of the repetitive rhyme scheme and chorus, which I thought I could imitate and because I think the misfortunes of the homeless make a sad story that seems to have no end, just like a sad ballad that goes on and on. I struggled with the line in the chorus, "To Mother's stew without the pain," because I didn't really like the effect of that wording, but I could not seem to come up with a better line that would express the emotional pain against something comforting like a mother's cooking. My favourite line was the figurative language in "It's ice within, that makes me sad." Other than that, I think my biggest challenge was expressing the ideas I had according to the form I had chosen.

METACOGNITION AND MAKING REVISIONS

In this third example from a fictional student's writing portfolio, the student was asked to revise a descriptive paragraph by creating a variety of sentence beginnings using different openers, such as adjectives, prepositional phrases, and past participles to replace the overused pattern of *the* plus a noun (subject). The original draft and the revised paragraph are reproduced below. A student reflection follows the two paragraphs, in which the student comments on the effect of the revision on the writing. Both drafts and the reflection would be kept in the student's portfolio. Take a look at the revisions, make a note of what has changed, and see if you prefer the revisions. What might you change about the original paragraph?

FIRST DRAFT OF DESCRIPTIVE PARAGRAPH

The room where I feel most relaxed is my bedroom. Mother and I painted it in my favourite color scheme, pale green and navy blue. The wide south window looks out over our sweeping back lawn with its massive weeping willow, where I once played as a child. I would play house, pretend it was a robbers' hideout, or even read a book under the umbrella of its cool shade on a hot July afternoon. The window is framed in white, with a softly draped sheer navy valance across its top. I like to sit by that window in my white wicker armchair during a thunderstorm, watching lightning stab the sky in jagged tears as angry raindrops pound against the glass. I feel cozy and secure. This is my own special place.

PARAGRAPH WITH REVISIONS

<u>Painted</u> in my favourite color scheme of pale green and navy blue, the room where I feel most relaxed is my bedroom. (Began sentence with a past participle) The wide south window looks out over our sweeping back lawn with its massive weeping willow where I once played as a child. <u>Under the umbrella of its cool shade</u> I would play house, pretend it was a robbers' hideout, or even read a book on a hot July afternoon. (Began sentence with two prepositional phrases) The window is framed in white, with a softly draped, sheer navy valance across its top. <u>In my white wicker armchair</u>, I like to sit by that window during a thunderstorm, watching lightning stab the navy sky with jagged tears as angry raindrops pound against the glass. (Began with a prepositional phrase) <u>Cozy and secure</u>, I burrow deeper into my chair. (Began with two adjectives) This is my own special place.

Student Reflection on Revisions

I thought my original draft was quite good, probably because I enjoy describing things and my room is a special place that I was able to share through precise description. When you taught us about sentence beginnings, I could see right away from your examples that this was a good way of adding variety to writing. It is hard to believe that we fall into the habit of repeating the same sentence pattern, even while using lots of effective descriptive phrases. Here is how I thought the revisions improved my writing with this paragraph:

1. Placing the participle *painted* at the beginning of the first sentence helped the reader to immediately see the color scheme, which is probably the most striking feature of the room.
2. The prepositional phrases in this sentence ("Under the umbrella of its cool shade") provided a good transition and link with the "weeping willow" that I had introduced in the preceding sentence.
3. This prepositional phrase ("In my white wicker armchair") provided a change from the more predictable beginning of the sentence just before it ("The window is…").
4. These two adjectives ("cozy and secure") describe the atmosphere of my room as well as how I felt there during the storm. By moving them to the beginning of the sentence, I was able to give the adjectives a more important status and to stress the mood in the room.

I liked the freedom to move words and phrasing around to add variety to my paragraph, without eliminating vocabulary that I had carefully chosen for the description. I thought the overall effect was much improved!

The applications of metacognition in this section are only examples. You can apply the language skills you have learned in many different ways. Reading out loud, reading with others, discussion, writing, and reworking texts are all useful. As you try different methods, you will begin to see which ones are the most effective for your learning style. The more information you can process and understand, the better able you will be to interact with and interpret the world.

Taking time to focus on metacognition will improve your skills in language arts. There is not one correct method for metacognition. It is best to use a variety of methods in order to determine how you learn best. Reflecting on how you learn should be an ongoing process. Metacognition is something that you can use throughout your life, in school, work, and other areas of your life. Examining how and why you do certain things gives you insight on how you can change and improve. Reflecting on how you read and write also helps you practise your reading and writing skills.

NOTES

Key Strategies for Success on Tests

KEY STRATEGIES FOR SUCCESS ON TESTS

Having a good understanding of effective test-taking skills can help your performance on any test. Being familiar with question formats can help you in preparing for quizzes, unit tests or year-end assessments.

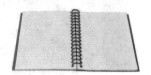

TEST PREPARATION AND TEST-TAKING SKILLS

THINGS TO CONSIDER WHEN TAKING A TEST

- It is normal to feel anxious before writing a test. You can manage this anxiety by thinking positive thoughts. Visual imagery is a helpful technique to try.
- Make a conscious effort to relax by taking several slow, controlled, deep breaths. Concentrate on the air going in and out of the body.
- Before you begin the test, ask questions if you are unsure of anything.
- Jot down key words or phrases from any oral directions.
- Look over the entire test to assess the number and kinds of questions on the test.
- Read each question closely and reread it if necessary.
- Pay close attention to key vocabulary words. Sometimes these words are bolded or italicized, and they are usually important words in the question.
- Mark your answers on your answer sheet carefully. If you wish to change an answer, erase the mark and then ensure that your final answer is darker than the one that you have erased.
- On the test booklet, use highlighting to note directions, key words and vocabulary that you find confusing or that are important to answering the question.
- **Double-check** to make sure you have answered everything before handing in your test.

When taking tests, some words are often overlooked. Failure to pay close attention to these words can result in an incorrect answer. One way to avoid this is to be aware of these words and to <u>underline,</u> circle or **highlight** these words while you are taking the test.

Even though these words are easy, they can change the meaning of the entire question and/or answer.

all	**always**	**most likely**	**probably**	**best**	**not**
difference	**usually**	**except**	**most**	**unlikely**	**likely**

Example

1. During the race, Susan is **most likely** feeling

   A. sad

   B. weak

   C. scared

   D. determined

HELPFUL STRATEGIES FOR ANSWERING MULTIPLE-CHOICE QUESTIONS

A multiple-choice question provides some information for you to consider and then asks you to select a response from four choices. There will be one correct answer. The other answers are distracters, which are incorrect.

Here are some strategies to help you when answering multiple-choice questions.

↗ Quickly skim through the entire test. Find out how many questions there are and plan your time accordingly.

↗ Read and reread questions carefully. Underline key words and try to think of an answer before looking at the choices.

↗ If there is a graphic, look at the graphic, read the question, and go back to the graphic. Then, you may want to circle the important information from the question.

↗ Carefully read the choices. Read the question first and then each answer with it.

↗ When choosing an answer, try to eliminate those choices that are clearly wrong or do not make sense.

↗ Some questions may ask you to select the "best" answer. These questions will always include words like **best, most strongly**, and **most clearly**. All of the answers will be correct to some degree, but one of the choices will be "best" in some way. Carefully read all four choices (A, B, C, D) before choosing the answer you think is the best.

↗ If you do not know the answer or if the question does not make sense to you, it is better to guess than to leave it blank.

↗ Do not spend too much time on any one question. Make a mark (*) beside a difficult question and come back to it. If you are leaving a question to come back to later, make sure that you also leave the space on the answer sheet.

↗ Remember to go back to the difficult questions at the end of the test; sometimes clues are given throughout the test that will provide you with answers.

↗ Note any negatives (Ex.: **no, not**) and be sure your choice fits the question.

↗ Before changing an answer, **be sure** you have a very good reason to do so.

↗ Do not look for patterns on your answer sheet.

HELPFUL STRATEGIES FOR ANSWERING OPEN-RESPONSE QUESTIONS

An open-response question requires you to respond to a question or directive such as **explain, predict, list, describe, use information from the text and your own ideas; provide the main idea and supporting details.** In preparing for open-response tasks you may wish to:

- Read and re-read the question carefully.
- Recognize and pay close attention to **directing words** such as **explain, predict, and describe.**
- <u>Underline</u> key words and phrases that indicate what is required in your answer such as <u>explain,</u> <u>summarize,</u> <u>mainly about,</u> <u>what is the meaning of,</u> <u>best shows…</u>
- Write down rough, point-form notes regarding the information you want to include in your answer.
- Think about what you want to say and organize information and ideas in a coherent and concise manner within the time limit you have for the question.
- Be sure to answer every part of the question that is asked.
- Stick to the question, be brief and only answer what is asked.
- Answer in full and correctly written sentences keeping your answer within the space provided.
- Re-read your response to ensure you have answered the question.
- **Think:** Does your answer make sense?
- **Listen:** Does it sound right?
- Use the appropriate subject vocabulary and terminology in your response.

TEST PREPARATION COUNTDOWN

If you develop a plan for studying and test preparation, you will perform well on tests.

Here is a general plan to follow seven days before you write a test.

Countdown: Seven Days Before the Test

1. Review important areas in which to gather information

    - areas to be included on the test
    - types of test items
    - general and specific test tips

2. Start preparing for the test at least seven days prior to the test-taking day. Develop your test preparation plan and set time aside to prepare and study.

Countdown: Six, Five, Four, Three, Two Days before the Test

1. Review old homework assignments, quizzes, and tests.
2. Rework problems on quizzes and tests to make sure you still know how to solve them.
3. Correct any errors made on quizzes and tests.
4. Review key concepts, processes, formulas, and vocabulary.
5. Create practice test questions for yourself and then answer them. Work out lots of sample problems.

Countdown: The Night Before the Test

1. The night before the test is for final preparation, which includes reviewing and gathering material needed for the test before going to bed.
2. Most important is getting a good night's rest and knowing that you have done everything within your means to do well on the test.

Test Day

1. Eat a healthy and nutritious breakfast.
2. Ensure that you have all the necessary materials.
3. Think positive thoughts: "I can do this!" "I am ready!" "I know I can do well!"
4. Arrive at your school early so that you are not rushing. A stressful, rushed morning can set a hurried or anxious pace for the test.

SUCCESS TIPS DURING THE TEST

The following strategies can be useful to use when writing your test.

↗ Take two or three deep breaths to help you relax.

↗ Read the directions carefully and underline, circle, or highlight any key words.

↗ Survey the entire test to get a flavour of what you will need to do.

↗ Budget your time.

↗ Begin with an easy question or a question that you know you can answer correctly rather than following the numerical question order of the test.

↗ If you draw a blank on the test, try repeating the deep breathing and physical relaxation activities first. Then move to visualization and positive self-talk to get you going.

↗ Write down anything that you remember about the subject on the reverse side of your test paper. This activity sometimes helps you to remind yourself that you do know something and you are capable of writing the test.

↗ Look over your test when you have finished and double-check your answers to be sure you did not forget anything.

NOTES

PREPARING TO WRITE THE PROVINCIAL EXAMINATION

Part One—Begin by looking at old exams.

---

1. **Google BC Ministry of Education Exams**

   On this page you will find

   • exam schedules
   • sample exams with key
   • reading categories
   • key words
   • scoring guides
   • sample responses

2. **Write a Response to the Sample Exams**

   Compare your response to the answer key provided at the website. This is a very effective method of improving your critical reading skills. This experience will also give you confidence.

Part Two—At the Examination.

---

1. **Look Through the Entire Exam**

   1.1 Understand that the exam directions are based on 2 hours, but you have 3 hours to complete the test, thus base your timing on 3 hours. If you have an IEP, you may have extra time above and beyond the 3 hours—check first with your learning assistance teacher.

   1.2 If writing online, familiarize yourself with the split screen and review features.

   1.3 Read the titles of each selection. You may see valuable connections in the titles.

2. **Multiple-Choice Questions**

   2.1 The stem of each question defines the task. Read the stem carefully. Many students highlight or circle the key word(s).

   2.2 Do not leave any multiple-choice responses blank.

Multiple choice questions often require you to make fine distinctions between correct and nearly correct answers. Consider the following suggestions:

- Read the question stem and formulate your own response before reading the available choices.
- Read the directions carefully, paying close attention to qualifying expressions like "the *best* answer," "*most* likely," and superlatives like "*never*, *always*, *all*, and *none*," which indicate that the correct response must be an undisputed fact.
- Use active reading techniques, such as underlining, circling, or highlighting critical words.
- Begin by answering only those questions for which you are certain of the correct answer.
- Be aware of distracters that may lead you to choose plausible but incorrect solutions.
- Use information from other questions to help you.
- Eliminate the responses you know are wrong, and then asses the remaining alternatives and choose the best one.
- Return to the questions you have skipped and consider them in again.
- Guess if you cannot decide between two arguably correct alternatives.

3. **Informational Text.** This section contains only multiple-choice questions. Read these carefully. Questions will be asked of textual and graphic material.

4. **Poetry**

   4.1 You may wish to read the open-ended response prior to reading the poem. This can help understand the intent of the poem and the task you are to perform.

   4.2 Read the title, then read the poem at least twice prior to beginning the questions. Write notes beside, or underline key lines in the poem, as you read.

   4.3 Open-ended question

   4.3.1 Find a few brief quotes from the poem that you can use in your response. These quotes are your proof.

   4.3.2 Your written response need not be multi-paragraph.

   4.3.3 Begin by illustrating, in your opening sentences, your understanding of the task required by the question.

   4.3.4 Integrate your quotes into your response in a logically organized manner.

   4.3.5 Upper-level papers avoid colloquial or conversational language. Upper-level responses also discuss how the quotes answer the question. This discussion is detailed and maintains a focus on this poem.

   4.3.6 This is literary analysis. Do not write literary criticism and avoid personal references.

5. Prose

5.1 As in poetry, an effective strategy is to read the open-ended question first. In prose there are two questions, and you select one to respond to.

5.2 Prose selections tend to focus on one critical incident. The resolution of this incident can be a key to the intent of the selection.

5.3 Open-ended question

5.3.1 Choose one.

5.3.2 As in poetry, select a few quotes that will be the foundation of your response. You may wish to find a quote from the opening of the selection, from the key incident or moment, and from the resolution (or denouement). Each quote should be the cornerstone of a separate paragraph.

5.3.3 Your response must be multi-paragraph (three or more paragraphs).

5.3.4 Upper-level responses illustrate an understanding of the task, of the reading selection, and of literary analysis. Your response must be precise, detailed, and formal.

5.4.5 This question, at 24 marks, counts for over 25 % of the final exam grade. It is wise to spend time thinking and organizing prior to writing.

Note: The open-ended responses are literary analysis, not literary criticism. It is also not appropriate to discuss personal stories or analogies at this time.

---

6. Composition

6.1 The original composition counts for over 25% of the exam.

6.2 This is an opportunity for you to be original and creative.

6.3 Use the techniques of good writing:

Vary your sentence lengths.

Be descriptive.

Vary your vocabulary.

Choose an appropriate and suitable topic or focus for an examination.

6.4 You may choose to write either a narrative, expository, or descriptive multi-paragraph composition.

Narrative: Limit the scope of the narrative—usually to one place and one time.

Describe in detail either the character, setting, or both. Write with a sense of audience, but do not be afraid of being creative.

The car drove by.

The red car drove by quickly.

The rusty, red '88 Hyundai Pony slowly drove by Gervin.

It appeared the rusty, red '88 Hyundai Pony with the bumper sticker "Free Tibet" was just going to drive by Gervin, when a can of Pepsi flew out the back window—narrowly missing his marvelous Rasta locks and the head they were flowing from.

After a few paragraphs, stop, think, and organize the ending.

Tension is important, but need not dominate.

Focus on showing the character doing something, rather than telling the audience what they should feel. Have the character do something, and make the audience figure out why they did it.

Expository: Again, limit the scope and choose a topic you know well.

> *I like the environment.*

> *I really like the environment here in British Columbia.*

> *The ancient Tamarac forest, deep in the Slocan Valley, is one of the most beautiful sights on earth. It was early in the morning on October 15, 1986. I was about to witness, for the first time, full scale clear-cut logging. The trees seemed to sense the doom as they began to move restlessly in the morning wind.*

6.5 Think. This is always a good place to start. Ponder the topic with your pen. Write all your ideas down—however haphazard they may seem. Do not just ponder—ponder with ink. People are visual learners—when you see your ideas on the page you will better connect and organize them.

6.6 Attitude. Try to avoid "perfect" characters. Life is complex. Show, when possible, a character or situation that is not a stereotype.

6.7 Avoid narratives that are inappropriate. This is an English 12 exam—be creative, yet remember the composition is for marks.

CHANGES TO THE PROVINCIAL EXAMINATION, 2008

I. New Examination Dates and Formats

1. Examinations in English Language Arts 12 are offered in

October	electronic session only
November	electronic session only
January	selected exams in print
April	electronic session only
May	electronic session only
June	electronic session only

   * August dates to be determined

2. Students may write the exam **twice** with the best mark the final mark.

3. Students may write the exam prior to completion of the course.

II. Types of Reading Passages

- ➢ poems
- ➢ short stories or excerpts
- ➢ novel excerpts
- ➢ newspaper and magazine articles, web pages, timelines, maps, charts, graphics, cartoons
- ➢ non-fiction prose (such as essays, journals, interviews, biographies)

III. The provincial examination is divided into four parts:

1. Reading Comprehension
2. Poetry
3. Prose
4. Original Composition

Overview of Important Changes to the Written Response
Students will still be required to produce 3 written responses:

Part A	Reading Comprehension	12 marks	New
Part B	Synthesizing Text	24 marks	New
Part C	Original Composition	24 marks	No change

Note: Each examination may be slightly different as to which section will serve as the 12 mark stand-alone written-response section (the other two sections will then contain the 24 mark synthesizing text written-response question). For example, the sample examination on the ministry website has the Reading Comprehension section as the stand-alone 12-mark written response section, the Poetry and Prose sections contain the 24-mark synthesizing text written-response question. Other exams may be different: Poetry may be stand-alone with Reading Comprehension and Prose containing the synthesis question. Students must be aware that each exam may be different.

Part A: Reading Comprehension—Stand-Alone Text *New*

The written response to the stand-alone text is new.
Samples are posted on the Ministry of Education website.
http://www.bced.gov.bc.ca/exams/search/

Students will read one text and respond to multiple-choice questions and one written-response question. The text may be informational, poetry, or literary prose. In answering the written-response question, students should be able to develop a unified and coherent paragraph of at least 150 words. Responses should be constructed using complete and effective sentences and adhere to the conventions of standard written English. Students will be provided with one question for response.

Part B: Reading Comprehension—Synthesis Texts 1 and 2 *New*

Students will read two texts and respond to multiple-choice questions on both. The texts may be informational, poetry, or literary prose.

This is similar to the Language Arts 10 question in format, but the marking rubric is far more rigorous. It is very important that students familiarize themselves with the new marking rubric for this section.

It is also very important for students to use the organization and planning page in preparing their response. This is a very sophisticated task. Students who have not taken the time to properly organize their response may produce written work that does not discuss the synthesis of ideas to the level necessary to attain upper level marks.

Students may wish to use a graphic organizer for this section. For example, a Venn diagram is a useful tool in helping organize a response to the synthesizing text question.

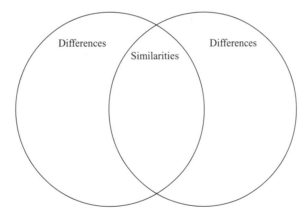

Part C: Reading Comprehension—Analysis of Synthesis Texts 1 and 2 *New*

Students will respond to two multiple-choice questions and one written-response question based on Synthesis Texts 1 and 2. The texts may be informational, poetry, or literary prose.

In answering the written-response synthesis question, students should be able to develop a multi-paragraph essay of at least 300 words. Students should be able to support a position or interpretation by citing specific details, features, and information from the texts. They should be able to generate and shape their ideas using varied sentences and an appropriate level of diction. They should also demonstrate an understanding of the conventions of standard written English by monitoring their spelling, grammar, punctuation, and syntax. Students will be provided with one question.

In interpreting informational text, students will be expected to demonstrate comprehension at the literal, inferential, and critical levels. Students should be able to identify and analyze ways of manipulating language to create a desired effect, such as presenting information, developing an argument, and supporting a thesis. Students will be asked to identify stylistic and persuasive techniques used by writers to achieve their purpose. Students will be expected to differentiate between subjective and objective language and between fact and opinion.

In interpreting poetry and literary prose, students will be expected to comprehend at the literal, inferential, and critical levels. As well, they should be able to demonstrate an understanding of the terms and devices relevant to the discussion of the work and be able to support a position or interpretation by citing specific details, features, and information from the poem or passage.

At least one graphic will be included to support texts in Part A, Part B, or Part C of the examination. The graphic may be placed with any of the three genres: informational, poetry, or literary prose. At least one question will be asked on the graphic.

A brief context statement may be provided above the reading passages where appropriate to give relevant information about the passage, source, or writer, including historical background and setting. As excerpts from longer works are sometimes used, context statements may explain the action or events that preceded the passage. For these reasons, students should be encouraged to read context statements.

IV. SCORING GUIDE FOR ANALYSIS OF SYNTHESIS TEXTS 1 AND 2

	This is a first-draft response and should be assessed as such.
	The response is assessed holistically.
6	This essay is superior, demonstrating an insightful understanding of the texts. The essay shows a sophisticated approach to synthesis, including pertinent references. The writing style is effective and demonstrates skillful control of language. Despite its clarity and precision, the essay need not be error-free.
5	This essay is proficient, demonstrating a clear understanding of the texts at an interpretive level. The essay clearly synthesizes the concepts within the texts. References may be explicit or implicit and convincingly support the analysis. The writing is well organized and reflects a strong command of the conventions of language. Errors may be present, but are not distracting.
4	This essay is competent. Understanding of the texts tends to be literal and superficial. Some synthesis is apparent. The essay may rely heavily on paraphrasing. References are present and appropriate, but may be limited. The writing is organized and straightforward. Conventions of language are usually followed, but some errors are evident.
3	This essay is barely adequate. Understanding of the texts may be partially flawed. An attempt at synthesis is evident. References to the texts are not clearly connected to a central idea or may be repetitive. The response may be underdeveloped. A sense of purpose may be evident, but errors can be distracting.
2	This essay is inadequate. While there is an attempt to address the topic, understanding of the texts or the task may be seriously flawed. Reference to only one text does not constitute synthesis. The response may be seriously underdeveloped. Errors are recurring, distracting, and impede meaning.

TABLE OF CORRELATIONS				
Strand	**General Outcome**	**Specific Outcome**		**Practice Test 1**	**Practice Test 2**
Students are expected to:					
Reading and Viewing	B Purposes	B1	read, both collaboratively and independently, to comprehend a wide variety of literary text		
		B2	read, both collaboratively and independently, to comprehend a wide variety of information and persuasive texts with increasing complexity and subtlety of ideas and form	1	
		B3	view, both collaboratively and independently, to comprehend a variety of visual texts with increasing complexity and subtlety of ideas and form	6	6
		B4	independently select and read, for sustained periods of time, texts for enjoyment and to increase fluency		
		B5	before reading and viewing, select, adapt, and apply a range of strategies to anticipate content and construct meaning		

		B6	during reading and viewing, select, adapt, and apply a range of strategies to construct, monitor, and confirm meaning		3
		B7	after reading and viewing, select, adapt, and apply a range of strategies to extend and confirm meaning, and to consider author's craft	11, 12, 13, 15, 17, 19, 20, 21	1, 4, 5, 7, 9, 12, 13, 17, 19, 20
	B Thinking	B8	explain and support personal responses to texts		
		B9	interpret, analyse, and evaluate ideas and information from texts	5, 9, 10	2, 18, 21
		B10	synthesize and extend thinking about texts	3, 8, 16, 18	15, 16
		B11	use metacognitive strategies to reflect on and assess their reading and viewing		
	B Features	B12	recognize and explain how structures and features of text shape readers' and viewers' construction of meaning and appreciation of author's craft	4, 7, 14	14
		B13	demonstrate increasing work skills and vocabulary knowledge	2	8, 10, 11

Writing	C Purposes	C1	write meaningful personal texts that elaborate on ideas and information	Written-Response Poetry	Written-Response Poetry
		C2	write purposeful information texts that express ideas and information	Written-Response Prose Written-Response Making Connections Written-Response Original	Written-Response Prose Written-Response Making Connections Written-Response Original
		C3	write effective imaginative texts to develop ideas and information	Written-Response Prose Written-Response Making Connections Written-Response Original	Written-Response Prose Written-Response Making Connections Written-Response Original
		C4	create thoughtful representations that communicate ideas and information	Written-Response Poetry Written-Response Prose Written-Response Making Connections Written-Response Original	Written-Response Poetry Written-Response Prose Written-Response Making Connections Written-Response Original
		C5	select, adapt, and apply a range of strategies to generate, develop, and organize ideas for writing and representing	Written-Response Poetry Written-Response Prose Written-Response Making Connections Written-Response Original	Written-Response Poetry Written-Response Prose Written-Response Making Connections Written-Response Original
		C6	select, adapt, and apply a range of drafting and composing strategies while writing and representing	Written-Response Poetry Written-Response Prose Written-Response Making Connections Written-Response Original	Written-Response Poetry Written-Response Prose Written-Response Making Connections Written-Response Original
		C7	select, adapt, and apply a range of strategies to revise, edit, and publish writing and representing	Written-Response Poetry Written-Response Prose Written-Response Making Connections Written-Response Original	Written-Response Poetry Written-Response Prose Written-Response Making Connections Written-Response Original

	C Thinking	C8	write and represent to explain and support personal responses to texts	Written-Response Poetry Written-Response Prose Written-Response Making Connections Written-Response Original	Written-Response Poetry Written-Response Prose Written-Response Making Connections Written-Response Original
		C9	write and represent to interpret, analyse, and evaluate ideas and information from texts	Written-Response Poetry Written-Response Prose Written-Response Making Connections Written-Response Original	Written-Response Poetry Written-Response Prose Written-Response Making Connections Written-Response Original
		C10	write and represent to synthesize and extend thinking	Written-Response Prose Written-Response Making Connections Written-Response Original	Written-Response Prose Written-Response Making Connections Written-Response Original
		C11	use metacognitive strategies to reflect on and assess their writing and representing		
		C12	use and experiment with elements of style in writing and representing, appropriate to purpose and audience, to enhance meaning and artistry	Written-Response Poetry Written-Response Prose Written-Response Making Connections Written-Response Original	Written-Response Poetry Written-Response Prose Written-Response Making Connections Written-Response Original
		C13	use and experiment with elements of form in writing and representing, appropriate to purpose and audience, to enhance meaning and artistry	Written-Response Poetry Written-Response Making Connections Written-Response Original	Written-Response Poetry Written-Response Making Connections Written-Response Original

PRACTICE TEST ONE

Part A: Informational Text

7 Multiple-Choice Questions   **Suggested Time: 15 minutes**

Value: 7%

> **Instructions:** Read the following selection, "The Finicky Shark," and answer the multiple-choice questions. For each question, select the **best** answer and record your choice on the **answer sheet** provided.

THE FINICKY SHARK

1. Few animals have the power to frighten people into the cold terror of being eaten alive. But the great white shark does so effortlessly. Its reputation for blood lust is rooted in images of jaws gleaming with rows of razor-sharp teeth, their edges nicely serrated to ease the job of tearing through bone and flesh.

2   Nature's great killing machine grows to lengths of six metres or more and is often viewed as crude and mindlessly malevolent, feeding just as heartily on humans as on fish, seals, whales and sea lions.

3   But new research is challenging that notion and shedding light on the hidden life of the great white, revealing a finicky eater that may find people unpalatable.

4   Though it is pitiless with prey, lunging and slashing in red-stained water, the species can be quite civil among its own. Scientists have found what appears to be a ritualized competition over kills in which two great whites will forego attacking with one another for a genteel bout of slapping tails on the sea's surface. The biggest splash decides the winner.

5   Such finesse stands in stark contrast to the raw violence among many predators, which can engage one another in bloody fights to the death.

6   Over all, scientists say, great whites have been badly misunderstood, wrongly making them the demons of movies and nightmares. Some research has even found evidence that the killers, when thwarted in feeding, get visibly frustrated and agitated, perhaps even sad and dejected.

7   "We're dispelling the myths and learning a lot about how they really live," said Dr. A Peter Klimley, a biologist at the University of California Bodega Marine Laboratory in Bodega Bay, California, who is a prominent expert on the infamous shark.

8   "They're not stupid feeding machines," he said. "They're exquisitely adapted."

9   Dr. Douglas J. Long, a fish scientist at the California Academy of Sciences who studies great whites, said the new insights, while substantial, still have a number of riddles.

10 "For instance," Long said, "we know virtually nothing about how and where they mate."

11 Even as scientists seek to unravel the great white's biology, behaviour and ecology, a political push is accelerating to protect the beast. The top predator of the sea, it appears to be declining in numbers because of assaults by sport fishermen as well as commercial interests serving a growing international market for white-shark jaws and teeth.

12 California, South Africa and Australia have taken steps to try to protect the great white and other states and countries are considering such conservation efforts.

Continued

13 "Its numbers will inevitably dwindle unless prudent controls are enacted," Dr. Richard Murphy, a marine biologist at the Cousteau Society in Chesapeake, Virginia, wrote in *Great White Sharks*, a collection of scientific reports published late last year by Academic Press.

14 "In addition to being increasingly rare," Murphy said, "they are majestic pre-eminent participants in a complicated food web which we, as yet, only partially understand."

15 "The willingness and ability of humans to protect the killer," Murphy said, "are indicators of the economic, political and sociological health of our own species."

16 The mythology of terror surrounding the great white is even wider and more ominous than the shark's jaws are in real life. In *Twenty Thousand Leagues Under the Sea*, Jules Verne tells how Professor Aronnax was taken by Captain Nemo for a global submarine tour, the two men finding themselves face to face with some of the razor-toothed giants during an underwater walk.

17 "The blood froze in my veins," the professor said, "as silver bellies and huge mouths bristling with teeth rushed out of the darkness."

18 After a narrow escape, the professor later told his companions of reports that fishermen had cut open the stomachs of great white sharks and found a buffalo head, a whole calf, and "a sailor still in uniform."

19 More recently, the beast achieved fame as the villain of *Jaws*, the best-selling book by Peter Benchley and the blockbuster movie by Steven Spielberg. Both featured a marauding great white that terrorized swimmers near crowded beaches.

20 The great white is "firmly ensconced in the pantheon of sea monsters," Richard Ellis wrote in *Monsters of the Sea* (Knopf, 1994). "It is the largest predator fish in the world," he said, "with some specimens weighing as much as a full-grown rhinoceros."

21 Sharks are ancient animals, long predating the dinosaur and myriad types of modern creatures. Carcharodon carcharias, or "ragged tooth" in scholarly Latin, is found in temperate waters throughout the world's seas. To find prey, it has acute sensors known as lateral-line organs that apparently can detect disturbances in seawater at ranges of 1,500 metres or more.

22 Closer to a victim (exactly how close is uncertain), its keen ears can hear thrashing, its sensitive nose can sniff blood, and its eerie black eyes can spy flesh. Powerful muscles send it lunging.

23 The triangular teeth grow to lengths of five or more centimeters and are extraordinarily strong. Three layers of enamel crisscross indifferent directions so the teeth can better withstand impact as well as twisting and bending. If a tooth is lost, a replacement directly behind it will rotate forward in a day or so. New teeth are constantly being formed in this replacement process.

24 Judging from stomach contents, the beast can indeed devour prey whole, including other sharks and seal lions. Though one of its nicknames is "man-eater" (another is "white death"), no one knows for certain whether people are in fact a preferred food.

25 Preliminary research suggests they are not. Klimley said white sharks might spit out humans, birds and sea otters because their bodies lack the energy-rich layers of fat possessed by animals like seals and whales.

26 "If they ingest something that's not energetically profitable, then they're stuck with that for a few days of slow ingestion," he said. "Fat has twice the energy and value of muscle."

27 Klimley noted three recent attacks along the northern California coast near Bodega Bay in which people had been quickly let go.

28 "Can you imagine?" he said. "These sharks are seizing people and holding them very gingerly to make this decision. They strike and hold and release—and that's for big sharks, three or four metres long."

29 Worldwide, great white sharks attack people four or five times a year, perhaps killing one of them.

—*by* William J. Broad

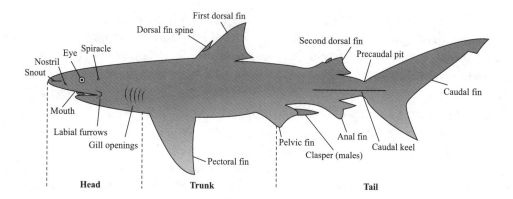

1. What does new research indicate about the great white shark?

   A. It is pitiless at all times.

   B. It is mindlessly malevolent.

   C. It has developed complex rituals to do with feeding.

   D. It will engage in bloody fights to the death with other sharks.

2. To what does "pre-eminent" refer (paragraph 14)?

   A. the shark

   B. Professor Aronnax

   C. Dr. Richard Murphy

   D. the Cousteau Society

3. In the context of the article, what is the **best** explanation for Dr. Klimley's view of the reason sharks may spit out humans?

   A. Humans are not energetically profitable.

   B. The shark cannot get a good grip on humans.

   C. The shark can easily mistake a human for a seal.

   D. Humans' wet suits produce a taste that discourages the shark.

4. Which method of presentation is **primarily** used in the article?

   A. anecdotal evidence

   B. chronological order

   C. quotes from experts

   D. cause-and-effect development

5. Which word **best** describes the tone of the article?

   A. assertive

   B. frustrated

   C. pessimistic

   D. informative

6. With reference to the diagram of a shark (Figure 1), what area of the diagram contains the **most** information ?

    A. tail

    B. head

    C. trunk

    D. caudal

7. In what form is the data in the quotation "no one knows for certain whether people are in fact a preferred food" presented?

    A. fact

    B. opinion

    C. statistical data

    D. anecdotal evidence

Part B: Poetry

Suggested Time: 30 minutes

7 Multiple-Choice Questions

1 Written-Response Question

Value: 23%

Instructions: Read the following poem, "The Writer," and answer the multiple-choice questions. For each question, select the **best** answer and record your answer on the **answer sheet** provided.

THE WRITER

1   In her room at the prow of the house
      Where light breaks, and the windows are tossed with linden[1],
      My daughter is writing a story.

      I pause in the stairwell, hearing
5   From her shut door a commotion of typewriter keys
      Like a chain hauled over a gunwale.

      Young as she is, the stuff
      Of her life is great cargo, and some of it heavy:
      I wish her a lucky passage.

10   But now it is she who pauses,
      As if to reject my thought and its easy figure.
      A stillness greatens, in which

Continued

---

[1]linden: an ornamental tree.

The whole house seems to be thinking,
And then she is at it again with a bunched clamor
15   Of strokes, and again is silent.

I remember the dazed starling
Which was trapped in that very room, two years ago;
How we stole in, lifted a sash

And retreated, not to affright it;
20   And how for a helpless hour, through the crack of the door,
We watched the sleek, wild, dark

And iridescent creature
Batter against the brilliance, drop like a glove
To the hard floor, or the desk-top,

25   And wait then, humped and bloody,
For the wits to try it again; and how our spirits
Rose when, suddenly sure,

It lifted off from a chair-back,
Beating a smooth course for the right window
30   And clearing the sill of the world.

It is always a matter, my darling,
Of life or death, as I had forgotten. I wish
What I wished you before, but harder.

—*by* Richard Wilbur

8. In the context of the poem, what do lines 22 to 24 imply about the bird?
    A. It is helpless.
    B. It is relentless.
    C. It is unconscious.
    D. It wants them to help.

9. What does the quotation "What I wished you before, but harder" suggest about the speaker?
    A. His rules are unbending.
    B. He worries about his daughter.
    C. He cares deeply about his daughter.
    D. His rules are hard but fair and will help her in times of life and death.

10. Which sound device is contained in the quotation "And how for a helpless hour"?
    A. assonance
    B. alliteration
    C. internal rhyme
    D. onomatopoeia

11. Which literary device is contained in the quotation "Like a chain hauled over a gunwale"?

    A. pun

    B. simile

    C. analogy

    D. metaphor

12. What is the extended metaphor in the poem ?

    A. a comparison of the father to a bird

    B. a comparison of the house to a bird

    C. a comparison of the house to a ship

    D. a comparison of the father to a ship's captain

13. What is the overall mood of the poem?

    A. ironic

    B. solemn

    C. playful

    D. serious

14. Which form of poetry is "The Writer"?

    A. ode

    B. epic

    C. sonnet

    D. narrative

Part B: Poetry

WRITTEN-RESPONSE QUESTION

Instructions: In paragraph form and in approximately **125 to 150 words**, answer question 1 in the **Response Booklet.** Write in **ink.** Use the **Organization and Planning** space to plan your work. The mark for your answer will be based on the appropriateness of the examples you use as well as the adequacy of your explanation and the quality of your written expression.

1. In paragraph form, and with specific reference to "The Writer," discuss the father's concern for his daughter.

Organization and Planning

Use this space to plan your ideas before writing in the Response Booklet.

WRITING ON THIS PAGE WILL NOT BE MARKED

Part C: Prose

8 Multiple-Choice Questions

1 Written-Response Question

Value: 40%

Suggested Time: 40 minutes

Instructions: Read the following Selection, "Saturday Climbing," and answer the multiple choice questions. For each question, select the **best** answer and record your answer on the **answer sheet** provided.

SATURDAY CLIMBING

1 Sixty feet up the cliff, the toe of his climbing boot resting on a ledge no wider than a dime, two fingers curled around a nubbin of rock, Barry was suddenly afraid that we would fall. "Rope," he called.

2 At the foot of the cliff, his daughter let out the golden line of rope that joined them. As Barry felt the rope go slack, he raised his right knee and pressed his toe into a shallow depression. Grunting with the strain, he stood up on his right leg, then paused, uncertain of his next move.

3 Six inches from his left hand there was a vertical crack that seemed hardly wider than a fingernail. Cautiously, he explored it with his fingers. Just within his reach it widened slightly. He ran his hand over his rack and unsnapped the smallest chock nut.

Continued

He forced the aluminum wedge deep into the crack. From the wedge there hung a wire loop and from that a carabiner[2]. Catching hold of the rope tied to his harness, he lifted it up, forced open the spring-loaded gate of the carabiner and fitted the rope into the aluminum oval.

4   Once the gate snapped shut, he sighed with relief. The chock nut, the wire loop, the carabiner, the rope, fragile as they looked, would hold ten times his weight. If he wanted to, he could let go and simply hang in space.

5   "You all right?" his daughter called. "Yeah," he lied. "Just resting."

6   His voice sounded faint and breathy. He was glad she could not see his momentary weakness. He could not control the trembling of his legs. The muscle of his right arm jerked spasmodically. Ever since his wife had left him, he had tried to compensate by providing unhesitating leadership for his daughter. He did his best to keep life simple and uncomplicated. It was, he thought, the way to provide security.

7   He glanced down. Among the scattered grey boulders, Moira's red hair gleamed like a burnished cap.

8   "You're doing fine," she hollered. The crosscurrents of air that played over the cliff face blurred her voice, making it seem farther away than it really was. To hear what she said, he had to strain toward the sound. "You've got another twenty feet to a big ledge. You can do it easy."

9   He was grateful for her confidence. Before they had started climbing, there had crept into his daughter's voice a constant note of disparagement and disappointment. The times he had managed to overcome his own insecurity and had asked her what was the matter, she had turned her back on him answering. "Nothing," with a tightly controlled voice.

10 Bewildered, he had sought the advice of women at work who had teenage daughters. They had been no help. Behind their competent, efficient professional selves, they too, he realized, were just as confused as he was. In desperation, he had gone so far as to pose the question of the relationship of fathers and daughters to his class. He had not been prepared for the reaction he got. From every corner of the room came cries of bitter disappointment and resentment.

11 For a moment, he suffered vertigo, and the cliff seemed to sway as if in an earthquake. He pressed his forehead to the cool stone and shut his eyes. Inside his flesh, his bones trembled.

12 Taking up rock-climbing had been an act of desperation. All the past activities Moira and he had done together—going to foreign films, visiting Seattle, beachcombing—she dismissed with a contemptuous shrug of her shoulders. At one time, they had played chess nearly every day. Lately, she pretended she had never seen the game. When he had noticed an advertisement for rock-climbing, he remembered that she had spoken admiringly of classmates who had hiked the West Coast Trail. He had registered them and paid their fees. Then he informed her.

13 He hoped she would be pleased. Instead, she was incensed that he had committed her to something without consent. He knew she was right to be angry but he was too frantic to care.

14 By emphasizing that the money was spent and there was no refund, he won the argument over rock-climbing. However, he took the car to the first class while she took her bike. She went prepared to sneer at everything, but once she saw her classmates, her attitude changed. Instead of Moira being isolated by her youth, Barry was isolated because of his age. Of the fifteen members, eleven were under twenty. The instructor still didn't need to shave more than once a week.

15 By the time the three hours were over and he realized that rock-climbing wasn't going to be rough hiking, it was too late to back out. There were only three girls in the class. In return for the attention of one-third of the young men, Moira was prepared to scale the Himalayas.

Continued

---

[2]*carabiner*: a D-shaped ring with a spring latch, used to fasten a rope.

16 Gradually, as a dozen Saturdays passed, what had seemed impossible was reduced to the merely difficult. Cliffs that had looked flat and smooth as polished marble became a series of problems and solutions. The names of the unfamiliar equipment became a part of his vocabulary. Young men in climbing boots frequented his backyard and kitchen. To his relief, Moira accepted him enough to spend an occasional hour practicing knot-tying with him.

17 This weekend there had been no class. In an attempt to heal a rift caused by an argument over her going away to college—she was two years ahead of herself in school and, therefore, in spite of being in grade 12 was only 16—he had offered to go climbing with her. To his surprise, she'd accepted.

18 "Climbing," he called.

19 "Climb on," Moira answered.

20 He stepped up, away from the safety of his perch. His life, he realized, was in her hands. If he fell, she was his protection.

21 Now, as he worked his way up toward the large ledge where he was to set up a belay station, it was as if Barry were in danger of being pulled backward by the sheer weight of his memories. It was with a sense of relief that he heaved himself onto the ledge. He paused to catch his breath, then anchored himself to a boulder.

22 "On belay[3]," he shouted down, giving Moira the signal that he was ready.

23 "Climbing," Moira answered.

24 "Climb on," he shouted.

25 From time to time, she paused to pull loose the chock nuts and pitons her father had left behind. These, since they would be needed later, she clipped to a sling that hung over her shoulder. Once, when she deviated from the route her father had taken, she became stuck at an overhang. Not having dealt with the obstacle himself, Barry could not help and has to leave her to find her own solution.

26 The climb seemed agonizingly slow, as if it would never be completed. Then, when it was over, and his daughter, grinning, breathless, was climbing over the edge, it was as if hardly any time had passed.

27 They sat side by side, sipping orange juice, their feet dangling in space.

28 "I thought you were in trouble," Moira said.

29 "I thought you were too," he replied, matching his weakness with hers. The, ashamed, he admitted, "I gripped."

30 Moira twisted about. Her red hair was snugged back with a rubber band. Being outside had sprinkled her nose with light freckles.

31 She studied the cliff face. It rose another hundred feet. There was a crack that ran more than halfway, then a small series of outcrops. He tried to see the route they should take, but the last ten or fifteen feet seemed impossible.

32 "I want to lead this pitch," Moira said.

33 Barry was startled. She has never led. Always before she'd been second or third on a rope.

34 "I was thinking of rappelling down," he answered. "I can't see a clear route up."

35 "There," she said. "There and there and there." She jabbed her fingertip at a series of holds.

36 "But where would you set your protection?"

—*by* W.D. Valgardson

---

[3]*belay*: secured by a rope.

15. What form of language is used in paragraph 3?

   A. jargon

   B. archaic

   C. colloquial

   D. conversational

16. What is the **most likely** reason Barry takes up rock-climbing ?

   A. He has a desire to overcome his lack of confidence.

   B. He has a desire to help his daughter become healthier.

   C. He wants to help his daughter meet people to improve her social life.

   D. He wants to rebuild his relationship with his daughter after his divorce.

17. Which literary device is contained in the quotation "Moira's red hair gleamed like a burnished cap"?

   A. simile

   B. metaphor

   C. foreshadowing

   D. understatement

18. What does the quotation "You all right" (paragraph 5) suggest about Moira's view of her father ?

   A. She is resigned to his childish behaviour.

   B. She is afraid he will fall because he is unfit.

   C. She is impatient with how slowly he is moving.

   D. She is becoming concerned that he is slowing down.

19. What is emphasized by the phrasing of the sentence "Her hand wove a series of stitches in the air" (paragraph 37)?

   A. She is fixing a rip in her clothing.

   B. She is nervous about the next climbing section.

   C. She is confidently describing the next climbing section.

   D. She is very unhappy at her father's lack of climbing skill.

20. What is the **primary** point of view in the story ?

   A. objective

   B. omniscient

   C. first person

   D. limited omniscient

21. Which of the following statements **best** describes the theme of the story ?

    A. Life offers many obstacles.

    B. Challenge can be overwhelming.

    C. People are drawn toward their destiny.

    D. Parents are often role models for their children.

You have Examination Booklet __. In the box above #1 on your Answer Sheet, ensure you filled in the bubble as follows.

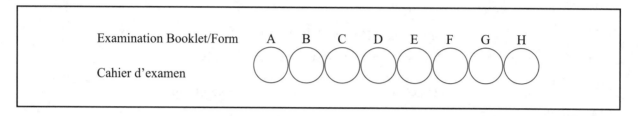

Part C: Prose

WRITTEN-RESPONSE QUESTION

Instructions: Answer one of the following questions in the **Response Booklet.** Write in **ink.** Using standard English, write a multi-paragraph **(3 or more paragraphs)** essay of approximately **300 words** based on one of the following topics. Use the **Organization and Planning** space to plan your work. The mark for your answer will be based on the appropriateness of the examples you use as well as the adequacy of your explanation and the quality of your written expression.

2. In multi-paragraph essay form and with reference to "Saturday Climbing," discuss the significance of rock climbing in the story.

3. In multi-paragraph essay form and with reference to "Saturday Climbing," discuss the character of the father.

Organization and Planning

Use this space to plan your ideas before writing in the Response Booklet.

WRITING ON THIS PAGE WILL NOT BE MARKED

Making Connections Through Reading

"The Writer" and "Saturday Climbing"

CRITERIA

Make sure your response
- clearly answers the question
- contains a discussion of both passages
- is well supported with relevant details

•••USE A PEN WITH BLUE OR BLACK INK•••

Question:

Discuss, with specific reference to the poem and the prose, the theme **"Our toughest struggles can be with ourselves."**

Organization and Planning

Use this space to plan your ideas before writing in the Response Booklet.

WRITING ON THIS PAGE WILL NOT BE MARKED

Part D: Original Composition

1 Written-Response Question

Value: 30%

Suggested Time: 35 minutes

Instructions: Using standard English, write in the **Response Booklet** a coherent, unified, multi-paragraph **(3 or more paragraphs)** composition of approximately **300** words on the topic below. In your composition, you may apply any appropriate method of development including exposition, persuasion, description, and narration. Use the **Organization and Planning** space for your work.

4. Write a multi-paragraph composition on the topic below. In addressing the topic, consider all possibilities. You may draw support from the experiences of others or from any aspect of your life—your reading or your experiences. Remember, you do not have to accept the basic premise of the statement.

Topic: Our friends and family are important.

Organization and Planning

Use this space to plan your ideas before writing in the **Response Booklet.**

WRITING ON THIS PAGE WILL NOT BE MARKED

END OF EXAMINATION

ANSWERS AND SOLUTIONS—PRACTICE TEST ONE

1. C	7. B	13. D	19. C
2. A	8. B	14. D	20. D
3. A	9. C	15. A	21. A
4. C	10. B	16. D	
5. D	11. B	17. A	
6. B	12. C	18. D	

PART A: INFORMATIONAL TEXT

1. **C**

   A. This refers to another paragraph, plus it is imprecise.

   B. Sharks are shown in paragraph 4 to not be "mindless."

   C. Paragraph 4 deals with dispelling the myth that sharks will fight each other over food. In this paragraph the sharks have a competition, in this case slapping tails, which is a social behaviour (i.e., a ritual).

   D. Sharks do not engage in bloody fights for food. They are pitiless but have not survived this long because they kill each other. They have learned, or have developed, a system of working together to survive.

2. **A**

   A. The topic of the paragraph is sharks.

   B, C, and D. These alternatives refer to people and groups named earlier in the article but do not relate to the topic of paragraph 14.

3. **A**

   A. This is based on the information that begins in paragraph 25 and concludes in paragraph 26: humans are not the type of fatty food sharks need to survive.

   B, C, and D. This information is either not discussed in the article or is wrong.

4. **C**

   A. There are few if any anecdotes—short amusing stories—contained in the article.

   B. The article does not follow a chronological order—the order events happen in time.

   C. Most information in the article comes from quotes from experts.

   D. Cause-and-effect—when one event brings about, or causes, another—is not employed here as a device.

5. **D**

   A. The writer is not presenting a confident or forceful argument.

   B. The writer may be frustrated by some aspects of the imprecise view some people have of the great white shark, but overall the article does not dwell on frustration; in fact, it is at times quite light-heartedly educational.

   C. The writer is concerned with the survival of the shark, but the overall tone is not pessimistic, as he does not discuss the survival of the shark population as being endangered.

   D. The article takes an informative look at the myths and truths surrounding the great white shark.

6. B

    A. In Figure 1, the tail has one less piece of information than the trunk.

    B. In Figure 1, the trunk and the tail both share the pelvic fin, thus giving the head more pieces of information. In reading charts and graphs, use other strategies of reading that are different from reading in a narrative manner.

    A student must understand the question, then read Figure 1 from right to left and left to right, bottom to top and top to bottom.

    C. In Figure 1, the trunk has very few pieces of information.

    D. The caudal is not an area of the shark as outlined at the bottom of the diagram.

7. B

    A. The statement is based on conjecture, not on fact, especially when the writer writes, "no one know for certain."

    B. There is no certainty in the statement. An opinion is a statement that reflects the writer's belief but cannot be proven.

    C and **D.** The quote and the entire article are a combination of formal and informal language.

PART B: POETRY

8. B

    A. There is no suggestion the bird is helpless. It is having difficulty, which is sad, but the bird is not helpless as it continues to attempt to find a way out.

    B. "Batter" implies that the bird is trying repeatedly—it is relentless in attempting to gain a way out of the room. It is also a metaphor for the daughter.

    C. The bird drops after hitting the wall, but is still conscious as it tries over and over again.

    D. Although the poet and his daughter have sympathy for the bird, they allow it to escape by itself.
They may want to help but allow the bird to escape by itself.

9. C

    A. The father's discipline is not a topic of this poem.

    B. The father worries about his daughter, as do all fathers, but he also gives her time and space to find her own way.

    C. The entire poem is about a daughter and how much her father cares about her. The incident involving the bird is a metaphor for how he cares for her. It may be inferred that the father wants to let her find her own way.

    D. This choice includes words from the poem in an attempt to trick a student who has not read the poem carefully.

10. B

    B. Alliteration is the repetition of initial consonants, as in *helpless* and *hour*.

11. B

    A. A pun is a joke exploiting the different possible meanings of a word.

    B. A simile compares two objects using the words *like*, *as*, or *than*. In this case, the "stuff" of her life is difficult, as difficult as it is to "haul" the heavy chain over the side of a boat.

    C. Analogy is a comparison of two or more items that does not use the key word *like*, *as*, or *than*.

    D. A metaphor is a direct comparison of two things that are essentially unlike.

12. C

    A. The bird may be considered a metaphor for the daughter, but not for the father.

    B. There is no comparison of the house to the bird; the bird has simply flown into the house and tries to escape.

    C. An extended metaphor is a metaphor that begins at the start of a poem and is used extensively in the poem. The poem begins at the "prow" of the house—a nautical term—then refers to the "gunwale" in stanza two and the "cargo" in stanza three.

    D. The father is not compared to a ship's captain at any time. The images of the ship all connect to the daughter's life.

13. D

    A. Irony involves a contrast between what is expected and what actually exists or happens.

    B. *Solemn* is defined as serious, but in a grave or religious manner.
The poem is not grave in its intent.

    C. The main incident and the main images from the poem are not playful. The bird striving desperately to escape from the room is not a playful event.

    D. Mood is the emotional tone pervading a section or whole of a literary work. In this case the father shows a calm attitude toward the difficulties faced by his daughter and the bird. He is serious in his concern.

14. D

    A. An ode is a complex and often lengthy lyric written in a dignified formal style.

    B. An epic poem is a narrative telling about the deeds and adventures of a great hero. This narrative is too short to be an epic, and the characters in the poem are ordinary people.

    C. A sonnet is a 14 line poem, and this poem is not 14 lines long.

    D. A narrative poem is a poem that tells a story. This poem tells the story of a father observing his daughter, who is writing a story.

POETRY WRITTEN RESPONSE: SOLUTION

1. **In paragraph form, and with specific reference to "The Writer," discuss the father's concern for his daughter.**

Before Beginning:

➢ This response need not be multi-paragraph.

➢ It is important to use specific references (quotes) from the poem.

➢ The question is not printed in the response booklet. A technique to stay on task is to begin by writing the question in the response booklet.

Possible Responses: This list is not exhaustive.

➢ He is concerned that she may be struggling with her writing, as it is "like a chain hauled over a gunwale."

➢ He is concerned that she is facing difficult issues, as her life is "great cargo."

➢ He wishes her "lucky passage"—he wants her to have a good life.

➢ The incident with the bird trapped in the room is a metaphor for her life and illustrates his concern not to be overbearing in her life, as they both were in allowing the bird to find its own way.

➢ He realizes that she is young and events often seem like they are more important or dramatic than they actually are: "It is always a matter, my darling, / Of life or death."

➢ He ends the poem repeating his wish for her to have a good life, but he is more emphatic.

PART C: PROSE

15. A

   A. *Jargon* is defined as special words or expressions used by a particular profession or group. In paragraph three, the writer uses words like "chock nut," "wedge," "carabiner," and "spring-loaded gate," which are terms specific to rock climbing and thus jargon.

   B. Archaic language is language that was commonly used in the past but is now less common.

   C and **D.** Colloquial, or informal, language and conversational language, which is very similar to colloquial language in that it is informal, are not used in this paragraph.

16. D

   A. Barry does lack confidence in connecting with his daughter, especially since the divorce. Barry does not take up rock climbing to increase his confidence.

   B. There is no implication that his daughter is not healthy. As the story progresses, you find out she is more athletic and fit than Barry is—she is healthier.

   C. There is no reason to believe she has no friends. She does meet people at rock climbing, but her father's intent is for the two of them to spend time together.

   D. As the story unfolds you learn that Barry has made many attempts to connect with his daughter. Rock climbing was "an act of desperation" to reconnect.

17. A

   A. A simile compares two objects using *like*, *as*, or *than*. In this case, Moira's hair is compared to a "burnished" (made smooth or bright) cap.

   B. A metaphor does not use *like* in its comparisons.

   C. This quote does not foreshadow any future events.

   D. An understatement expresses an idea with less emphasis or in a lesser degree than is the actual case. The quote is more likely an overstatement, or hyperbole.

18. D

   A. There is no implication that he is childish.

   B. You can assume he is fit for his age, as he is leading the climb. Even if he is unfit, there is no reason to believe she is afraid. You do come to realize that she is more fit and athletic than he is, but this does not automatically mean she is impatient.

   C. It may be implied that young people in general are impatient, but in the context of the story and from the limited omniscient point of view, you do not know this to be true.

   D. In paragraph 5 Moira is simply expressing her concern that her father is doing okay. He is still leading the climb at this point in the story.

19. C

   A. Her clothing is not ripped.

   B. Barry is nervous, not his daughter.

   C. Moving her hand in such a manner illustrates how she has planned the next climbing move. She is confident and is ready to continue the climb.

   D. There is no indication that she is unhappy, nor that she questions her father's climbing skill.

20. D

A. The objective point of view does not present any perspective.

B. The omniscient point of view uses the third person in giving the thoughts and feelings of more than one character. In this story, only Barry's thoughts are given. The daughter's actions are described, but you are not told what she is thinking.

C. The first person point of view uses *I*. *I* may be used in dialogue in the limited omniscient point of view, but not at any other time.

D. The limited omniscient point of view narrative presents the story from a single character's perspective and gives the thoughts and feelings of that character only. This story is presented from the point of view of the father, Barry: "Barry protested, surprising himself..." and "Below her, her father, ever watchful, full of fear."

21. A

A. The theme of a piece of fiction is the message the writer suggests by the actions of the characters. In this case Barry has obstacles in connecting with his daughter, in keeping up with his daughter on a difficult climb, and with self-confidence. The daughter also takes on obstacles, in this case rock-climbing and dealing with her father's decisions.

B. The challenge in this story does not overwhelm but actually provides a vehicle for the father and daughter to connect.

C. This story is not about destiny, or the "hidden power" believed by some to control future events.

D. The story does not imply that Barry is a role model. If anything, it implies that the daughter becomes the role model for the father by taking charge of the situation and leading by example.

PROSE OPEN-ENDED RESPONSE: SOLUTIONS

Before Beginning:

➢ This response must be multi-paragaph (3 or more paragraphs).

➢ It is important to use specific references from the story.

➢ The question is not printed in the response booklet—a technique to stay on task is to begin by writing the question in the response booklet.

2. In multi-paragraph essay form and with reference to "Saturday Climbing," discuss the significance of rock climbing in the story.

Possible Responses: This list is not exhaustive.

➢ Rock climbing is the activity, or vehicle, the writer uses to have the father and daughter connect.

➢ Rock climbing helps illustrate the fact that the daughter is growing up, as she becomes the leader in the climb, which may parallel their relationship.

➢ Rock climbing is dangerous and creates fear in the father, similar to his fear of how to connect and rebuild his relationship with his daughter.

➢ They must communicate and work together to climb safely and successfully, which is parallel to the rebuilding of their relationship.

➢ Rock climbing, like relationship building, demands trust.

➢ The plot of the story is significant, as the father takes the first action by signing them up for rock climbing, which the daughter at first resists but then begins to enjoy.

3. In multi-paragraph essay form and with reference to "Saturday Climbing," discuss the character of the father.

Possible Responses: This list is not exhaustive.

➢ He lacks confidence in how to rebuild the relationship with his daughter.

➢ He is somewhat desperate to rebuild their relationship.

➢ He is ambitious and daring in taking up rock climbing at his age.

- He cares very much about his daughter's safety as illustrated by the story about the young climber who "grounded out."
- He realizes the climb is becoming dangerous but is willing to take the risk to build the relationship.
- He is more cautious than his daughter.
- He is struggling with the physical challenge of climbing but is willing to continue.
- He is somewhat bewildered by how to connect with a teenage daughter.
- He is a good listener, as one reason he signed them up for rock climbing was that he had remembered how she had spoken admiringly of classmates who had hiked the west-coast trail.

SOLUTION TO THE MAKING CONNECTIONS QUESTION

Discuss, with specific reference to the poem and the prose, the theme "**Our toughest struggles can be with ourselves.**"

Before Beginning:

- This response must be multi-paragraph (3 or more paragraphs).
- It is important to use specific references from both selections to attain full marks.

- The question is not printed in the response booklet—a technique to stay on task is to begin by writing the question in the response booklet.

Possible Responses: This list is not exhaustive.

"The Writer" and "Saturday Climbing"

- Look to similarities and differences in the poem and the story.
- Both fathers care deeply about their daughters.
- The poet is helping his daughter, as they have a strong relationship.
- The poet realizes his daughter must find her own path.
- The protagonist in "Saturday Climbing" is less sure of himself and is attempting to reconnect with his daughter.
- The protagonist in "Saturday Climbing" is desperate.
- The protagonist in "Saturday Climbing" seems more hesitant to allow his daughter her independence but comes to a realization that she is ready.
- Both fathers, at the end of the poem and the story, are watching their daughters closely—both are also ready to give them their independence.

PRACTICE TEST TWO

Part A: Informational Text

7 Multiple-Choice Questions

Suggested Time: 15 minutes

Value: 7%

Instructions: Read the following selection, "Herbal Remedies: Buyers Beware," and answer the multiple-choice questions. For each question, select the **best** answer and record your choice on the **Answer Sheet** provided.

---

adapted from HERBAL REMEDIES: BUYERS BEWARE

1 Janet Ouellette was at her wit's end. The 46-year-old homemaker from Sardis, BC, was plagued by frequent and debilitating migraine headaches. She had tried every conventional medication. Nothing seemed to work.

2 As a last resort, her brother, Dr. Robin Marles, a biochemist, suggested that she try a herbal remedy known as feverfew.

3 Mrs. Ouellette gave it a whirl. Almost immediately, the severity of the migraines diminished; then gradually, the number of attacks.

4 Feverfew, she says, changed her life for the better. She continues to take it twice daily. "I might get one migraine every three months. It means I can function."

5 Mrs. Ouellette's experience illustrates both the promise and pitfalls of herbal remedies, which have swelled into a $2-billion-dollar-a-year industry in North America, and are growing by an estimated 15 percent a year.

6 Some herbal remedies do appear to provide benefit for some people with a variety of ailments. But, with no strict regulatory controls, many herbal remedies are of questionable quality. Not everyone, after all, has a big brother to tell them which product is effective.

7 "Quality control is our central issue," said Frank Chandler, director of the college of pharmacy at Dalhousie University and head of the new advisory panel. "You've got people out there who are selling fraudulent products, some of them knowingly, some of them unwittingly."

8 "Buying a herbal remedy in Canada is a 'crap shoot,'" he said.

9 Under existing Canadian laws, any commercial product that is meant to be ingested through the mouth is regulated as either a food or drug. That means herbal producers have a great deal of flexibility in how they market most of their products.

10 But if a company wants to claim that a herb can cure serious illnesses—such as heart disease—it must provide the same type of scientific studies required of a new prescription drug. Those studies can cost millions of dollars.

11 As a result, many labels do not mention what a supplement might be used for—or warn of possible side effects. The sellers rely on word of mouth to generate interest in their remedies or use marketing language that hints at potential uses.

12 Nonetheless, the free-for-all in the marketplace has not dampened consumer interest in herbal remedies. "When the populace gets disillusioned with traditional medicine, they go back to their roots," said Ian Cameron, professor of family medicine at Dalhousie University.

Continued

13 Indeed, public suspicion of synthetic drugs has led many to turn to alternative medicines, which are perceived to be "natural" and therefore presumed to be "good".

14 And without doubt, folkloric tradition—as well as some modern research—suggests that certain herbal remedies have merit. To some degree, modern medicine can trace its own roots back to herbal remedies that likely evolved through trial and error.

15 "Many contemporary western remedies were really used in folk history for many years," noted Dr. Ronald Carr, professor of medicine at Dalhousie University. "For example, digitalis, the powerful heart medication, is derived from the foxglove plant."

16 But the similarity between pharmaceutical drugs and traditional herbs can be taken only so far.

17 Modern pharmacology came about through the development of standardized products containing a fixed amount of a known active ingredient. Herbal remedies, by contrast, can contain a multitude of different ingredients, and their so-called active compounds may not even be known. Potency can vary from batch to batch, depending upon where and how the plant has grown and processed.

18 Some companies take great care in the selection and processing of their herbs to try to ensure some consistency in potency. But others buy their raw material from a variety of domestic or foreign sources and often lack the in-house expertise to know what they are getting. It may be a stale batch or not the real thing.

19 Herbal remedies can be risky when used incorrectly, despite the popular myth that so-called natural products are safe.

20 "Just because it's a natural product doesn't mean it's not dangerous," said Tim Lee, an immunologist at Dalhousie University. "Poison ivy's a natural product and hemlock's a natural product."

21 Some herbs (chaparral and comfrey) are considered so toxic that they are banned outright by Health Canada. A few (including ephedra) are so strong they cannot be sold without a DIN (drug identification number). And experts advise pregnant women to avoid many herbal remedies because it is often not know how they might affect a developing fetus.

22 Dr. Marles noted that herbal remedies can sometimes interact with prescription and non-prescription drugs. Using ginseng in combination with certain antidepressants has been know to cause headaches and insomnia.

23 Another concern is that a product may contain more than just the herb. Ground-up ginseng roots can include the dirt in which they were planted, warned Michael Atkins, who grows ginseng in Waterford, Ontario, and is president of the Ginseng Growers Association of Canada. "There is a risk that the earth might contain potentially harmful bacteria," he said. "If you buy a capsule and the powder in it is very brown looking….I would be very worried about the amount of dust that's in it."

24 Occasionally, the consequences of herbal misuse can be catastrophic.

25 In the United States, where the rules are more lax than in Canada, 18 deaths and thousands of injuries have been caused by herbal diet remedies containing ephedra. Mixed with caffeine, it can accelerate the heart beat, causing a heart attack and stroke. Misuse can damage the liver.

26 In Canada, ephedra can be sold only as a nasal decongestant, and remedies that combine the herb with other stimulants are strictly forbidden.

27 Despite tighter rules, there still have been two reported cases of Canadians suffering from ephedra toxicity.

28 Ephedra mishaps grab headlines, but herbalists say most of their products are much safer than many pharmaceutical products.

Continued

29　On the other hand, Micheline Ho, chief of the product information division of Heath Canada's health protection branch, said there are no reliable figures on how many people suffer ill effects from herbal remedies. She added that most of the federal government's enforcement is at the manufacturing, distribution and large importation level. "Our activities are not at the retail level, so that could be why we haven't spotted them."

30　Yet even when companies apply for DIN's, there is no guarantee that the bottle contains what it is supposed to. "There is no actual product submission or testing that is involved with getting a DIN," said Don Beatty, head of regulatory affairs and quality assurance for Quest Vitamins. "It's just really a paper process and the government relies on honesty, I guess, and good faith. In a perfect world, that would be sufficient, but it doesn't always work that way."

31　So, then, how should herbal remedies be regulated?

32　Dr. Varro Tyler, the retired dean of pharmacy at Purdue University in West Lafayette, Indiana, believes that it would be wrong to put herbal remedies in their own category and let them be sold solely on the strength of folkloric tradition. "Some research should still be required of herbal manufacturers," he insisted. He remains committed to the idea that people cannot act solely on faith. Much of the common knowledge of herbs comes from anecdotal evidence.

33　He believes that Germany has the best rules for herbal remedies and other countries would be wise to follow its example. Germany set up a special commission to review herbal remedies, and companies are required to apply for the right to sell them. They must show beyond a reasonable doubt that the product is safe and some evidence that the product really works.

34　This approach fosters some research, but does not require that a company spend vast sums usually needed for a brand new pharmaceutical drug. "It is a happy medium that reflects the unique status of herbal remedies," Dr. Tyler said. "Keep in mind that these old herbals have been used for hundreds, if not thousands, of years."

35　Dr. Tyler thinks that research can pay off big time. In Germany, a herb known as St. John's wort, used to treat mild depression, is a bigger seller than Prozac. In Germany, herbal products are covered by state insurance.

36　"And yet, in Canada, the industry has a credibility problem," Dr. Beatty concluded. "Change of some sort is needed," he added.

37　As Dr. Marles put it: "People are spending incredible amounts of money on this and they have a right to get something that works."

—by Paul Taylor

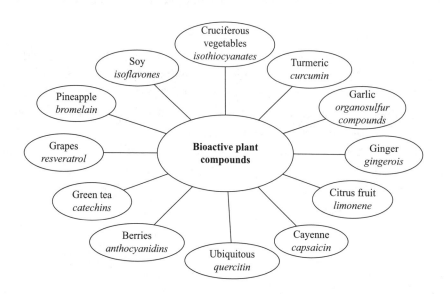

1. What is the **primary** purpose of paragraphs 5 to 7?

   A. to inform of Mrs. Ouellette's herbal cure

   B. to examine how quickly the herbal industry is growing

   C. to question the quality control standards in the herbal industry

   D. to inform the general public that herbal remedies are not a good, viable choice

2. In the quotation "buying a herbal remedy in Canada is a 'crap shoot,'" the phrase "crap shoot" is an example of what type of language?

   A. jargon

   B. archaic

   C. colloquial

   D. conversational

3. In the context of the article, what country **best** regulates herbal remedies?

   A. USA

   B. China

   C. Canada

   D. Germany

4. Which of the following methods of presentation is **primarily** used in the article?

   A. anecdotal evidence

   B. chronological order

   C. quotes from experts

   D. cause-and-effect development

5. Which of the following words **best** describes the tone of the article?

   A. amusing

   B. optimistic

   C. concerned

   D. pessimistic

6. What form of organization is used in the diagram of bioactive plant compounds (Figure 1)?

   A. random

   B. alphabetical

   C. chronological

   D. cause and effect

7. In what form is the data in the quotation "there are no figures for how many people suffer ill effects from herbal remedies" presented?

A. fact

B. opinion

C. formal language

D. informal language

Part B: Poetry

7 Multiple-Choice Questions   **Suggested Time: 30 minutes**

1 Written-Response Question

Value: 23%

> **Instructions:** Read the following poem, "What Shall He Tell That Son?" and answer the multiple-choice questions. For each question, select the **best** answer and record your answer on the **Answer Sheet** provided.

WHAT SHALL HE TELL THAT SON?

A father sees a son nearing manhood.
What shall he tell that son?
"Life is hard; be steel; be a rock."
And this might stand him for the storms
5   and serve him for humdrum and monotony
and guide him amid sudden betrayals
and tighten him for slack moments.
"Life is soft loam; be gentle; go easy."
And this too might serve him.
10   Brutes have been gentled where lashes failed.
The growth of a frail flower in a path up
has sometimes shattered and split a rock.
A tough will counts. So does desire.
So does rich soft wanting.
15   Without rich wanting nothing arrives.
Tell him too much money has killed men
and left them dead years before burial:
and quest of lucre beyond a few easy needs
has twisted good enough men
20   sometimes into dry thwarted worms.
Tell him time as a stuff can be wasted.
Tell him to be a fool every so often
and to have no shame over having been a fool
yet learning something out of every folly

Continued

25   hoping to repeat none of the cheap follies
        thus arriving at intimate understanding
        of a world numbering many fools.
        Tell him to be alone and get at himself
        and above all tell himself no lies about himself,
30   whatever the white lies and protective front
        he may use amongst other people.
        Tell him solitude is creative if he is strong
        and the final decisions are made in silent rooms
        Tell him to be different from other people
35   if it comes natural and easy being different.

        Let him have lazy days seeking his deeper motives.
        Let him seek deep for where he is a born natural.
        Then he may understand Shakespeare
        and the Wright brothers, Pasteur, Pavlov,
40   Michael Faraday and free imaginations
        bringing changes into a world resenting change.
        He will be lonely enough
        to have time for the work
        he knows as his own.

—*by* Carl Sandburg

8. In the context of the poem, what does the quotation "Brutes have been gentled where lashes failed" imply?

    A. Punishment is not always necessary.

    B. It is difficult to control strong people.

    C. Gentle people can best control strong people.

    D. A tough will and a strong desire can help control a situation.

9. Which literary device is contained in the quotation "and serve him for humdrum and monotony / and guide him amid sudden betrayals / and tighten him for slack moments"?

    A. simile

    B. metaphor

    C. repetition

    D. onomatopoeia

10. What does the quotation "Tell him too much money has killed men / and left them dead years before burial" suggest?

    A. Rich men have short life spans.

    B. Rich men need to be fools once and a while.

    C. The pursuit of too much money can change people.

    D. The pursuit of too much money can force sudden betrayals between friends.

11. What does the quotation "Tell him to be alone often and get at himself" (line 28) suggest?

    A. He wants the son to get fit.

    B. He wants the son to find new friends.

    C. He wants the son to lie to other people.

    D. He wants the son to find his own true self.

12. Which of the following figures of speech is contained in the quotations "Life is hard; be steel, be a rock" and "Life is soft loam; be gentle; go easy"?

    A. simile

    B. paradox

    C. hyperbole

    D. onomatopoeia

13. Which of the following literary devices is used in the quotation "Then he may understand Shakespeare / and the Wright brothers, Pasteur, Pavlov, / Michael Faraday and free imaginations"?

    A. satire

    B. irony

    C. allusion

    D. personification

14. Which form of poetry is "What Shall He Tell That Son"?

    A. ode

    B. epic

    C. sonnet

    D. free verse

Part B: Poetry

WRITTEN-RESPONSE QUESTION

> **Instructions:** In paragraph form and in approximately **125 to 150 words**, answer question 1 in
> the **Response Booklet.** Write in **ink.** Use the **Organization and Planning** space
> to plan your work. The mark for your answer will be based on the appropriateness
> of the examples you use as well as the adequacy of your explanation and the
> quality of your written expression.

1. In paragraph form, and with specific reference to "What Shall He Tell That Son," discuss the father's
   advice to his son.

Organization and Planning

Use this space to plan your ideas before writing in the Response Booklet.

WRITING ON THIS PAGE WILL NOT BE MARKED

Part C: Prose

8 Multiple-Choice Questions

1 Written-Response Question

Value: 40%

Suggested Time: 40 minutes

Instructions: Read the following selection, "The Firewood Gatherers," and answer the multiple-choice questions. For each question, select the **best** answer and record your answer on the **Answer Sheet** provided.

THE FIREWOOD GATHERERS

1 Our camp had been pitched at the foot of a great, bleak, ragged hill, a few feet from the swirling waters of the Kazan River. The two small green tents, pegged down tight with heavy rocks, shivered and rippled under the faint touch of the northern breeze. A thin wisp of smoke rose from the embers of the fire.

2 Eleven o'clock and the sun had just set under a threatening bank of clouds far away to the northwest. It was the last day of June and daylight still. But the whole country seemed bathed in grey, boulders, moss, sand, even the few willow shrubs scattered far apart in the hollows of the hills. Half a mile away, upstream, the caribou-skin topeaks of an Eskimo settlement, fading away amid the background, were hardly visible to the eye.

3 Three small grey specks could be seen moving slowly above our camp. Human shapes, but so puny, so insignificant-looking against the wild rocky side of that immense hill! Bending down, then straightening up, they seemed to totter aimlessly through the chaos of stone, searching for some hidden treasure.

4 Curiosity, or perhaps a touch of loneliness, suddenly moved me to leave camp and join those three forlorn figures so far away above me near the sky line.

5 Slowly I made my way along the steep incline, following at first the bed of a dried-up stream. Little by little the river sank beneath me, while the breeze, increasing in strength, whistled past, lashing and stinging my face and hands. I had lost sight momentarily of the three diminutive figures which had lured me on to these heights. After a while a reindeer trail enabled me to leave the coule[1] and led me again in the right direction, through a gigantic mass of granite which the frost of thousands of years had plucked from the summit of the hill and hurled hundreds of feet below.

6 At last I was able to reach the other side of the avalanche of rocks and suddenly emerged comparatively in the open, on the brim of a slight depression at the bottom of which a few dead willow bushes showed their bleached branches above the stones and the grey moss. There I found the three silent figures huddled close together, gathering one by one, the twigs of the precious wood. Two little girls, nine or ten years old, so small, so helpless, and an aged woman, so old, so frail, that my first thought was to marvel at the idea of their being able to climb so far from their camp to that lonely spot.

Continued

---

[1] a dry stream bed.

7   An Eskimo great-grandmother and her two great-granddaughters, all three contributing their share to the support of the tribe. Intent on their work, or most probably too shy to look up at the strange white man whom, until then, they had only seen at a distance, they gave me full opportunity to watch them.

8   All were dressed alike, in boots, trousers, and coats of caribou skin. The children wore little round leather caps reaching far over their ears, the crown decorated with beadwork designs. One of them carried on the wrist, as a bracelet, a narrow strip of bright red flannel. Their faces were round and healthy, the skin sunburned to a dark copper color, but their cheeks showed a tinge of blood which gave them, under the tan, a peculiar complexion like the color of a ripe plum. Their little hands were bare and black, the scratches caused by the dead twigs showing plainly in white while their fingers seemed crapped with the cold.

9   The old woman was bareheaded, quite bald at the top of the head, with long wisps of grey hair waving in the wind. The skin of her neck and face had turned black, dried up like an old piece of parchment. Her cheeks were sunken and her cheek bones protruded horribly. Her open mouth showed bare gums, for her teeth were all gone, and her throat, thin and bare as a vulture's neck, showed the muscles like cords. Her hands were as thin as the hands of a skeleton, the tip of each finger curved in like a claw. Hey eyes, once black, now light grey, remained half closed, deep down in their sockets.

10 She was stone blind.

11 Squatting on her heels, she held, spread in front of her, a small reindeer skin. As soon as the children dropped a branch beside her, she felt for it gropingly; then, her hands closing on it greedily, like talons, she would break it into small pieces, a few inches long, which she carefully placed on the mat at her feet.

12 Both little girls, while searching diligently through the clumps of dead willows for what they could break off and carry away, kept absolutely silent. Not only did they never call to one another when one of them needed help, but they seemed to watch each other intently whenever they could. Now and then, one of them would hit the ground two or three times with the flat of her hand. If the other had her head turned away at the time, she appeared to be startled and always wheeled around to look. Then both children would make funny little motions with their hands at one another.

13 The little girls were deaf and mute.

14 After a while they had gathered all the wood the reindeer skin could contain. Then the children went up to the old woman and conveyed to her the idea that it was time to go home. One of them took her hands in hers and guided them to two corners of the mat, while the other tapped her gently on the shoulder.

15 The old, old woman understood. Slowly and carefully she tied up the four corners of the caribou skin over the twigs, silently watched by the little girls. Groaning, she rose to her feet, tottering with weakness and old age, and with a great effort swung the small bundle over her back. Then one little girl took her by the hand, while the other, standing behind, grasped the tail of her caribou coat. Slowly, very slowly, step by step they went their way, following a reindeer trail around rocks, over stones, down, down the hill, straight toward their camp, the old woman carrying painfully for the young, the deaf and mute leading and steering safely the blind.

—*by* Thierry Mallci

15. What is emphasized by the phrasing of the quotation "Our camp had been pitched at the foot of a great, bleak, ragged hill"?

    A. the danger of the landscape

    B. the inhospitable beauty of the landscape

    C. the narrator's view that the landscape is boring

    D. the narrator's view that the landscape is monotonous

16. What is the **most likely** reason the narrator desires to leave camp?

    A. He is bored.

    B. He is lonely.

    C. He wants to explore the countryside.

    D. He wants to help the Eskimo (now called Inuit) people.

17. Which figure of speech is contained in the quotation "frost of thousands of years had plucked from the summit"?

    A. simile

    B. metaphor

    C. hyperbole

    D. personification

18. What does the quotation "too shy to look up at the strange white man?" (paragraph 7) suggest about the narrator?

    A. He is arrogant.

    B. He is prejudice.

    C. He is intent on watching them without being seen.

    D. He is attempting to understand the firewood gatherers.

19. What is the tone at the end of the passage?

    A. ironic

    B. happy

    C. admiring

    D. condescending

20. What is the **primary** point of view in the story?

    A. objective

    B. omniscient

    C. first person

    D. limited omniscient

21. Which of the following statements **best** describes the theme of the story?

    A. People accept defeat easily.

    B. People can overcome adversity.

    C. People from different races can work together.

    D. Grandparents are often role models for their children.

You have Examination Booklet __. In the box above #1 on your Answer Sheet, ensure you filled in the bubble as follows.

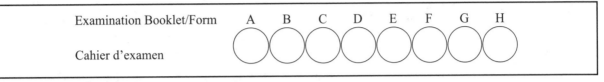

Examination Booklet/Form	A	B	C	D	E	F	G	H
Cahier d'examen	○	○	○	○	○	○	○	○

Part C: Prose

WRITTEN-RESPONSE QUESTION

Instructions: Answer one of the following questions in the **Response Booklet**. Write in **ink**. Using standard English, write a multi-paragraph (**3 or more paragraphs**) essay of approximately **300 words** based on one of the following topics. Use the **Organization and Planning** space to plan your work. The mark for your answer will be based on the appropriateness of the examples you use as well as the adequacy of your explanation and the quality of your written expression.

2. In multi-paragraph essay form and with reference to "The Firewood Gatherers," discuss the character development of the narrator.

3. In multi-paragraph essay form and with reference to "The Firewood Gatherers," discuss the impact of the setting on the Inuit characters.

Organization and Planning

Use this space to plan your ideas before writing in the Response Booklet.

WRITING ON THIS PAGE WILL NOT BE MARKED

Making Connections Through Reading

"What Shall He Tell That Son" and "The Firewood Gatherers"

CRITERIA

Make sure your response

➢ clearly answers the question

➢ contains a discussion of both passages

➢ is well-supported with relevant details

••• USE A PEN WITH BLUE OR BLACK INK •••

QUESTION

Discuss the view of life presented in "What Shall He Tell That Son" and "The Firewood Gatherers."

Organization and Planning

Use this space to plan your ideas before writing in the Response Booklet.

WRITING ON THIS PAGE WILL NOT BE MARKED

Part D: Original Composition

1 Written-Response Question

Suggested Time: 35 minutes

Value: 30%

Instructions: Using standard English, write in the **Response Booklet**, a coherent, unified, multi-paragraph **(3 or more paragraphs)** composition of approximately **300** words on the **topic** below. In your composition, you may apply any appropriate method of development including exposition, persuasion, description, and narration.

Use the **Organization and Planning** space for your work.

---

4. Write a multi-paragraph composition on the topic below. In addressing the topic, consider all possibilities. You may draw support from the experiences of others or from any aspect of your life—your reading or your experiences. Remember, you do not have to accept the basic premise of the statement.

TOPIC

There are moments in life that can change our destiny.

Organization and Planning

Use this space to plan your ideas before writing in the **Response Booklet**.

WRITING ON THIS PAGE WILL NOT BE MARKED

END OF EXAMINATION

ANSWERS AND SOLUTIONS—PRACTICE TEST TWO

1. C	7. A	13. C	19. C
2. C	8. A	14. D	20. C
3. D	9. C	15. B	21. B
4. C	10. C	16. B	
5. C	11. D	17. D	
6. A	12. B	18. D	

PART A: INFORMATIONAL TEXT

1. **C**

   A. Incorrect. Mrs. Ouellette's story is simply an interesting narrative to begin the selection.

   B. Incorrect. Paragraph 6 does comment on how quickly the industry is growing, but this is not the central focus of the selection.

   C. Correct. Paragraph 7 states "Quality control is our central issue."

   D. Incorrect. The essay questions all aspects of the industry, but never passes judgment on the viability of herbal remedies.

2. **C**

   A. Incorrect. Jargon is terminology that relates to a specific activity, profession, or group.

   B. Incorrect. Archaic language involves words and phrases that were once used frequently in a language in the past but now are less common.

   C. Correct. "Crap shoot" is an example of colloquial language, which is similar to slang in that a colloquialism is an expression not used in formal speech.

   D. Incorrect. Conversational language is simply the language of everyday speech.

3. **D**

   A and **C.** Incorrect. Canada and the USA are mentioned in the article as having outdated rules for regulating herbal remedies.

   B. Incorrect. China's government policy on pharmaceuticals is not mentioned in the article.

   D. Correct. In paragraph 33 Dr. Tyler states that Germany has the best rules for herbal remedies.

4. **C**

   A. Incorrect. There are few if any anecdotes—short amusing stories—contained in the article.

   B. Incorrect. The article does not follow a chronology—the order events happen in time.

   C. Correct. The majority of information in the article comes from quotes from different experts. The article is organized around a series of quotes from experts, many from Dalhousie University.

   D. Incorrect. Cause and effect—when one event brings about, or causes, another—is not employed here as a device.

5. C

   A. Incorrect. The topic of the article is too serious to be amusing.

   B and **D.** Incorrect. The focus of the article is to express concern and to inform. There is no optimistic or pessimistic focus, although there are aspects of the article that inform of the best and worst cases in the industry—the optimistic and pessimistic aspects.

   C. Correct. The article takes an informative look at the herbal remedy industry and is concerned as to the impact these remedies are having on patients.

6. A

   A. Correct. A simple process of elimination is required to arrive at the answer, *random*.

   B. Incorrect. Figure 1 is not organized alphabetically.

   C. Incorrect. There is no time sequence to Figure 1 (*chronological*—the order events happen in time).

   D. Incorrect. There is no cause-and-effect relationship in Figure 1.

7. A

   A. Correct. There is certainty in the statement. The quotation "there are no figures" can be proven and as such is a fact.

   B. Incorrect. An opinion is a statement that reflects the writer's belief but cannot be proven.

   C and **D.** Incorrect. The quote, and entire article, is a combination of formal and informal language.

PART B: POETRY

8. A

   A. Correct. The quotation "Brutes have been gentled where lashes failed" infers that it is not always effective to "lash" or punish a person to have them change or adapt.

   B. Incorrect. The quote does not discuss a need to control anyone or anything.

   C. Incorrect. The quote is not discussing gentle people, rather gentle actions.

   D. Incorrect. The quotation refers to a different aspect of what the father wishes to tell his son and is irrelevant to using force or gentle actions in certain situations.

9. C

   A. Incorrect. There is no use of *like, as,* or *than* in the quote, thus simile is incorrect.

   B. Incorrect. There is no direct comparison of two essentially unlike things, thus there is no metaphor.

   C. Correct. The repetition of *and* makes this a very straightforward question.

   D. Incorrect. And there is no onomatopoeia—imitation of a sound.

10. C

   A. Incorrect. The person with "too much money" is still alive.

   B. Incorrect. This alternative refers to another aspect of the father's advice in lines 22–26.

   C. Correct. When the father says "dead years before burial," he implies that too much money changed the people and they were no longer "alive" and vibrant. The pursuit of too much money is not a path to happiness.

   D. Incorrect. This alternative refers to other advice the father is giving about growing up.

11. D

A and **B.** Incorrect. The quote does not discuss physical fitness or finding new friends.

C. Incorrect. The father does discuss the topic of the son lying to himself, but does not advise his son to lie to others, even though the father realizes that the son may tell lies to others to protect himself.

D. Correct. The father wants his son to "be alone" and "get at himself"—he wants his son to get to know himself.

12. B

A. Incorrect. There is no use of simile (a comparison using *like*, *as*, or *than*).

B. Correct. This alternative is the best answer taken in context of the two lines. A *paradox* is an apparent contradiction—in this case "life is hard" and "life is soft."

C. Incorrect. This is not the best answer even though the first line does use hyperbole in the phrases "be steel" and "be a rock." The second line does not use hyperbole, and the question asks for the best answer.

D. Incorrect. There is no onomatopoeia (imitation of a sound).

13. C

A. Incorrect. Satire holds up the weakness of an individual or group to ridicule.

B. Incorrect. Irony involves a contrast between what is expected and what actually exists or happens.

C. Correct. An allusion is a reference to a person, a place, or an event that the poet expects the reader to recognize. Shakespeare, the Wright brothers, Pasteur, and Pavlov are famous names from history.

D. Incorrect. You cannot personify people.

14. D

A. Incorrect. An ode is a complex and often lengthy lyric written in a dignified formal style.

B. Incorrect. An epic poem is a narrative telling about the deeds and adventures of a great hero. This narrative is too short to be an epic, and the characters in the poem are ordinary people.

C. Incorrect. A sonnet is a 14-line poem, and this poem is not 14 lines long.

D. Correct. Free verse poetry is verse that has either no metrical pattern or an irregular pattern. This poem does not have a consistent rhyme or rhythm.

POETRY WRITTEN-RESPONSE QUESTION: SOLUTION

1. **In paragraph form, and with specific reference to "What Shall He Tell That Son," discuss the father's advice to his son.**

Before beginning

➢ This response need not be multi-paragraph.

➢ It is important to use specific references (quotes) from the poem.

➢ The question is not printed in the response booklet—a technique to stay on task is to begin by writing the question in the response booklet.

Possible Responses—This list is not exhaustive.

➢ The son must be "hard, be a rock" and "soft"—the father's advice is at times paradoxical.

➢ The father does not want the son to be too greedy.

➢ The father wants the son to know himself—"get at himself."

➢ The father wants his son to have a tough will and desire.

➢ The father wants him to be foolish once in a while, but to learn from his foolishness.

➢ The son should be alone at times.

➢ The son should make his own decisions, but not until he has had time to think.

➢ The father wants the son to be different from other people, but only if it is natural to him.

PART C: PROSE

15. B

   A. Incorrect. The emphasis is not only on the danger of the "ragged hill" but also its majesty.

   B. Correct. *Bleak* is the key word in the quote, as it implies barren or exposed, and thus inhospitable, wilderness. The "great" and "ragged hill" refers to the beauty of the area.

   C and **D.** Incorrect. There is no implication that the narrator is either bored or finds the landscape monotonous—if anything, he is excited and finds the landscape impressive.

16. B

   A. Incorrect. The narrator is not bored, but is curious.

   B. Correct. You learn in paragraph 4 that the narrator has "a touch of loneliness."

   C. Incorrect. He probably does want to explore the area, but this is not the main reason he wants to leave camp.

   D. Incorrect. The narrator has not as yet met the Inuit people, so he cannot assume they need his help.

17. D

   A. Incorrect. There is no use of *like*, *as*, or *than* in the quotation, nor is there a comparison.

   B. Incorrect. There is no comparison contained in the quotation.

   C. Incorrect. Hyperbole is a figure of speech that uses exaggeration for effect. Nothing in the quotation is exaggerated.

   D. Correct. Personification is a figure of speech in which something non-human is given human characteristics—in this case, the frost is personified.

18. D

   A, B, and **C.** Incorrect. In the story the narrator is never arrogant, prejudice, or intent on hiding from the Inuit people.

   D. Correct. He is attempting to understand them, which connects to paragraph four and his "curiosity." As the story progresses he becomes more impressed by their ability to survive despite the obvious physical challenges the three Inuit characters face.

19. C

   A. Incorrect. This story is not intent on providing an ironic view of the Inuit people.

   B. Incorrect. This is not a happy or sad story.

   C. Correct. Tone is the attitude a writer takes toward his or her subject, character, or audience. The narrator is surprised and impressed by the ability of the Inuit characters to gather firewood in this desolate land.

   D. Incorrect. The story is never condescending, as the narrator never implies his superiority over the Inuit characters; it is more correct to imply that he is in awe of them.

20. C

   A. Incorrect. The objective point of view does not present any perspective and is rarely used, if ever, on a provincial examination.

   B. Incorrect. The story is not told in the third person.

   C. Correct. The first person point of view uses *I* in telling a story directly. Paragraphs 5 and 6 begin with the quotations "Slowly I" and "At last I."

   D. Incorrect. The limited omniscient point of view narrative presents the story from a single character's perspective and gives the thoughts and feelings of that character only.

21. B

A. Incorrect. No one is defeated in the story.

B. Correct. The theme of a piece of fiction is the message the writer suggests by the actions of the characters. In this case the narrator is curious and bored and finds a group of Inuit people gathering firewood. As the story unfolds, it becomes apparent that the narrator is surprised and in awe of their ability to overcome the adversity presented by not only their physical challenges, but by the harsh environment in which they live.

C. Incorrect. The narrator does not help or work with the Inuit people.

D. Incorrect. As much as the grandmother is a hard worker, the three Inuit characters work together. You do not know if she is a role model.

PROSE OPEN-ENDED RESPONSE: SOLUTIONS

Before beginning

➢ This response must be multi-paragraph (3 or more paragraphs).

➢ It is important to use specific references from the story.

➢ The question is not printed in the response booklet—a technique to stay on task is to begin by writing the question in the response booklet.

2. In multi-paragraph essay form and with reference to "The Firewood Gatherers," discuss the character development of the narrator.

Possible Responses—This list is not exhaustive.

Note: For character questions, look to character traits. In character development questions, discuss how the character appears to evolve during the story. They need not go through a dramatic change from good to evil, but you should discuss how they develop or learn.

➢ He is curious.

➢ He is somewhat bored.

➢ He is observant.

➢ He learns more about the local people.

➢ He is intrigued by their struggle and their ability to work together.

➢ He does not want to intrude.

➢ There is no indication he is prejudice.

➢ He is quite captivated by their challenges.

➢ He does seem like a very nice person.

3. In multi-paragraph essay form and with reference to "The Firewood Gatherers," discuss the impact of the setting on the Inuit characters.

Possible Responses—This list is not exhaustive.

Note: It is important to discuss both the setting and the Inuit characters.

➢ The area is bleak.

➢ There is not much firewood.

➢ It is a challenging place to live.

➢ The characters have physical challenges that make the setting even more difficult to survive in.

➢ The characters have adapted to the setting and survive despite all the challenges presented.

➢ Students may discuss how the characters have learned to communicate.

SOLUTION TO THE "MAKING CONNECTIONS" QUESTION

Discuss, with specific reference to the poem and the prose, the view of life presented in "What Shall He Tell That Son" and "The Firewood Gatherers."

Before beginning

➢ This response must be multi-paragaph (3 or more paragraphs).

➢ It is important to use specific references from both selections to attain full marks.

➢ The question is not printed in the response booklet—a technique to stay on task is to begin by writing the question in the response booklet.

Possible Responses—This list is not exhaustive.

"What Shall He Tell That Son" and "The Firewood Gatherers"

➢ Look to similarities and differences in the poem and the story.

The poet is giving direct advice to his son—all related to the struggle to become an adult.

➢ The poet looks at the paradoxical aspect of life—sometimes you need to be gentle, and sometimes you need to be forceful.

➢ The poet looks at how a young person must be alone in order to find out who they are.

➢ The poet advises the son to not lie to himself.

The narrator looks to the struggles he sees in the Inuit people.

➢ The narrator sees them as "puny shapes" in the distance as compared to the landscape.

➢ The narrator sees them originally as quite helpless, but then realizes they have overcome the adversity of their challenges and the adversity of the landscape.

➢ The narrator's emotions begin somewhat with pity, turn to awe, and end with humility at how these people have overcome their struggles.

NOTES

Appendices

LITERARY TERMS

Abstract	Not physical. Ideas and emotions are abstract, as are love, justice, and honour. Both abstract and concrete things are real.
Active Voice	In sentences written in active voice, the subject performs the action expressed in the verb; the subject acts. In sentences written in passive voice, the subject receives the action expressed in the verb; the subject is acted upon.
Allegory	A story or visual image with a second distinct meaning partially hidden. It involves a continuous parallel between two or more levels of meaning so that its persons and events correspond to their equivalents in a system of ideas or chain of events external to the story. Often, characters, actions, or settings represent abstract ideas or moral qualities. As an example, characters may be named Christian, Hope, or Despair.
Alliteration	Repetition of initial consonant sounds. For example, as T.S. Eliot wrote in *The Love Song of J. Alfred Prufrock*, **S**cuttling across the floors of **s**ilent **s**eas.
Allusion	Indirect or passing reference to some person, place, or event; possibly biblical, historical, literary, artistic, etc. The nature of the reference is not explained because the writer relies on the reader's familiarity with it.
Anachronism	A person, place, event, or thing that appears out of order, or in the wrong time sequence. Anachronisms are often things that belong to an earlier time and appear out of place. A flashback is an example of an anachronism.
Analogy	A comparison between things intended to show the similarities between them.
Anecdotal Evidence	Evidence based on personal experience that has not been tested.
Anecdote	A brief story of an interesting incident.
Antagonist	A force or person opposing the protagonist. An antagonist may also be a rival.
Antecedent Action	Action that takes place before the story line opens.
Anticlimax	A disappointing conclusion, often ironic because of the difference between what is expected and what happens.
Antithesis	A contrast or opposition of ideas, usually by the balancing of phrases. One of the most famous examples is from Alexander Pope's *Essay on Criticism*: "To err is human, to forgive divine."
Apathy	A lack of interest.
Apostrophe	A speech addressed to a dead or absent person or an abstract object. (Do not confuse this use of apostrophe with the punctuation mark.) This often takes a vocative form and can be seen in our national anthem and many other cases in which the subject is addressed with an "O," as in *O Canada*.
Archaic Language	A word, phrase, or style of language that is no longer in everyday use but is sometimes used to impart an old-fashioned flavour.
Argumentative Essay	An assertive, brief composition that attempts to advance, substantiate, or prove a thesis.
Aside	A remark, usually in a play, that is intended to be heard by the audience but is supposed to be unheard by the other characters.
Assonance	Repetition of similar or identical vowel sounds (a, e, i, o, u) in a line or series of lines of poetry. For example, "Our echoes grow for ever and ever."
Atmosphere	The mood or feeling of a literary work. Atmosphere is often developed through setting.
Autobiography	A person's account of his or her own life. Often found in the form of diaries, journals, or memoirs.

Ballad	A narrative poem that tells a story, often in a straightforward and dramatic manner and often about such universals as love, honour, and courage. Ballads were once songs, and literary ballads often have the strong rhythm and plain rhyme scheme of songs. (Songs are still written in ballad form, some old ballads are still sung, and some literary ballads have been set to music.) Samuel Taylor Coleridge's *The Rime of the Ancient Mariner* is an example of a literary ballad.
Ballad Stanza	Generally found as a quatrain, or a four-line stanza, within a ballad.
Bias	An inclination or prejudice toward or against a person, group, or idea; a concentration on or interest in a single particular area or subject.
Biography	A detailed account of a person's life written by another person.
Blank Verse	Is written in unrhymed iambic pentameter (a light beat followed by a heavy beat, five times per line). Of all the English verse forms, it is the most fluid and comes closest to the natural rhythms of English speech. The following is an example from William Wordsworth's *Lines Composed a Few Miles Above Tintern Abbey*: With some uncertain notice, as might seem, Of vagrant dwellers in the houseless woods, Or of some hermit's cave, where by his fire…
Cacophony	The use of harsh or unmusical sounds, as in *truncheon* and *cataract*.
Caricature	A caricature involves the use of exaggeration or distortion to make a person or public figure appear comic or ridiculous.
Case Study	A study of a single event or instance.
Catastrophe	The ending or denouement of a drama. Often a catastrophe is tragic and causes great suffering or damage.
Cause and Effect	An organisational pattern in writing in which the result (effect) is directly related to a cause (often an event). Causes always come first.
Character	The qualities distinctive to an individual; the distinctive nature of something.
Characterisation	The means by which a writer reveals the qualities of a character: – through actions – through speech and thoughts – through physical description – through the opinions that others have about the character – through a direct statement made by the writer
Character Foil	A person or thing that contrasts strongly with another and, in doing so, makes the qualities of the other person or thing more obvious.
Chorus	A part of a poem that is repeated. A chorus can also refer to a group of characters in a play that provides commentary on the events of the play.
Chronological Order	The order of a literary work based on time—on what happened first, second, etc.
Chronology	The measurement of time or the ordering of events.
Cliché	A phrase or opinion that is overused and betrays a lack of original thought.
Climactic Order	An order in a story or essay in which a series of events, thoughts, or statements is arranged in order of increasing importance with a climax at the end.
Climax	The point of greatest intensity or suspense in a narrative. It is the point at which it is revealed whether the protagonist triumphs or fails.
Colloquial	Informal; suitable for everyday speech but not for formal writing.
Colloquial Language	The use of familiar or conversational language.

Comedy	In general, a literary work that is light and often humorous or satirical in tone and tends to resolve the conflict happily. It is distinct from tragedy, which is generally concerned with unhappy or disastrous endings.
Comic Relief	Humorous content in a dramatic or literary work intended to offset more serious episodes or events.
Compare and Contrast	To find similarities and differences.
Comparison	A consideration or estimate of the similarities or dissimilarities between two things or people.
Concrete	Solid, physical; not theoretical or abstract. Trees, copper, and kangaroos are all concrete things. Both concrete and abstract things are equally real. See *abstract*.
Conflict	A struggle between two opposing forces or characters in a work of literature. Conflict can be internal or external and it can take one of these forms: (1) a person against another person (2) a person against society (3) a person against nature (4) two elements within a person struggling for control
Connotation	The feelings suggested by a word or phrase. It is the opposite of denotation, which is the literal meaning of a word or phrase. A connotation of a maple leaf might be the symbolic identity of Canada; in terms of denotation, it would literally be a leaf from a maple tree.
Consonance	The repetition of similar consonant sounds in a group of words. Alliteration is a form of consonance. For example, Theodore Roethke's *Praise to the End* uses consonance in the following line: Now the water's low. The weeds exceed me.
Contrast	Compare in such a way as to emphasize differences. For example, "She was tall in contrast to her older sister, who couldn't even reach the top of the bookshelf."
Couplet	Two consecutive lines of poetry that rhyme, as in this line from Shakespeare's *King Henry V*: Then brook abridgment, and your eyes advance, After your thoughts, straight back again to France.
Deduction	A conclusion reached by logic or reasoning, or by examining all the available information.
Denotation	The explicit or direct meaning or set of meanings of a word or expression. These are the meanings listed in dictionaries. See also *connotation*.
Denouement	The outcome of a plot in which all of the conflict and mystery is explained or concluded.
Descriptive Essay	An essay that portrays people, places, things, moments, and theories with enough vivid detail to help the reader create a mental picture of the subject.
Dialect	A form of language that is particular to a specific region or social group.
Dialogue	The words in a conversation.
Diary	A book in which one keeps a record of personal events and experiences.
Diction	A writer's choice of words, particularly in terms of clarity and precision.
Didactic	A form of poetry that has as its primary intention the teaching of some lesson or moral, or the making of some critical statement about society.
Dilemma	A difficult situation in which a choice has to be made between two or more undesirable alternatives.
Direct Presentation	In direct presentation, the reader is told exactly what a character is like. For example, "She is a very caring person."
Discrepancy	Distinct difference between two things that should not be different or that should correspond.
Dissonance	Harsh sound or discordance. Dissonance can be emotional or intellectual.
Drama	A play for theatre, radio, or television.
Dramatic Form	A dramatic form is simply something structured as a play.
Dramatic Irony	A situation in which a reader or an audience becomes aware of something that a character in the story or play does not know.

Dramatic Monologue	A form of narrative poem in which one character speaks to one or more listeners whose replies are not given.
Dynamic Character	A character that undergoes a change or development during the course of a narrative, be it from good to bad, from bad to good, from bad to worse, etc.
Editorial	And article expressing the editor's opinion.
Elegy	A poem of mourning, usually over the death of an individual.
Emotional Appeal	An attempt to persuade an audience or reader by making subjective or emotional appeals.
Epic	A long poem that is often about a heroic character. The style is elevated and the poetry often represents religious or cultural ideals. *Beowulf* and the *Odyssey* are examples of epics.
Epigram	A short, witty statement.
Epilogue	A final address to the audience, often delivered by a character in a drama.
Epiphany	A moment of significant illumination or insight.
Epitaph	An inscription on a tombstone, or a short poem written in memory of someone who has died.
Euphemism	A mild expression or indirect word substituted for another word or term that is considered to be too blunt or harsh.
Euphony	Sounds that are pleasing to the ear.
Expert Testimony	Using the ideas and/or words of an expert to advance an argument or position within a piece of writing.
Exposition	A comprehensive explanation of an idea or theory in a piece of writing.
Expository Essay	The function of an expository essay is to explain a body of knowledge.
Extended Metaphor	A metaphor (a comparison of two things that are dissimilar) that is extended throughout a piece of literature.
External Conflict	The conflict a character undergoes in relation to other characters, nature, fate, or any other force outside of the character's own personality and emotions.
Fable	A brief story told to present a moral or practical lesson.
Falling Action	The action in a narrative that occurs after the climax.
Fantasy	A literary genre. As a rule, fantasy contains events, characters, or settings that would not be possible or that would not be found in real life.
Farce	A type of comedy based on ridiculous situations, often with stereotyped characters.
Figurative Language	Language that is not intended to be interpreted in a literal sense. Figurative language includes such figures of speech as *hyperbole*, *metaphor*, *metonymy*, *oxymoron*, *personification*, and *simile*.
First Person Point of View	In the first person point of view, the story is told by one of the characters involved in the events in his or her own words, using the pronoun *I*.
Flashback	A scene in a narrative that interrupts the action to show an event that happened earlier.
Flat Character	A flat character is presented only in outline without much individualising detail and so can readily be described in a single phrase or sentence.
Foil	A person or thing that contrasts strongly with another, and therefore makes the qualities of that other more salient and obvious.
Foreshadowing	A technique whereby an event or incident is indicated beforehand when the writer includes hints or clues about the main events of a story.
Form	The literary shape of a piece of literature, be it drama, essay, poetry, or prose.
Formal Essay	A formal essay has a serious tone and intent and uses technical words and organisation in a conservative fashion.
Formal Language	Language in speaking or writing characterised by conservative and/or technical terms.
Free Verse	Is usually written in variable rhythmic cadences. It may be rhymed or unrhymed, but the rhymes are likely to be irregular and may not occur at the end of lines.
Genre	A style or category within a literary form. For example, *haiku* constitute a genre of poetry, while science-fiction is a genre of drama, prose, or novels.

Graphic Text	Text and text inserts that use visual art or specialised lettering.
Hero	A person who is admired for his or her courage, outstanding achievements, or noble qualities.
Historical Reference	A reference or mention of an event or person from the past.
Hyperbole	A figure of speech that uses exaggeration for effect. Like a metaphor, it is not intended to deceive.
Iambic Pentameter	A poetic line consisting of five verse feet with each foot featuring an unstressed syllable followed by a stressed syllable, as in Milton's *Paradise Lost*: Too well I see and rue the dire event,
Idiom	A form of expression or group of words natural to a language, person, or group of people; the meaning of which cannot be understood from literally interpreting the words, as in *over the moon* to represent happiness or *keeping tabs on someone* to represent close supervision.
Image	A word or sequence of words that refers to a sensory experience.
Imagery	Words or phrases that create pictures or images in the reader's mind, as in Ezra Pound's *In a Station of the Metro*: The apparition of these faces in the crowd; Petals on a wet, black bough.
Imitative Harmony	A series of words that seem to imitate the sounds to which they refer. "The crash, hiss, and whisper of the rolling sea foam" is an example of imitative harmony. Not to be confused with *onomatopoeia*, which refers to individual words imitating specific sounds.
Indeterminate Ending	An indeterminate ending is an uncertain, ambiguous, or unresolved conclusion to a plot or sequence of events.
Indirect Presentation	When a writer uses indirect presentation, he or she depicts a character or event, and the reader or listener must interpret meaning. This is in contrast to direct presentation, wherein the writer explicitly states meaning and significance.
Informal Essay	A short literary composition on a single subject, usually presenting a personal view using conversational language mixed with formal language.
Informal Language	Relaxed, unofficial, or colloquial words.
Interior Monologue	Conversation-like thoughts of a character.
Internal Conflict	The conflict a character experiences within him or herself.
Internal Rhyme	A rhyme that occurs within a line of verse, such as in Percy Bysshe Shelley's *The Cloud*, I bring fresh **showers** for the thirsting **flowers**, From the seas and the streams; I bear light **shade** for the leaves when **laid** In their noon-day dreams.
Irony	The key element of irony is discrepancy. There is always a notable difference between appearance and reality, between expectation and fulfillment, or between what is intended and what results. Writers use irony for both serious and humorous effects. Irony can also be a technique for indicating, through character or plot development, the writer's own attitude toward some element of the story.
Jargon	Special vocabulary of a particular group or activity. Sometimes used for confusing or unintelligible language.
Justification	The giving of reasons or support; for example, giving an argument or reason that shows that an action or belief is reasonable or true.
Juxtaposition	The deliberate contrast of characters, settings, or situations for effect. The effect may result in a demonstration of character or heightening of mood.
Legend	A traditional story sometimes popularly regarded as historical, but not authenticated.

Limited Omniscient	A narrative told from a third person point of view but restricted to the thoughts and experiences of a single character. In unlimited omniscient narratives, the narrator can comment on the thoughts, feelings, and actions of any or all of the characters.
Literal Language	Use of words in their most basic sense without any additional meanings, references, or subtext. Literal language does not employ any metaphor, irony, exaggeration, or allusions.
Lyric	A short poem that expresses the private emotions or thoughts of the writer. Originally, lyrics were poems intended to be sung. *Sonnets*, *odes*, and *elegies* are examples of lyrics. As the poetic genre developed, it retained the melodic and musical quality. (In modern use, *lyrics* (always plural) are the words of a song.)
Melodrama	A drama containing stereotypical characters, exaggerated emotions, and a conflict that pits an all-good hero or heroine against an all-evil villain.
Metamorphosis	An alteration in appearance or character. Generally used to refer to physical change, but can also refer to character development and emotional growth, particularly if the character changes very significantly.
Metaphor	A figure of speech that makes a comparison between two things that are fundamentally dissimilar. The simile "George is like a mad dog when he's angry" is a comparison using like; the same idea in a metaphor would be "George is a mad dog when angry."
Metonymy	Figure of speech that replaces the name of one thing with the name of something closely associated with it. For example, *the White House* generally means the American government. Metonymy is closely related to synecdoche, in which a part of something is used to represent the whole, as in "Many hands make light work," where *hands* represents people.
Metre	A generally regular pattern of stressed and unstressed syllables in poetry.
Metrical poetry	Is written in regular, repeating rhythms and may be rhymed or unrhymed. Rhymes are regular, like the rhythm, and are often found at the end of the line.
Monologue	A literary form: an oral or written composition in which only one person speaks. A kind of soliloquy: a speech or narrative presented by one person.
Mood	In a story, the atmosphere. When a writer orders the setting, action, and characters of a story so as to suggest a dominant emotion or patterns of emotions, you can say that this emotional pattern is the mood of the story. Also a person's state of mind or complex of emotions at any given time.
Motif	A recurring theme, situation, incident, idea, image, or character type that is found in literature.
Mystery	A profound secret; something wholly unknown or something kept cautiously concealed, therefore exciting curiosity or wonder; something that has not been or cannot be explained.
Myth	A story, often about immortals and sometimes concerned with religious rituals, intended to give meaning to the mysteries of the world.
Narration	The act of giving a spoken or written account of a story.
Narrative	A piece of literature that tells a story.
Narrator	One who narrates or tells a story. The word *narrator* can also refer to a character in a drama who guides the audience through the play, often commenting on the action.
Objective Language	Language that does not attempt to influence the attitudes of others through the use of personal feelings or opinions. Objective language only considers the facts of the matter.
Objective Point of View	The writer tells a story in third person but avoids including any thoughts or feelings and focuses only on what the characters say or do.
Octave	An eight-line poem or stanza. An octave can also refer to the first eight lines of an Italian (or Petrarchian) sonnet.
Ode	A poem expressing lofty emotion. Odes often celebrate an event or are addressed to nature or to some admired person, place, or thing. An example is *Ode to a Grecian Urn* by John Keats.

Omniscient Point of View	The narrative is written in the third person point of view, and the thoughts and feelings of more than one character are revealed through the narrator's perception.
Onomatopoeia	Words that seem to imitate the sounds to which they refer, such as *buzz*, *bang*, or *hiss*.
Oxymoron	A combination of two usually contradictory terms in a compressed paradox. For example, *the living dead*. An oxymoron is like a metaphor in that it expresses some truth in words that cannot be understood literally. *Truthful lies* is an oxymoron that describes metaphors.
Parable	A short, often simple story that teaches or explains a lesson, often a moral or religious lesson.
Paradox	An apparently self-contradictory statement that is in fact true.
Parallelism	The arrangement of similarly constructed clauses, verses, or sentences, suggesting some correspondence between them.
Parenthetical	A word, phrase, or passage (sometimes within parentheses) that explains or modifies a thought.
Passive Voice	In sentences that are written in passive voice, the subject receives that action expressed in the verb; the subject is acted upon. In sentences written in active voice, the subject performs the action expressed in the verb; the subject acts.
Pastoral	A type of poem that deals in an idealized way with shepherds and rustic life.
Pathos	The quality in a work of art that arouses the reader or listener's feelings of pity, sorrow, or compassion for a character.
Personal Essay	A short piece of writing in which the writer relates biographical details and private perceptions as a means of illuminating an issue or conflict.
Personification	The giving of human attributes to inanimate objects.
Persuasive Essay	The purpose of a persuasive essay is to convince a reader of the value or validity of an argument. A good writer may present emotional as well as rational appeals in order to sway the reader's opinion.
Persuasive Technique	A writer uses the techniques of persuasion, including appeals to emotion, use of statistics, quotations from experts, and graphic representations.
Plot	The sequence of events in a narrative.
Point of View	The vantage point from which a narrative is told. Most writing uses two basic points of view: first person and third person (omniscient).
Precedent	Something that serves as an example or justification for subsequent situations.
Pro and Con Argument	An essay or section of writing structured around evidence in support (pro) and against (con) a thesis.
Prologue	An introduction to a play, often delivered by the chorus (in ancient Greece, a group, but in modern plays, one actor) who plays no part in the following action.
Propaganda	Information, especially of a biased or misleading nature, used to promote a political cause or point of view. The appeals are primarily to the emotions and are designed to convince and persuade groups or individuals to action.
Protagonist	The central character of a drama, short story, or narrative poem.
Proverb	A short, well-known saying that states a general truth or piece of advice.
Pun	A humorous expression that depends on a double meaning, either between different senses of the same word or between two similar-sounding words: for example, "Santa's helpers are subordinate Clauses."
Purpose	The reason for which something is done or created. The purpose is the writer's intention within a piece of literature.
Quatrain	A stanza of four lines, usually with alternating rhymes.
Question and Answer	An essay or section of a piece of writing structured around questions and answers in support of a thesis and designed to advance details of that thesis.
Refrain	A word, line, phrase, or group of lines repeated regularly in a poem, usually at the end of each stanza.
Repetition	The action of repeating something that has already been said or written.
Research	The systematic investigation into and study of materials and sources in order to establish facts and reach new conclusions.

Rhetoric	The art of speaking or writing.
Rhetorical Question	A question for which a reply is not required or even wanted. The question is asked for effect; often a rhetorical question is a way of making a statement: *Is there anyone who does not believe in freedom?* really means *Everyone believes in freedom.*
Rhyme	The repetition of sounds in two or more words or phrases that appear closely to one another in a poem. For example, Alan Moore's *Vicious Cabaret* has the following lines: There's a girl who'll push but will not *shove* And she's desperate for her father's *love* She believes the hand beneath the *glove* May be one she needs to hold.
Rhyme Scheme	A rhyme scheme is a pattern of rhymes in a poem.
Rhythm	The arrangement of stressed and unstressed syllables into a pattern. Rhythm is most apparent in poetry, though it is a part of all good writing.
Ridicule	Contemptuous laughter or derision (contempt and mockery). Ridicule may be an element of satire.
Rising Action	The events of a dramatic or narrative plot that precede the climax.
Round Character	A round character is a complex and fully realised individual and is therefore difficult to describe in one or two sentences.
Sarcasm	The use of irony to mock or convey contempt.
Satire	A form of writing that exposes the failings of individuals, institutions, or societies to ridicule or scorn in order to correct or expose some evil or wrongdoing. The word is sometimes used as a synonym for *ridicule*.
Sestet	The last six lines of an Italian (or Petrarchian) sonnet. The first six lines of an Italian sonnet (the octave) often contain a problem, whereas the last six (the sestet) contain a solution or resolution.
Setting	The time and place in which the events in a short story, novel, play, or narrative poem occur.
Simile	A comparison of two things through the use of a specific word of comparison, such as *like, as, than,* or *resembles*.
Slang	Words or phrases that are regarded as very informal, are more common in speech than in writing, and are typically restricted to a particular context or group of people.
Soliloquy	A speech by a character who is alone on stage or whose presence is unrecognized by the other characters. The purpose is to make the audience aware of the character's thoughts or to give information concerning other characters or about the action.
Sonnet	A lyric poem fourteen lines long and usually in iambic pentameter. The Shakespearean sonnet consists of three quatrains (four-line stanzas) and one couplet (two lines) all written to a strict end-rhyme scheme (*abab cdcd efef gg*). The development of the poet's thoughts is also structured. There are several methods; one method is to use each quatrain for different points in an argument and the couplet for the resolution of the argument. Because of the complexity of the sonnet, poets sometimes find it a suitable form for expressing the complexity of thought and emotion.
Speaker	Separate from the writer, it is the person whose voice or identity dictates the poem or story.
Stanza	A stanza is a segment within the formal pattern of a poem, distinguished from other stanzas by clearly indicated divisions.
Static Character	A static character does not change or develop over the course of a narrative. That character's responses and characteristics do not vary at any point, in contrast with a dynamic character, which can move from one attitude or way of behaving to another.
Statistical Evidence	Numerical information acquired through research that substantiates or advances an argument based on scientific and mathematical methods.
Stereotype	A commonplace type or character that appears so often in literature that his or her nature is immediately familiar to the reader.

Stock/Stereotypical Character	Stereotypes, also called stock characters, always look and behave in the same way and reveal the same traits of character.
Stream of Consciousness	A style of writing that attempts to imitate the natural flow of a character's thoughts, feelings, reflections, memories, and mental images. Often, a stream of consciousness method of narration will ignore conventions of grammar and punctuation in order to simulate a flow of thoughts.
Style	A writer's characteristic way of writing, determined by the choice of words, the arrangement of words in sentences, and the relationship of the sentences to one another.
Stylistic Technique	The techniques or methods a writer uses, particularly insofar as they define his or her style.
Subjective (language, tone, etc.)	Language based on emotion, feeling, or opinion. The opposite of objective language, which is not influenced by emotion and feeling.
Surprise Ending	An unexpected or unforeseen ending.
Suspense	The quality of a story or drama that makes the reader uncertain or tense about the outcome of an event or series of events. Suspense makes a reader or member of the audience anxious about what will happen next.
Syllogism	A form of logical argument that derives a conclusion from two premises. For example: *All men must die. Socrates is a man. Therefore, Socrates will die.*
Symbol	Anything that stands for or represents something other than itself. In literature, a symbol is a word or phrase referring to an object, scene, or action that also has some further significance associated with it. For example, a rose is a common symbol of love. Many symbols, such as flags, are universally recognized. Other symbols are not so universally defined. They do not acquire a meaning until they are defined by how they are used in a story. They may even suggest more than one meaning. For example, snow might be used to symbolize goodness because of its cleanness or cruelty because of its coldness. Symbols are often contained in story titles; in character and place names; in classical, literary, and historical allusions and references; in images or figures that appear at important points in a story; and in images that either receive special emphasis or are repeated.
Symbolism	The use of symbols to represent ideas or qualities.
Synecdoche	Figure of speech that replaces the name of something with the name of a part of that same thing. *Many hands make light work.*
Syntax	The way the words of a sentence are organised and arranged. A sentence with good syntax has been assembled using the laws of grammar.
Theme	The general idea or insight about life that a writer wishes to express in a literary work.
Thesis	A statement that is made as the first step in asserting an argument or a demonstration.
Thesis Statement	A statement or theory put forward and supported by arguments.
Third Person Point of View	In the third person (omniscient) point of view, the writer can describe and comment on all of the thoughts and feelings within the characters. In a third person (limited) point of view, the speaker can only observe and relate the thoughts and emotions of a single individual within the narrative.
Tone	A particular way of speaking or writing. Tone may also describe the general feeling of a piece of work. It can demonstrate the writer's attitude toward characters, settings, conflicts, and so forth. The many kinds of tone include *thoughtful, chatty, formal, tragic,* or *silly*; tone can also be a complex mixture of attitudes. Different tones can cause readers to experience such varying emotions as pity, fear, horror, or humour.
Tragedy	In general, a literary work in which the protagonist meets an unhappy or disastrous end.
Understatement	The presentation of something as being smaller, less good, or less important than it really is.
Voice	The tone, syntax, and characteristics of the speaker within a work of literature.
Wit	The capacity for inventive thought and quick, keen understanding—often with the intent of producing humorous responses. Cleverness.

KEY WORDS

The following list of key words has been taken from the English 12 Examination Specifications, September 2002,[1] where it was introduced with these important points:

> *Students frequently lose marks by not addressing the question as given.*
>
> *When markers evaluate answers to questions using these words, they generally have the*
> [definitions in the following list] *in mind.*

If a written-response assignment includes a key word from this list, then part of the instructions is not actually written down. That part of the instructions is found in the definition of the key word. For example, *discuss* means "present the various points of view in a debate or argument"; "write at length about a given subject"; "engage in written discourse on a particular topic." Study this list and be prepared to follow the unwritten instructions fully.

KEY WORD	DEFINITION
AGREE OR DISAGREE	Support or contradict a statement; give the positive OR negative features; express an informed opinion one way or the other; list the advantages for OR against.
ASSESS	Estimate the value of something based on some criteria; present an informed judgment. Command words such as *assess* strongly suggest to the student that two schools of thought exist about a given subject. These questions often involve weighing the relative merit of conflicting points of view; e.g., negative vs. positive, strong vs. weak components, fundamental vs. immediate, etc.
COMPARE	Give an estimate of the similarity of one event or issue to another; give an estimate of the relationship between two things. Often used in conjunction with CONTRAST.
CONTRAST	Give an estimate of the difference between two things. See COMPARE.
DESCRIBE	Give a detailed or graphic account of an object, event, or sequence of events.
DISCUSS	Present the various points of view in a debate or argument; write at length about a given subject; engage in written discourse on a particular topic.
EXPLAIN	Give an account of what the essence of something is, how it works, or why something is the way it is. This task may be accomplished by paraphrasing, providing reasons or examples, or by giving a step-by-step account.
IDENTIFY	Clearly establish the identity of something based on an understood set of considerations; recognize the unique qualities of something and state the criteria used to identify it; simply provide the name of something.
ILLUSTRATE	Give concrete examples to clarify a point or an idea.
LIST	Give a catalogue, in some specified order, of names, ideas, or things that belong to a particular class of items.
OUTLINE	Give a written description of only the main features; summarize the principal parts of a thing, an idea, or an event.
SHOW (THAT)	Give facts, reasons, illustrations, or examples to support an idea or proposition.
STATE	Give the key points with supporting reasons.
SUGGEST	To identify and propose; to present viable alternatives, options, and solutions.
SUPPORT	Defend or agree with a particular, predetermined point of view; give evidence, reasons, or examples.
TRACE	Outline the development; describe the specified sequence.

CONJUNCTIVE ADVERBS

These adverbs can be used with a semicolon to join independent clauses into compound sentences. (This is not the only use.)		
accordingly	incidentally	on the contrary
as a result	indeed	on the other hand
at the same time	instead	otherwise
consequently	likewise	similarly

finally	meanwhile	so far
for example	moreover	still
for instance	namely	thereafter
furthermore	nevertheless	therefore
hence	next	thus
however	nonetheless	undoubtedly
in fact	of course	

SUBORDINATING CONJUNCTIONS

Subordinating conjunctions introduce a subordinate clause.
Some of the most common subordinating conjunctions are shown in this chart.

after	before	that	when
although	even though	though	where
as	if	unless	whether
as if	than	until	while
because			

USEFUL LINKING VERBS

A linking verb can be used in either of two sentence patterns:

noun + linking verb + adjective (My new car is black.)
noun + linking verb + noun (His uncle is the ombudsman.)

Linking Verbs Expressing State	Linking Verbs Expressing a Change in State
taste	turn
appear	become
be	get
feel	grow
lay	fall
look	prove
remain	run
seem	
smelled	
sound	
stay	

---

[1] Published by the Student Assessment and Program Evaluation Branch of the British Columbia Ministry of Education (http://www.bced.gov.bc.ca/exams/specs/pdfs/enspec.pdf)

CREDITS

The publishers wish to thank all those who assisted in the creation of this publication.

Efforts have been made to provide proper acknowledgement of the original sources and to comply with copyright law. However, some attempts to establish original copyright ownership may have been unsuccessful. If copyright ownership can be identified, please notify Castle Rock Research Corporation so that appropriate corrective action can be taken.

Reading and Viewing

"Sonnet VIII", by William Shakespeare

"When I Heard the Learn'd Astronomer", by Walt Whitman

"Before Two Portraits of my Mother", by Émile Nelligan

Excerpts from the plays, Romeo and Juliet, Hamlet, MacBeth, Julius Caesar, Taming of the Shrew, by William Shakespeare

"The Short Story and Novel", by Emily Dickinson

Excerpt from "The Hard Life" by James Fallows, published in The Atlantic 263 n3 (March 1989) © James Fallows.

Photograph by Amy Toensing. "Why We Pulled the Taffeta." In National Geographic, March 2003.

Poster by Holger Matthies. In Persuasive Images: Posters of War and Revolution, by Peter Paret, Beth Irwin Lewis, and Paul Paret. Princeton: Princeton University Press, 1992.

Reading and Viewing Practice Questions

"Follower" by Seamus Heaney, published in "Death of a Naturalist" by Seamus Heaney, Faber and Faber, 1966

"The Answer is Blowin' in the Wind" from Points of View by Rex Murphy © 2003. Published by McClelland & Stewart Ltd. Used with permission of the publisher.

"Snow" excerpted from Belonging by Isabel Huggan. Copyright © 2003 Isabel Huggan. Reprinted by permission of Knopf Canada."

"The Myth of the Cave" from The Republic by Plato

Reading and Viewing Unit Test

"Sonnet 116" by William Shakespeare

Excerpt from "Dr. Jekyll and Mr. Hyde" by Robert Louis Stevenson

Metacognition

"Dragon Night" by Jane Yolen. Copyright © 1980 by Jane Yolen. Currently appears in HERE THERE BE DRAGONS, published by Harcourt Brace and Company. Reprinted by permission of Curtis Brown, Ltd.

Practice Test One

"The Finicky Shark" by William J. Broad, The Times Colonist. from New York Times News Service. Sunday, August 10, 1997. Copyright © 1997 by The New York Times.

"The Writer" from New and Collected Poems" by Richard Wilbur, published by Harcourt Brace, 1988. Copyright © 1969 by Richard Wilbur. All rights reserved.

"Saturday Climbing" by W.D. Valgardson

Practice Test Two

Adapted from "Herbal Remedies: Buyer Beware" by Paul Taylor, published in The Globe and Mail. Tuesday, September 23, 1997, pg. A.1

"What Shall He Tell That Son?" from THE PEOPLE, YES by Carl Sandburg, copyright © 1936 by Harcourt Brace Jovanovich, Inc. Copyright © 1964 by Carl Sandburg

"The Firewood Gatherers" by Thierry Mallci

NOTES

ORDERING INFORMATION

INDIVIDUAL ORDERS	SCHOOL ORDERS
ORDER ONLINE at www.castlerockresearch.com or contact Castle Rock Research BC Toll-free: 1.866.882.8246 Fax: 250.868.9146	School and school jurisdictions are eligible for our **educational discount** rate. Contact Castle Rock Research BC for more information.

THE KEY Study Guides are specifically designed to assist students in preparing for unit tests, final exams, and provincial examinations.

KEY Study Guides – $29.95 each plus G.S.T.

SENIOR HIGH		JUNIOR HIGH	ELEMENTARY
Biology 12 Chemistry 12 English 12 Geography 12 History 12 Physics 12 Principles of Math 12	Biology 11 Chemistry 11 English 11 Physics 11 Principles of Math 11 Social Studies 11 English 10 Principles of Math 10 Science 10	Language Arts 9 Math 9 Language Arts 7 Math 7	Math 6 Language Arts 4 Math 4

Student Notes and Problems (SNAP) Workbooks contain complete examinations of curriculum concepts, examples, and exercise questions.

SNAP Workbooks – $29.95 each plus G.S.T.

SENIOR HIGH		JUNIOR HIGH	ELEMENTARY
Chemistry 12 Physics 12 Principles of Math 12	Chemistry 11 Physics 11 Principles of Math 11 Principles of Math 10 Science 10	Math 9 Science 9 Math 8 Math 7	Math 6 Math 5 Math 4 Math 3

For students in the following courses, we have available the following corresponding resources which are correlated to the B.C. curriculum.

B.C. COURSE NAME	CORRESPONDING RESOURCE
Applications of Math 12	*THE KEY* – Math 30 Applied
Applications of Math 12	**SNAP** – Math 30 Applied
Applications of Math 10	**SNAP** – Math 10 Applied
Calculus 12	**SNAP** – Math 31

Visit our website for a "tour" of resource content and features, or order online at www.castlerockresearch.com

#4-1905 Evergreen Court
Kelowna, BC V1Y 9L4
E-mail: learnbc@castlerockresearch.com

Phone: 250.868.8384
Toll-free: 866.882.8246
Fax: 250.868.9146

ORDER FORM

ORDER ONLINE AT www.castlerockresearch.com

THE KEY	Price	Quantity	Total
Biology 12	$29.95		
Chemistry 12	$29.95		
English 12	$29.95		
Geography 12	$29.95		
History 12	$29.95		
Physics 12	$29.95		
Principles of Math 12	$29.95		
Biology 11	$29.95		
Chemistry 11	$29.95		
English 11	$29.95		
Physics 11	$29.95		
Principles of Math 11	$29.95		
Social Studies 11	$29.95		
English 10	$29.95		
Principles of Math 10	$29.95		
Science 10	$29.95		
Language Arts 9	$29.95		
Math 9	$29.95		
Language Arts 7	$29.95		
Math 7	$29.95		
Math 6	$29.95		
Language Arts 4	$29.95		
Math 4	$29.95		
		Subtotal 1	

SNAP WORKBOOKS	Price	Quantity	Total
Chemistry 12	$29.95		
Physics 12	$29.95		
Principles of Math 12	$29.95		
Chemistry 11	$29.95		
Physics 11	$29.95		
Principles of Math 11	$29.95		
Principles of Math 10	$29.95		
Science 10	$29.95		
Math 9	$29.95		
Science 9	$29.95		
Math 8	$29.95		
Math 7	$29.95		
Math 6	$29.95		
Math 5	$29.95		
Math 4	$29.95		
Math 3	$29.95		
		Subtotal 2	

Total Cost

Subtotal 1

Subtotal 2

Subtotal 3

Cost Subtotal

Shipping and Handling
(Please call for current rates)

G.S.T

Order Total

For students in the following courses, we recommend the corresponding Alberta resources which are highly correlated to the B.C. curriculum.

B.C. Course NAME	Alberta Resource	Price	Quantity	Total
Applications of Math 12	THE KEY-Math 30 Applied	$29.95		
Applications of Math 12	SNAP-Math 30 Applied	$29.95		
Applications of Math 10	SNAP-Math 10 Applied	$29.95		
Calculus 12	SNAP-Math 31	$29.95		
			Subtotal 3	

Significant discounts for school orders. Prices subject to change.

Please complete the shipping and payment information.
Name: _____
Mailing Address: _____
City: _____ Postal Code: _____
Telephone: _____ School: _____
Visa/MC card number: _____ Expiry Date (mm/yy): _____
Name on Card: _____

ORDERING OPTIONS
On-line: 250.868.8384 or 866.882.8246
Fax: 250.868.9146
E-mail: learnbc@castlerockresearch.com
Mail: #4-1905 Evergreen Court,, Kelowna, BC V1Y 9L4
OR CONTACT YOUR DISTRICT REPRESENTATIVE
(Visit our website for the name of the representative in your area)